AN INTRODUCTION TO THE CRUSADES

COMPANIONS TO MEDIEVAL STUDIES
series editor: Paul Edward Dutton

AN INTRODUCTION TO THE CRUSADES

S.J. Allen

UNIVERSITY OF TORONTO PRESS

Copyright © University of Toronto Press 2017
Higher Education Division

www.utppublishing.com

Allen, S.J. (Susan Jane), 1959–, author
    An introduction to the crusades/S.J. Allen.

(Companions to medieval studies series)
Includes bibliographical references and index.
Issued in print and electronic formats.
ISBN 978-1-4426-0023-2 (softcover).—ISBN 978-1-4426-0024-9 (hardcover).
—ISBN 978-1-4426-0027-0 (HTML).—ISBN 978-1-4426-0025-6 (PDF)

    1. Crusades. I. Title. II. Series: Companions to medieval studies series.

D151.C76 2017   909.07   C2017-902666-6
                                C2017-902667-4

We welcome comments and suggestions regarding any aspect of our publications—please feel free to contact us at news@utphighereducation.com or visit our Internetsite at www.utppublishing.com.

North America
5201 Dufferin Street
North York, Ontario, Canada, M3H 5T8

2250 Military Road
Tonawanda, New York, USA, 14150

ORDERS PHONE: 1-800-565-9523
ORDERS FAX: 1-800-221-9985
ORDERS E-MAIL: utpbooks@utpress.utoronto.ca

UK, Ireland, and continental Europe
NBN International
Estover Road, Plymouth, PL6 7PY, UK
ORDERS PHONE: 44 (0) 1752 202301
ORDERS FAX: 44 (0) 1752 202333
ORDERS E-MAIL: enquiries@
nbninternational.com

Every effort has been made to contact copyright holders; in the event of an error or omission, please notify the publisher.

Maps by Robert Cronan of Lucidity Information Design

The University of Toronto Press acknowledges the financial support for its publishing activities of the Government of Canada through the Canada Book Fund.

Printed in the United States of America.

For Emilie Amt

CONTENTS

ILLUSTRATIONS AND MAPS

TEXT BOXES

ACKNOWLEDGMENTS

I am indebted to the University of Toronto Press for the opportunity to write this companion book to *The Crusades: A Reader*, second edition. I am especially grateful for the support and guidance provided by the Series Editor, Paul Edward Dutton, UTP's History Editor, Natalie Fingerhut, and copy editor Martin Boyne. This book would simply not have been possible without their professional direction and sympathetic assistance. Any shortcomings of the work are, of course, my own. I would also like to offer my heartfelt thanks to the University of Toronto Press production team, especially for their work on the book's index, maps, and illustrations. The Open University Library staff were instrumental in the research stage of the book, as was my *Crusades* reader co-editor, Emilie Amt. Finally, particular thanks must be given to my son Giles for his encouragement and patience and to my husband Stephen, whose British civil-service skills proved invaluable on more than one occasion during the writing of *An Introduction to the Crusades*.

PREFACE

The word "crusade" conjures up an array of conflicting images and emotions. Popular impressions of this movement range from that of a chivalric expression of piety to a violent example of human greed and intolerance. Modern curiosity about the Crusades owes much to our post-9/11 world and the current dialogues and tensions surrounding western and Islamic ideologies.

Our early twenty-first century has seen popular interest in the Crusades matched by a corresponding surge of academic research. The ideas put forward by professional historians, however, are often found to be in conflict with the views of the general public. This is perhaps understandable, given the density of current crusade scholarship and the prevalence of romantic or overtly political interpretations of the movement. The Crusades' perceived significance to today's society was emphasized in the Preface to *The Crusades: A Reader*, second edition (which Emilie Amt and I edited): "It could be argued that the Crusades, more than any other medieval event, have become inextricably linked to present-day political and religious debates" (Allen and Amt 2014: xii). Whether popular or academic, it is true to say that never before has this movement received such widespread attention and deliberation.

An Introduction to the Crusades, as part of the *Companions to Medieval Studies* series, aims to provide students with a concise introduction to the subject and to current discussions and debates within crusade studies. It has been designed as an interactive text, with opportunities to engage with original source material while developing a critical approach to the period and its events. To this end, *An Introduction to the Crusades* contextualizes many of the primary documents found in the companion sourcebook, *The Crusades: A Reader*, second edition. Although the *Introduction* can be read as a stand-alone work, its use with the *Reader* should lead to a deeper appreciation of the subject and its related issues.

As with any academic study, the Crusades generate intense debate among scholars concerning their origins, development, and import. Therefore, a key objective of this volume is to raise awareness not only of how this history has been constructed, but also of the means by which it continues to be reviewed and evaluated. Efforts have been made to encourage students to assess and reinterpret both primary evidence and secondary research, with the aim of generating a better understanding of the material and the historical problems associated with the topic.

PLACE AND PERSON NAMES

All names are anglicized with the aim of providing the most common English spellings. Please be aware, however, that quoted sources may exhibit some variation.

IN-TEXT REFERENCES

References to primary documents in *The Crusades: A Reader* are given as *CR*, preceded by the title of the document as it appears in the reader. References to secondary sources are in a shortened in-text style, with the full citation appearing in the Bibliography at the end of the book.

ABBREVIATIONS

BCE/CE   Before the Common Era/Common Era (the modern alternative to BC and AD). Dates without an abbreviation should be read as CE.

CR   *The Crusades: A Reader*, second edition (2014)

ca   *circa*, about; approximately (indicating that the exact dates are not known)

fl.   *floruit*, flourished (indicating that exact dates of a person's life are uncertain or signifying the period when the person was most active)

r.   reign or tenure of office (indicating the ruling dates of a king, emperor, caliph, sultan, pope, or other leader)

d.   died (used if only the date of death is known)

b.   born (used if the person referred to is still living at the time of the work's publication)

CHAPTER ONE

THE CRUSADES– A BRIEF HISTORY

PROLOGUE: DEFINING THE CRUSADES

It may be surprising to learn that the word "crusade" did not exist at the time of the campaigns we now associate with this term. It is used today, without apology, by respected historians and is entrenched in our western psyche. Yet at the time of the First Crusade (1096), there were many ways to define the event and its participants. These included the Latin for journey or pilgrimage (*iter, peregrinatio*) and, later, names associated with the cross that was sewn onto the shoulders of crusaders (such as *crucesignati*, meaning "persons signed by the cross"). The wearing of the cross was a recognized emblem of Christian pilgrims, and the link between pilgrimage and crusading was strong from the outset. Both were seen as penitential activities, providing forgiveness for an individual's sins and paving one's way to heaven (see box 1.1). As for Islamic terminology, the eastern recipients had no word for these campaigns; nor did they mark them as a distinct movement. The wars that we in the west see so clearly as crusades were just another of the many territorial disputes of the time and region. Phrases such as "the cross wars" did not come into Islamic use until the mid-nineteenth century, and even then were adapted from European sources.

BOX I.I *Pilgrimage*

Pilgrimage was an established religious activity in the Middle Ages. It involved journeying to sacred sites or relics with the aim of gaining God's forgiveness for sins or help in adversity. Although such penitential acts could be the result of the sinner's own initiative, the Church offered direction for the pilgrim's journey and defined degrees of forgiveness. The notion of indulgences—that is, the Church's full or partial lessening of the punishment of sin—came into its own later, around the time of the Fourth Crusade (1204).

The goal of every medieval Christian was heaven, yet the accumulation of sin over a lifetime meant that the soul would be required to "work off" these transgressions in purgatory. Pilgrimage was specifically a penitential act. Within Europe, pilgrimage usually centered on the resting place of saints' relics. Those individuals recognized by the Church as being holy in life were in death believed to intercede for earth-bound Christians (Sumption 2002, 22–4). Some of the most popular pilgrimage sites housed objects and remains of those related to the life of Christ. It is for this reason that Jerusalem was regarded as the greatest of all pilgrimage destinations, for it contained the most sacred of Christian sites, the Church of the Holy Sepulcher, the assumed location of Christ's crucifixion and burial.

Pilgrimage to the Holy Land was a well-established activity by the time of the First Crusade, and there are numerous medieval accounts of travels to the Holy Land and guides to the sacred sites (see, for example, "The Pilgrimage of Etheria" and "John of Würzburg's Pilgrim Guide," *CR*).

The ambiguity of crusade terminology is compounded by debates on what constitutes a crusade and when they occurred. In the past, scholars of the Crusades have fallen into either "Traditionalist" or "Pluralist" camps. The Traditionalist's definition of a crusade is that of a military campaign called by the papacy with the aim of gaining the Holy Land and, in particular, Jerusalem. The more accepted view is that of the so-called Pluralists, those who define a crusade by how it was motivated, organized, and legally legitimized. By this definition, crusades are those campaigns motivated by perceived threats to the papacy and the Church. This stands as the primary reason for crusading, as opposed to the more specific goal of gaining the Holy Land.

As a result of these wider criteria, the Crusades of the Pluralists cover a broader temporal and geographic sphere. This book takes a Pluralist stance, and in doing so it considers not only the traditional crusades, but also how the notion of crusading evolved to include campaigns against Muslims in Islamic Spain, pagans in eastern Europe, home-grown heretics, and even Christian political enemies of the pope. Again, the key distinguishing factors are those individuals, groups or ideologies that were seen to threaten the papacy and Church, and the ways in which the campaigns themselves were organized and authorized by ecclesiastical rituals and grants of penance.

As always with definitions, there are exceptions. Popular movements, such as the Children's Crusade or the Crusades to Egypt, rather than the Holy Land, have led many historians to see a strict Traditionalist/Pluralist debate as irrelevant and outdated. And if we accept that the Crusades went beyond 1291, when did they end? There are those who will push for a definition that takes crusading right up to our own century. Yet we need to distinguish crusading activity from crusade rhetoric or memory. As the historian Christopher Tyerman warns, "[h]aving previously wreaked so much havoc, the Crusades should not be recruited to the battlegrounds of the 21st century ..." (Tyerman 2004, 146).

This book concentrates on the Crusades of the Middle Ages, while taking into consideration their legacy and place in modern memory. On the labeling of individual crusades, the use of numbers or names is, of course, a modern convention. Historians generally refer to the campaigns of the Middle East using numbers, while those outside this area are given titles reflecting the crusade's participants or region. There are also lesser European crusades centered on perceived threats to papal authority, which are given the name *passagium particulare*. These are sometimes called the "Political Crusades," although the line between politics and religion was a fine one during this period.

SETTING THE SCENE

It is important to understand the background of the three great players of the crusading era—the Byzantine Empire, Christian Europe, and the Islamic States. Some consideration should also be given to the part played by Jewish communities within each of these entities.

Byzantium

In response to a variety of pressures, the Late Roman Empire was effectively split into two distinct regions by 300 CE. From the Roman era through to the medieval period, the eastern region evolved into what we today call the Byzantine Empire or Byzantium. Of the two regions, Byzantium was the more obvious heir to the Roman Empire. The first Christian emperor, Constantine the Great (273–337), had moved the capital from Rome to the eastern side of the Empire in 324. "New Rome," as it was first titled, was situated between the Black Sea and the Sea of Marmara. Building on the old Greek city of Byzantium, Constantine created a capital worthy of his name: Constantinople. Not only was its peninsular location perfect for defense but it also stood at the crossroads of numerous trade routes, thus ensuring its economic viability.

It is this economic success that came to distinguish Byzantium from western Europe in the first half of the medieval period. The eastern Roman Empire had always surpassed the western region in trade, manufacture, and urban populations. Eastern cities were wealthy, multicultural centers, and this continued to be the case long after the fall of Rome. Byzantine's emperors were recognized as heads of the eastern Church. As we will see, the western region's development of church authority took a different path, thus leading to the rise of two Christian churches: western Catholic and eastern Orthodox.

Western Europe

The history of western Europe, from the late Roman Empire through the early medieval period, demonstrates the religious, political, military, and social trends that were to shape the crusading mentality. In contrast to the eastern empire, the west was more rural in its economy and less developed in terms of commercial activity. There were many reasons for this, including, in part, the make-up of the west's European population. From the time of Rome's first expansion, this region had been populated by a variety of tribally organized peoples. Farming was the economic base for these groups, and the majority lived in small, rural settlements. On the northern frontier of the Empire, numerous Germanic tribes began to infiltrate Roman territory in the third century. The exact nature of this movement and its consequences for Rome are matters of ongoing debate, but whether peaceful or violent, these Germanic peoples came to assume secular control as the empire lost its grip. It is generally agreed that by the close of the fifth century, the Roman Empire had been replaced by settled Germanic kingdoms. The one surviving element was the Christian Church, which provided religious leadership, administrative structure, literacy, and the language of the Church—Latin.

The depth of religious feeling and the prominence of its place within medieval society cannot be overstated. Germanic kings and their nobles would come to rely on the Church and churchmen to provide help with governance and to legitimize their rule. The clergy itself became an accepted career path for the Germanic ruling class, which in turn strengthened the power and wealth of the Church. Rich or poor, the Church defined and directed the people of western Europe from their birth to the afterlife.

The Church supported the social hierarchy of the period, asserting that one's place was divinely ordained. Most of the population were of the laboring class, and of these, nearly all worked the land of their lord. Within this class were many tiers, ranging from slaves to serfs to freemen. Serfs did not normally engage in military activity, nor did they have any great say in their conditions or management. The rise of towns and the commercial class would allow for some social mobility, but this development did not occur until just before the Crusades. Prior to that time, all wealth, power, and status stemmed from the possession of land. At the top were the landed classes. Lands were exchanged for loyalty and service, most often military, as the ability to gain and maintain these territories required force of arms. Thus the landed class was a military class, with much of its identity tied to militaristic culture and activities. The system of land for military service was not, however, as straightforward or regulated as it might seem. Divided loyalties, land grabs, inter-family wars, and the ever-present change of fortune made for an often unstable and violent society.

As noted above, churchmen played an important role within medieval government. Bishops and lesser clergy wielded power and influence at royal courts and nobles' halls. Aristocratic control of monastic establishments also paid dividends in the form of lucrative career opportunities, a safe deposit for lands, and an institution that would offer perpetual prayers for oneself and one's kinsmen. Well before the crusading period, the Church had accepted and worked alongside the martial class, yet the juxtaposition of military and religious authority is often difficult for us to comprehend. In trying to determine the motivation and rationale of seemingly religious people undertaking brutal actions, we often opt for *either* religion *or* personal gain as being the one "true" cause or incentive. This period, however, shows us that violent individuals could also be deeply devout in their Christian belief and practice, and that the Church could, when needed, sanction violence as spiritually justified.

It fell to the bishop of Rome, the "pope" (from *papa*, Latin for "father"), to lead the western Church. The supremacy of the bishop of Rome was based on the city's imperial role and its link to saints Peter and Paul. Deteriorating relations with Byzantium also strengthened the papacy's hand. On Christmas Day 800, Pope Leo III (r. 795–816) crowned the Frankish king Charlemagne (r. 768–814) "Roman Emperor of the West." The creation of this title in the early Middle Ages makes plain the authority of the papacy in legitimizing secular rulers. It also shows the desire of both rulers and popes to create an imperial Christian past that rivaled that of Byzantium.

The Islamic States

Of the two regions, it was the western one that would survive into the modern period. Reasons for this are varied and complex, but few would disagree that the long decline of Byzantium owes much to the rise of our third political and religious entity, the Islamic States. Islam began in the Arabian peninsula with Muhammad, a merchant born in the city of Mecca around the year 570. The Islamic faith teaches that Muhammad began to receive revelations from God (Arabic: *Allah*) in 610. These continued up to Muhammad's death in 632 and were later gathered together to create the religion's holy book, the *Qur'an*. The faith itself became known as Islam, meaning "submission to God," and followers of Islam are called Muslims. Islam sprang from a Judeo-Christian tradition and shares with these religions many key personages and prophets, including Abraham, Moses, Mary, and Jesus (Jesus is taken to be a prophet, although Muhammad is believed to be the last and greatest of the prophets. See Khalidi 2003, 5–9). Muhammad waged a war on Mecca, conquering the city in 630. Under Muhammad and his followers, the Ka'ba was declared to be a shrine built by Abraham and his son Ishmael. It became the most holy of Islamic sites and remains so today. Sacred also is Jerusalem, because it is the place of the prophet's "Night Journey," an event in which Muhammad was said to have been miraculously transported to Jerusalem and to have ascended from there into heaven.

The rise and spread of early medieval Islam were remarkably swift. By 750, Islamic rule ranged from the Indus River in the east to Spain in the west. Islamic armies had fought and defeated Byzantine forces, taking Jerusalem from them in 638. From Spain they launched forays into France but were unsuccessful in gaining a permanent foothold ("al-Baladhuri on Early Muslim Conquests," *CR*). Leadership was held by the caliphs—recognized successors to Muhammad who wielded both political and spiritual authority. The question of who should succeed Muhammad, however, was a source of conflict that resulted in the emergence of two Islamic sects, Sunni and Shi'a (box 1.2).

BOX 1.2   *Islam: Sunni and Shi'a*

With the death of Muhammad in 632, arguments arose among his followers as to who should succeed him. This was not, however, a question of a new prophet, as Muhammad was acknowledged to be the last of these. The dispute centered on whether the office should be restricted to descendants of Muhammad or chosen by merit from Muhammad's close followers. Each faction sought to justify its choice as the will of Muhammad, with the terms "Sunni" and "Shi'a" used to distinguish each.

The majority of the Prophet's companions chose from their group Abu Bakr, seeing his designation by Muhammad as leader of community prayers proof of his right to succession. The smaller Shi'a group looked to Muhammad's cousin and son-in-law Ali as the natural successor. The first three caliphs were Sunni; Ali became the fourth caliph in 656 but was killed in a war over the caliphate in 661. By this point Islamic rule had spread into the wider Middle East with the Sunni Umayyads, the first great dynastic caliphate (r. 661–750). The discord between Sunni and Shi'a further intensified, however, in 680 when Hussein (Ali's youngest son and grandson of Muhammad), was attacked and killed along with his family and supporters by the forces of the Umayyad caliph, Yazid.

As the period progressed, Sunni and Shi'a sects developed differing beliefs and practices concerning secular and religious rule. Today, Sunni Muslims remain the largest and most widespread of the Islamic sects (87–90 per cent), with Shi'a Muslims concentrated primarily in Iran, Pakistan, India, and Iraq.

Early medieval Islamic society was characterized by a mixture of religious practices, tribal customs, and, in comparison to the west, a more sophisticated network of towns, trade, and markets. The Islamic world that developed in the centuries leading up to the Crusades was economically industrious, multicultural, and learned. It was also more affluent than the west, with a flourishing agricultural economy, a stable currency, and a thriving trade in luxury goods. This is not to deny economic fluctuations or setbacks, but taken as a whole, and again in comparison to the west, the Islamic States were a more highly developed economic entity. Islamic cities and towns hosted Muslims, Christians, and Jews from across Europe, Africa, and the Middle East (Cobb 2014, 22). Islamic culture valued and contributed greatly to the gathering of knowledge and promotion of scholarship. The universal language of Arabic, combined with networks of trade, facilitated the spread of learning and the exchange of ideas. Damascus and later Baghdad became major intellectual centers, attracting scholars and providing the means by which hundreds of ancient texts were translated, studied, and disseminated.

The scholastic, commercial, and multicultural aspects of Islamic rule all served to create a society where coexistence was possible among those of differing faiths and cultures. Jews and Christians, in particular, were recognized as part of Islam's religious tradition and were accorded the title "People of the Book" or "Scripture People." By Islamic custom, Jews and Christians were given protected status (*dhimmis*, meaning "protected people") and allowed to practice their respective religions. This was not, however, without restriction, as they were required to pay a tax for the privilege, the *jizya*, and could be subject to other regulations (see "The Pact of Omar," *CR*).

Jewish Communities

The history and status of Jewish populations in the late Roman and early medieval periods is often overlooked in crusade studies, yet their development and settlement are also a part of the story. Following the Jewish Revolt against the Romans (132–135), Jews had been exiled from Jerusalem and denied any degree of autonomous rule. Jews continued to live in the region surrounding Jerusalem and other Roman provinces, but their dispersal, coupled with the non-proselytizing nature of the religion, meant that their congregated numbers remained small.

In the west, church law forbade Christians from marrying Jews or converting to Judaism. Other laws, both secular and religious, served to isolate Jews and Jewish communities from their Christian neighbors. Generally prohibited from holding land and with no centralized leadership, Jewish communities were typically urban and locally organized. Records show that Jews of this era were involved with scholarship, medicine, trade, markets, and finance (including usury, as church law did not allow Christians to lend money at interest) (Chazan, 2006, 58–62). We associate anti-Semitic violence in western Europe with the crusading era, but this was by no means its first appearance. Forced conversions and attacks on individuals and communities occurred throughout the early medieval period. Recent scholarship, however, has questioned the picture of communities under constant attack. As Jonathan Elukin proposes, "[i]nstead of persecution and suffering, it is more important to understand how and why Jews survived in societies whose dominant theology increasingly cast them in the role of deicides" (2007, 5–6).

It is generally held that Jews and Jewish communities fared better within Islamic states than under Christian rule. David Wasserstein (2012) has gone so far as to claim that "Islam saved Jewry," in particular by providing

> a new context in which they [Jews] not only survived, but flourished, laying foundations for subsequent Jewish cultural prosperity.... Along with legal near-equality came social and economic equality. Jews were not confined to ghettos, either literally or in terms of economic activity.

Jews under Byzantine rule did find themselves at times the subject of harsh legislation and forced conversions. Overall, however, their situation was comparable to, or in some cases better than, the Jews of western Europe. Despite restrictions, Byzantine Jews could be found living and working within the main cities of the empire. In addition to economic activity, Jewish society also saw developments

MAP I.I   Europe and the Middle East in the eleventh century.

in religious practices as well as a rise in poetry, literature, and other scholarly activities (Sharf 2007, vol. 4, 326–27).

ON THE EVE OF THE CRUSADES:
THE ELEVENTH CENTURY

The Islamic States

The late tenth and eleventh centuries witnessed many changes in the Islamic world. The once powerful Abbasid dynasty was in decline, which allowed Byzantium to take back previously lost territory. The gains, however, did not include the Holy Land, as this was seized in 969 by the Fatimids, an Egyptian-based Shi'a force. In 1009, the then-Fatimid caliph al-Hakim (r. 996–1021) ordered the total destruction of Jerusalem's Church of the Holy Sepulcher. Al-Hakim is described in non-Fatimid sources as being unstable, but whatever his mental state, this action, along with his persecution of Christians and Jews, had far-reaching consequences. Christian pilgrimages were effectively halted—a situation that provoked rage in the west. Rumors spread that Jews recently settled in

9

France had encouraged al-Hakim in this deed (Whalen 2011, 166–69). Many of these Jewish communities were subsequently attacked and their populations slaughtered. This violent reaction created a link between European Jews and events in the Holy Land. Thus, a pattern was set for the later anti-Semitic massacres that preceded so many crusading movements.

With the death of al-Hakim in 1021 relations between eastern Christians and Muslims improved. Byzantine builders were allowed to restore the Church of the Holy Sepulcher, and the pilgrimage trade was re-established. The peace was short lived, however, as a new force, the Seljuk Turks, arrived in the region in the 1050s. The Seljuk Turks, who originated in central Asia, had converted to the Sunni sect of Islam. They captured Baghdad in 1055 and took Jerusalem from the Fatimids in 1070. At first hostile to Jews and Christians, they became more tolerant of the multicultural nature of the region. Tales of their initial persecutions, however, had already made their way back to Christian Europe. Moreover, pilgrims of this period often found themselves caught between warring Islamic factions, which made their journeys difficult and dangerous.

Still, the period saw a steady stream of pilgrims, spurred on in part by the apocalyptic expectations of the millennium. In 1064–65 a group of at least 7,000 set out from Germany as, according to Christian tradition, the co-occurrence of the dates of Good Friday and the Annunciation would herald the end of the world (Whalen 2011, 175–80). Attacked by bands of robbers and thieving armies (in both Christian and Muslim lands), the German pilgrimage eventually reached Jerusalem, although many had suffered and perished along the way. This was one of many eleventh-century apocalyptic prophecies that continued beyond the year 1000, each promoting the popularity of pilgrimage during the century. Their stories of hardship, however, would drift back to Christian Europe, where they would spark anger and a sense of injustice (Rubenstein 2011, 11–12).

While an intermittent evil for western pilgrims, the volatile situation in the Middle East was beginning to pose a more serious threat to Byzantium.

Byzantium

On 19 August 1071, the year after the Turks had taken Jerusalem, Byzantine forces met and were defeated by the Seljuk Turks in what has come to be known as the Battle of Manzikert. Successive emperors watched the steady advance of Turkish forces into Byzantine territory, at least until the ascension of Alexius I Comnenus (r. 1081–1118).

Alexius's troubles did not begin and end with the Turks. He also faced difficulties in the north from aggressive pagan tribes, and from the west with the advance of the Normans. The Normans were descendants of Viking stock who had settled in France. Under the leadership of Robert Guiscard (ca 1015–85, *guiscard* meaning "cunning"), the Normans spent over 30 years fighting for Byzantine lands in Italy and the Balkans. Alexius had scrambled to put together a mercenary force to repel the invasions, and in doing so he initiated links with various western powers. Through a combination of force of arms, back-room scheming, and a bit of luck, Alexius was able to fend off the Norman threat. Relations between the east and the west had also greatly improved due to Alexius's overtures to an assortment of secular and ecclesiastical leaders, including the pope. The Turks remained an issue, but one that Alexius now felt he could manage, especially with the help of his new western allies.

Western Europe

The story of eleventh-century Europe is one of reform, consolidation, and vision. For many centuries, lords had ruled independently, weathering the storms of Viking and Magyar invasions and the rapaciousness of their armed Christian neighbors. Bishops and abbots directed their affairs outside the constraints of papal authority, while popes themselves did well to maintain their home ground in central Italy.

Yet this fragmented, violent society was changing. The growth of towns and cities not only ushered in greater economic stability but also created conditions for a class of burghers or townsmen. Long-distance trade generated wealth and development, putting urban centers and their merchants in touch with the markets of Byzantium and the Islamic States. Knowledge of foreign shores and the riches found there tempted some, such as the Normans, to try their luck. In Spain, Christian lords began what would come to be termed the *Reconquista*—the "reconquest"—of Muslim-held lands. Historians believe that these early incursions into Muslim Spain were spurred by economic rather than religious motivations, although later campaigns would come to develop a crusading veneer.

Within Christian Europe, kings and emperors worked to create a stronger central government and a tighter web of lordly obligations. This included control over their regional churches and churchmen; however, in this they met with opposition from a new breed of popes and their promotion of a new idea of Christendom. Prior to this period, Christendom had loosely referred to the community of the faithful. Beginning with Pope Leo IX (r. 1048–54), however, the term took on a more directorial meaning. Leo was the first of the "papal monarchs," a series of popes intent on establishing their authority over both spiritual and secular matters (Whalen 2009, 12). The most influential of the eleventh-century papal monarchs was Gregory VII (r. 1073–85). To popes such as Gregory, the establishment of Christendom meant submission of secular rulers to the papacy and its policies. Peacekeeping ventures such as the Peace of

God banned attacks on clergy and non-combatants, while the proclaimed Truce of God called for the cessation of fighting on Sundays and other holy days of the year ("Declaration of the Truce of God," *CR*). Yet Gregory went beyond these peace policies and in doing so set a precedent for the crusading popes that followed. In 1074, he made a controversial plea for a military force to "liberate" the Byzantine or eastern Christians from a "pagan race" ("Gregory VII's Call for Assistance to the Greeks," *CR*). Included in this plan was the offer of heavenly rewards and the hint of reconciling the eastern and western churches.

A state of formal excommunication between the two churches had been decreed in 1054 by Pope Leo IX and Michael I Cerularius (r. 1043–59), the patriarch of Constantinople, a declaration that would remain in place until 1965. Gregory's call to arms in aid of Byzantium was made with the aim of healing this division and paving the way for a united Christian Church. In the end, it came to naught as the pope's struggles with the German emperor dominated the final years of his rule. Yet Gregory's ambitions were not wholly in vain, for watching all this with a critical eye was the Cardinal bishop of Ostia—the man who was to become Pope Urban II, the author of the First Crusade.

THE FIRST CRUSADE

In late November 1095, Pope Urban II (r. 1088–99) gave a sermon in a field outside the French city of Clermont. The event was a church council, and here he is reported to have called for a force to free Jerusalem's Church of the Holy Sepulcher from Muslim control. This was not a pro forma plea on the part of Urban, nor was he unprepared for such a venture. Born of a noble family, he understood the minds and workings of the European military class who would respond to his call. As Pope Gregory VII's legate (a pope's foreign envoy for diplomatic missions), Urban had defended church interests against King Henry IV of Germany (r. 1056–1105). As pope, he continued Gregory's work, fighting for ecclesiastical rights and taking active steps to heal the divisions between the western and eastern churches. To this latter end he opened a dialogue with the emperor Alexius I. In March 1095, Alexius had sent an envoy to an Italian church council, where he was offered help by the pope and secular leaders (Somerville 2011, 55). Urban's call in Clermont came eight months after this council.

Evidence for Urban's Clermont sermon is taken from accounts written by churchmen ("Urban's Call for a Crusade," *CR*). The accounts themselves, however, were penned after the fall of Jerusalem to crusader forces in 1099. Because of this, historians have been wary of taking the whole of these reports at face value, citing that they may well have been embellished in light of the success of this first campaign. Yet the unequivocal call to holy war and the penitential nature of the venture are echoed in the pope's own contemporary decrees and letters: "Whoever for devotion alone, not to obtain honor or money, sets out to liberate the church of God in Jerusalem, this [act] will be counted for all his penance" (qtd. in Somerville 1972, 74).

The preaching of the crusade has been likened to an evangelical revival in terms of its drama and effect. Along with sanctioned calls to arms from bishops and clerics, there were also less-tempered appeals made by inflammatory preachers. Such was the fever whipped up by these itinerant speakers that many were recruited who had no business taking up arms. Military activity was generally restricted to the landed classes and their military retinues, but the message was strong and the Church struggled to control the poorest members of society from joining in the cause. This produced results that were both ludicrous and tragic. The German cleric Albert of Aachen (*fl.* 1100) poured scorn on the popular response, calling this gathering of people on foot "stupid and insanely irresponsible." He further cited an incident in which a group "claimed that a certain goose was inspired by the Holy Ghost and a she-goat was filled no less with the same, and they made them their leaders for this holy journey to Jerusalem" (Edgington 2013, 41). The story may be the exaggeration of an annoyed cleric against what he saw as an ignorant peasantry, but if so, it is one that was repeated both by the abbot and historian Guibert of Nogent (ca 1064–ca 1125) and the Jewish chronicles of the period.

The most successful of the popular preachers was a man known as Peter the Hermit (ca 1050–1115). Peter was a charismatic figure who might have been preaching the crusade even before Clermont. Revered and ridiculed in turn, he was instrumental in raising the first crusader force, which is known today as the Peasants' or People's Crusade. Traditionally this movement has been portrayed as a violent, disorganized mob of men, women, and children from the lower orders. Historians of late, however, have had another look at the composition of Peter's forces, with many concluding that although at times undermined by its large non-combatant contingent, it also had a "strong knightly element" (Riley-Smith 2014, 49). Whatever its faults, this was not simply a rabble of destitute peasants with pitchforks.

Yet the People's Crusade is a movement associated with infamous acts and ultimate failure. A large part of its failure has been attributed to the eagerness of its participants to set out in April 1096, four months before the official start date and at a time of famine. In all, nearly 30,000 embarked for the Holy Land under the direction of Peter and a knight called Walter Sans Avoir (d. 1096). Peter and Walter arranged to meet at Constantinople before heading south with their armies to Jerusalem. Walter arrived at the Byzantine capital in July, although not without some conflict due to his forces' pillaging in Hungary. Peter's army, less organized and with fewer military leaders, traveled from France to the Rhineland, where off-shoots of this force turned on the Jewish communities settled there.

BOX I.3   *The Crusades and Attacks on Jewish Communities*

We have seen how Jewish communities in France were attacked following the destruction of the Church of the Holy Sepulcher in 1009. Persecution of Jews began again in France soon after Pope Urban's call, but the most brutal attacks took place in the German Rhineland. Here Jewish communities in the cities of Cologne, Mainz, Trier, and Worms were subject to pillage and mass slaughter at the hands of crusading bands following in the wake of Peter the Hermit ("Albert of Aachen on the Peasant's Crusade" and "Solomon bar Samson on the Massacres of Jews," *CR*).

Both Christian and Jewish sources tell of the most persistent and cruel persecutor, Count Emich of Flonheim, describing him as a man who "pulverized God's people like the dust in threshing" (qtd. in Hallam 2000, 69). While Christian fanaticism accounts in part for the actions of Emich and his kind, we must also acknowledge that this was a large force lacking in supplies and with a long journey ahead of them. The Jewish communities of the Rhineland were relatively prosperous, being composed primarily of craftsmen, traders, and moneylenders. As such, they were a tempting target.

The Church itself was pledged to protect Jews, and many bishops of the region tried to intervene, offering shelter against both crusaders and hostile locals. Most bishops, although initially helpful, gave way to overwhelming numbers and fled their posts. Both Jewish and Christian sources provide grim details of the subsequent massacres, noting that many of the victims, seeing no way out, opted for suicide. Tales of husbands killing their wives and of mothers slaying their children rather than letting them fall prey to the crusaders make for harrowing reading. The destruction of synagogues, the desecration of holy books, and the wholesale pillaging of Jewish quarters for valuables and coinage accompanied the butchery.

Prior to this episode, evidence suggests that Jewish settlements in the region were thriving and that there was at least a degree of integration and tolerance between them and their Christian neighbors. The attacks of the first crusaders must, therefore, have come as a terrible surprise. The fact that so few fled in the face of the threat may be a sad indication of the faith that many Jews put in both their Christian neighbors and the Church, although Jewish chronicles also relate instances of some Christian townspeople offering a hiding place for their Jewish friends

(Elukin 2007, 76, 81–84). None of the armies that attacked Jewish communities made it to the Holy Land, or even to Constantinople. Emich and his forces fought and plundered their way to the borders of Hungary, where they were defeated and disbanded.

Later crusades would prompt further attacks, yet despite the appalling outcome of these events, Rhineland Jewish communities survived, rebuilt, and continued.

Peter's army arrived in Constantinople on 1 August and settled with Walter's forces on the outskirts of the city. Unable to afford the market prices, Peter's followers began to raid the suburbs and countryside, prompting the emperor to ferry them across the Bosporus on 6 August. It was at this point that what little unity there was in Peter's force further disintegrated. The army split in two, consisting of a French contingent and another made up of German and Italian crusaders. The two forces were soon locked in a game of one-upmanship raiding. Anna Comnena (1083–ca 1153), the daughter of the emperor, recorded how they plundered and murdered both Turks and eastern Christians, neither knowing nor caring to know the difference ("Anna Comnena's *Alexiad*," CR). Successful pillaging of the French outside the sultan's capital of Nicaea goaded the German and Italian forces into capturing a castle. Unfortunately, there was no water supply within its walls and after eight days of thirst they surrendered to the Turks. When the French heard of this defeat, they went out to meet the Turkish forces and marched straight into an ambush. The bulk of the army perished, while the rest were killed in a Turkish raid on their camp. Peter the Hermit survived, but with no crusade left to lead he had little choice but to return to Constantinople and wait for the official force.

The armies of the First Crusade began to arrive at the gates of Constantinople in late autumn of 1096. The crusade combined the leadership of seven senior nobles and a papal legate, Bishop Adhemar (d. 1098). Adhemar had been a knight before taking holy orders, and Urban envisioned that he would serve as the crusade's ecclesiastical leader. The seven nobles brought with them their own armies, as well as leagues of non-combatants. These included wives, children, servants, and other retainers. The total number of this force continues to be a subject of debate, but it may have been as many as 50,000 armed men and just as many civilians.

The leaders of the crusade undoubtedly considered material gains when they took the cross, but this did not lessen their sense of pious duty. Crusaders might have differed over who was to lead and benefit most from the campaign, yet all were in agreement on its spiritual purpose and goal. It was not, however, a vision shared by the Emperor Alexius. This religious war with its emphasis on penance and, at times, fanatical devotion was not the measured military response he had expected. One can only imagine his growing horror as wave after wave of crusaders looted their way to Constantinople and, once there, demanded to be received as heroes.

Alexius's experience of the People's Crusade had made him wary of the conduct of crusaders, and so, to avoid further pillaging in his own lands, he arranged for these new crusaders to be given supplies and an armed escort from the moment they set foot on his territory. The emperor also demanded that each of the nobles swear an oath of loyalty (fealty) to him. This included the promise to surrender any captured lands previously under Byzantine rule. Although this act of homage was unpopular with the crusade leaders, it was not an unreasonable request. Pope Urban had, after all, envisioned that the western armies would join up with the Byzantine forces under the supreme command of Alexius. The emperor, however, had no intention of leaving Constantinople and, having gained their oath, he quickly ferried each leader and their entourage across the Bosporus. By late spring 1097, the western force had gathered at the Byzantine military camp of Kibotos, just 25 miles from Nicaea, the proclaimed capital of the Turkish sultan Kilij Arslan I (r. 1092–1107).

Without Alexius, the First Crusade had no designated military commander. Each of the seven nobles had his own expectations of the crusade and where they stood with regard to its leadership. Count Raymond of Toulouse (ca 1041–1105) was the most formidable of the senior crusaders in terms of wealth, lands, and the size of his army. Bishop Adhemar had been assigned by Urban II to accompany the count, and this also lent authority to his role. Raymond's nearest rival was the Norman prince Bohemund of Taranto (1050–1111). Bohemund was the son of Robert Guiscard and had fought with his father against the Byzantine Empire. Included in Bohemund's forces was his nephew, Tancred of Hauteville (d. 1112), who commanded the prince's southern Italian army. Godfrey of Bouillon (d. 1100) had been an ally of the German emperor in his conflicts with the papacy, but the calling of the crusade had caused him to switch sides. With his brother Baldwin of Boulogne (d. 1118), Godfrey departed for Constantinople, bringing with him a combined force from Germany, Lorraine, and Lotharingia.

A crusade leader who found himself on the right side from the outset was Count Robert II of Flanders (1065–1111). Robert's father, Robert I, was a friend and supporter of Alexius and had earlier sent the emperor 500 of his knights to help with his fight against the Turks. His son now wished to carry on this family tradition with the help of his Flemish army. Robert was joined by his kinsmen, Count Stephen of Blois (1045–1102) and Duke Robert of Normandy (1054–1134). Duke Robert was the son of William the Conqueror while Stephen of

Blois was Duke Robert's bother-in-law. The last member of this elite group was Count Hugh of Vermandois (1057–1102). Hugh was the brother of the then-king of France, Philip I (r. 1060–1108). King Philip had been excommunicated for remarrying without first divorcing his wife, and it seems that Hugh's crusade was meant, in part, to ease his difficulties with the papacy.

The crusade force headed out toward Nicaea, as this was a city that could not be left in Muslim hands if they were to proceed. Its ruler, Kilij Arslan, was away dealing with a rival sultan, and the crusaders were besieging the city in late May when the sultan arrived back with his force. In the ensuing battle, Kilij Arslan suffered a resounding defeat and was forced to flee, leaving behind his wife, children, and treasure inside the city. The crusaders continued their siege, lobbing the heads of enemy prisoners over the walls and seeing their own captured comrades' heads flung back. This went on for weeks, until the crusaders sent word to Alexius asking for help. Alexius stepped in with ships and supplies but, unknown to the crusaders, negotiated a surrender with the Nicaeans, taking the city for himself. Afterwards the emperor offered the crusade leaders gifts and praise, but many were not pleased with the outcome.

As for the Muslims of the region, it would appear that they did not recognize the crusaders as a force separate from Byzantium and certainly not one that was intent on conquest in its own right. Muslim leaders were accustomed to seeing western soldiers in the employ of a Byzantine emperor, many of whom were to be found stationed on the borders of Turkish territory. Muslim rule was also fragmented at the time of the First Crusade. The sultanates of Rum (Kilij Arslan's region), Syria, and Palestine were fiercely contested lands fought over by would-be sultans and minor warlords alike. This was to be the crusader's pathway to Jerusalem.

Alexius returned to Constantinople, fearing revolt if he was away for too long. In his place he offered his general Tatikios as a guide, along with a small Byzantine force. The crusaders, having split into two forces, began their march south through Anatolia. It took many months for the crusaders to pass through this region and on to Antioch. In that time they suffered the heat of summer, hunger, thirst, disease, not to mention hostile inhabitants who decimated lands and settlements along their route. Many of the knights' warhorses died, and the crusader leaders were forced to ride oxen and donkeys, while sheep, goats, and dogs carried their provisions.

The challenges of maintaining unity with so disparate an army became evident when Baldwin of Boulogne abandoned the crusade altogether to carve out his own territory. In southwest Anatolia he met with sympathetic Armenian Christians, who offered support, augmenting his military force. There then came an invitation from Thoros, the prince of Edessa, to come to the city and become his heir. Baldwin arrived on 6 February 1098 and was duly adopted. By 9 March, Thoros was dead, killed by a mob, and Baldwin stepped into his place. This was the first crusader state, and while it was a betrayal to the aims of the crusade, Baldwin's new position enabled him to offer supplies to the main army while serving as a barrier between the Turks and Antioch. The episode was, however, an early warning to Byzantium, as Baldwin made no effort to fulfill his oath to return to the emperor the lands he had gained.

The main crusader army had arrived outside Antioch on 21 October 1097. Antioch was a well-fortified city encircled by a wall several miles long with hundreds of towers. The only way to subdue such a formidable target was by means of a lengthy siege. Lacking equipment and manpower to blockade the city effectively, the crusaders settled in for a long wait. Over seven months, disease, starvation, and the winter cold took their toll. Supplies would occasionally arrive from Byzantium, but not enough for 40,000 men-at-arms. Crusaders were dying, and many were deserting (including Peter the Hermit, who was caught and brought back). In February, Tatikios left the siege with the excuse of searching out and bringing back supplies. He never returned. Stephen of Blois, who had boasted to his wife that he had been made "commander-in-chief" of the crusade, also deserted the day before the city fell.

In the end, Antioch succumbed not to military might but through the betrayal of one of its tower captains. Bohemund and his Norman soldiers gained the captain's tower and opened the gates of Antioch to the crusaders on 3 June 1098. Unfortunately, they soon found themselves besieged by a reinforcing Muslim army, and it was at this point that the crusaders realized just how well they had brought the city to the edge of starvation. Desertion continued, and of those who escaped, some were able to join Stephen's retreating entourage. On his way home Stephen had sought out Alexius, marching south with his army, to tell him that the situation was hopeless. Alexius had enough to do defending his newly retrieved lands in Anatolia and so turned his army around and headed back to Constantinople. That, for the crusaders of Antioch, was the final straw. In their eyes Alexius had broken his side of the oath of allegiance/fealty by failing to provide aid to his vassals, forfeiting his right to any lands and spoils that might come their way.

As the hope for military aid waned, it was replaced by prayers and visions. A cleric, Peter Bartholomew (d. 1099), claimed to have found the Holy Lance, the spear that had pierced Christ's side. Encouraged by the relic, the crusaders chose to launch an attack, and although superior in numbers, internal divisions had led many Muslim leaders to withdraw, granting the crusaders a surprising victory ("Anselm of Ribemont on Events at Antioch," *CR*). The crusaders had learned their lesson on marching through desert terrain in high summer and decided to postpone their journey to Jerusalem until November. During this time, disease (possibly typhoid) took hold of the city and many died, including

Bishop Adhemar. This was not good news for the unity of the crusade. Adhemar had kept the crusade leaders in check, resolving disputes and reminding them of their crusading vows. Without him, divisions widened ("Ralph of Caen on Divisions among the Crusaders," *CR*). Riley-Smith characterizes the leadership of the crusade as one "run by committees and assemblies," concluding, "not one of the princes was strong enough to dominate the others" (2014, 62–63).

These committees met and argued throughout the winter, pressured by the rank and file of the crusade to start the march to Jerusalem. The first to leave was Raymond, who was given the title of commander-in-chief. This was in consolation for the loss of Antioch to Bohemund, who remained in the city. Although not without its hardships and perils, the crusaders' passage was eased by fighting between the Turks and the Fatimid dynasty of Egypt. The Fatimids had just that year ousted the Turks from many of the cities of Palestine, including Jerusalem. Their misreading of the western army now advancing on their newly acquired territory is shown by their offer to the crusaders of an alliance against the Turks. The offer was refused, and the crusaders, numbering around 14,000, arrived outside Jerusalem on 6 June 1099.

The crusaders built siege towers, a battering ram, and several trebuchets to hasten the city's fall. The Fatimid governor of Jerusalem, Iftikhar al-Dawla (*fl.* 1099), had expelled the Christians from the city, lest there be a repeat of the treachery seen at Antioch. He also ordered the poisoning of the wells outside the walls. His hopes lay primarily with the Egyptian relief force, which was expected within four weeks. The crusader attack began on 13 July, and for two days it met with fierce resistance. On 15 July, however, Godfrey of Bouillon's forces succeeded in bringing their siege tower up to a point in the wall just east of Herod's Gate. There they entered the city and opened the Damascus Gate. Others gained entry through a breach in the walls made by a battering ram. The crusaders poured into Jerusalem.

The sacking of fallen cities and the slaughter of their inhabitants was common practice for both Christian and Muslim forces. Historians disagree on the numbers killed by the crusaders, with figures ranging from 3,000 to 10,000. The expulsion of Christians by al-Dawla and the influx of refugees seeking safety make it difficult to offer any clear conclusions, although both Muslim and Christian sources offer passionate accounts of the massacre. While phrases such as "men rode in blood up to their knees and bridle reins" are clear exaggerations, there is little doubt concerning the brutality of the crusaders toward the besieged population ("Raymond of Aguilers on the Fall of Jerusalem," *CR*). That the slaughter carried on over two days is a testament to both unbridled and calculated cruelty. Many defenders fled to the Temple Mount, but were hunted down and killed. Those that took refuge in the al-Aqsa mosque were initially offered protection but were killed the next day. Jews who had barricaded themselves inside the synagogue were burned alive. This was not, however, a total massacre. Al-Dawla and others took refuge in the Tower of David, later negotiating with Raymond for safe conduct to the coastal city of Ascalon. A letter dated some nine months after the fall by elders of the Karaite Jewish community describes how they collected ransom money to release Jews and Jewish relics being held in Jerusalem by the crusaders. Not all captives were freed, however. Al-Rumayli, a well-known Muslim religious scholar, was ransomed for 1,000 dinars but was stoned to death when the sum failed to materialize (Friedman 2001, 151).

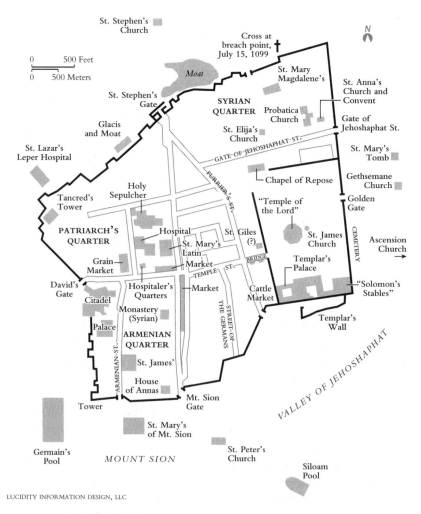

LUCIDITY INFORMATION DESIGN, LLC

MAP I.2   **Jerusalem, 1099–1187.**

What astounds and horrifies modern sensibilities is the violence of the crusaders coupled with their evident religious devotion. One eyewitness account from a crusade chaplain exclaimed, "Indeed, it was a just and splendid judgment of God that this place should be filled with the blood of the unbelievers" ("Raymond of Aguilers on the Fall of Jerusalem," *CR*). There was no contradiction in the eyes of the crusaders or their supporters; they sincerely believed they were instruments of God's will. They were also soldiers, and medieval warfare was a brutal enterprise.

With Jerusalem under control, there remained the question of who would rule the city. The title of king of Jerusalem was offered first to Count Raymond, but he refused, saying he would not wear a crown where Christ had worn a crown of thorns. The post was then offered to Duke Godfrey, who, on acceptance, tempered his status with the less exalted title of "Advocate of the Holy Sepulcher." The new ruler of Jerusalem soon faced a test of his leadership when the Egyptian relief army arrived at the port city of Ascalon. However, the Egyptians were quickly defeated by Godfrey, who met them with a force of around 10,000 on 12 August.

At this point many of the crusaders went home, having fulfilled their vows. Given the original number of 50,000 (not counting non-combatants), the First Crusade had lost two-thirds of its fighting force. True, some had deserted, but many more were the victims of disease, starvation, and the hazards of warfare. New recruits would have to be found. Pope Urban II died on 29 July, before news of the victory reached him. He was succeeded by Paschal II (r. 1099–1118), who praised the crusaders while threatening excommunication to deserters and those who had not yet set out for the Holy Land ("Letter of Pope Paschal on the Capture of Jerusalem," *CR*). Stephen of Blois was compelled to take up the cross again along with other, less illustrious deserters. Many who had taken the vow in the first flush of Urban's call also responded and were joined by eager new recruits. It is believed that this "third wave" of the First Crusade was as large as the first official force. The armies began their trek to Constantinople in the autumn of 1100 and were ferried across the Bosporus by an anxious Alexius. There were three main armies, but each met with a disastrous end at the hands of Muslim forces (including that of Stephen, who died at the second battle of Ramla in May 1102). Crusaders would continue to take the cross, but the region would not see another major crusade for the next 47 years.

As for what the Muslim population made of the fall of Jerusalem, there is, as Niall Christie notes, a problem with the sources:

> the earliest sources for the period give us some insight into how the Frankish attacks were perceived among some poets and religious scholars, but those works are far less useful in helping us to understand the reactions of the politico-military elites, who were most able to mount, opposition to the crusades. (2014, 21)

21

Some chronicles provide more detail, but these were written decades after the First Crusade and reflect the anti-crusade sentiment of a later period. There is, however, 'Ali ibn Tahir al-Sulami's *The Book of the Jihad* (*CR*; Christie 2015). Al-Sulami was a religious scholar whose work, written in 1105 and read in public, was to serve as a unifying call to *jihad* against the Franks (Christie 2014, 23).

What is clear is that the fragmented state of Islamic rule was a significant factor in the absence of a united response to the crusaders. Wars raged between Sunni and Shi'a factions, while the political wrangling of the Turkish warlords blinded them to the crusade agenda. Some, as has been noted, may not have even recognized the Crusades as a western phenomenon, seeing them as an extension of Byzantine expansion. Others viewed the crusaders as just another contender for territory and were willing, if necessary, to make alliances with them against their Muslim neighbors. This was the situation that characterized the first half of the eleventh century, and it lasted just long enough to allow the crusaders to settle into their newly conquered lands.

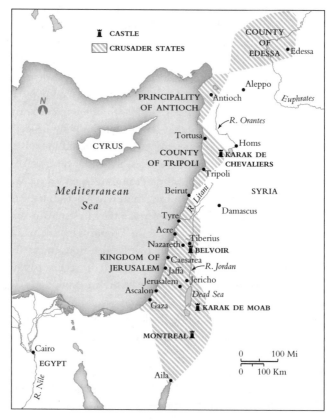

MAP I.3   **The Latin States (ca 1102 to 1140).**

THE CRUSADER STATES

The crusader regimes were not pre-planned. Pope Urban II had no strategy with regard to the governing of territories once Jerusalem was gained. In the years that followed the taking of Jerusalem, the crusaders forged four Latin states—the kingdom of Jerusalem (1099), the counties of Edessa (1098) and Tripoli (1102), and the principality of Antioch (1098) (Barber 2012, xiii–xiv). The whole region would become known as the "Levant" (the east), or "Outremer" (the land beyond the sea). It was a tenuous occupation given the crusaders' reduced numbers, and while there were periodic reinforcements from Europe, these were never enough to ensure a stable core. The crusaders were, however, fortunate that the region enjoyed a certain degree of economic prosperity. The crusader lands were second only to Egypt in productivity, while coastal towns served as ports for a lucrative luxury trade. Moreover, the fragmentation of Islamic power facilitated alliances and treaties based on political expediency rather than religious ideology.

The situation was not, however, without difficulties. The crusaders struggled to expand eastwards, and Aleppo and Damascus remained firmly in Muslim hands. Harried from the north and west, the fledgling Crusader States also faced periodic attacks from Egyptian forces using the port city of Ascalon as their base. The conquest of the coastal region and its ports became a major concern for the Latin kings of Jerusalem. They were aided in part by smaller crusades, such as those led by King Sigurd of Norway (1109–10), Fulk V of Anjou (1112 and 1128), and the doge of Venice (1123–24). While many of the surviving crusaders from these campaigns returned home afterwards, the Italian city states of Venice, Genoa, and Pisa set up commercial centers in the captured ports. In this they were welcomed, as the original crusade had no navy. By 1153, all of the coastal ports were under the control of the Crusader States.

Through the early years of the Crusader States, the leadership of this coastal conflict fell to the kings of Jerusalem. Upon Godfrey's death in 1100, Daimbert (1050–ca 1107), the newly arrived papal legate, attempted to bypass secular rule and establish himself in Godfrey's place. This alarmed the nobles, who offered the rule to Godfrey's brother, Baldwin. This was the same Baldwin who had left the crusade to create the first of the Latin States, the County of Edessa. Daimbert himself was banished by Baldwin, ending any future challenge from churchmen for rule of the Crusader States. Under Baldwin's leadership (1100–18), the first of the military orders, the Knights of the Hospital of St. John of Jerusalem, was recognized by the papacy. This was a religious order of fighting knights who had taken monastic vows of poverty, chastity, and obedience. The founding of the Knights Templar followed in 1120. Both played vital roles in the maintenance and defense of the Crusader States. More, however, will be said of these and other military orders in Chapter Three.

The Crusader States were independent of any European leader or realm. The Kingdom of Jerusalem was given honorary prominence, but each territory developed its own governance, laws, and customs based on what its leaders had been accustomed to back home. The rulers of these states offered lands, money, and protection in exchange for military or governmental service, just as it would have been done in Europe. The highest military and government positions were, not surprisingly, reserved for the crusaders themselves, but the general administration was undertaken, with some alterations, by local Muslim and/or eastern Christian officials. Amid the military skirmishes and political wrangling life went on, although it is fair to say that the society created by the Latin Kingdoms was neither truly integrated nor strictly segregated.

THE SECOND AND THIRD CRUSADES

As Outremer neared the midpoint of the twelfth century, its states were as stable as any other in the region. All this changed, however, in 1144 with the fall of Edessa to the Turkish warlord Imad ad-Din Zengi (r. 1127–46). Zengi had no grand plan to undermine Latin rule; in 1128 he had gained the city of Aleppo and for the next 16 years focused his attacks primarily on the Muslim rulers of Syria and Iraq. The fall of Edessa, however, was the first major setback to the crusaders, and the shock of its loss prompted calls for a second crusade.

The Second Crusade

The call came from Pope Eugenius III (r. 1145–53) in the same year as his election, 1145. The crusade's guiding light, however, was Bernard, abbot of Clairvaux (ca 1090–1153). Bernard and his fellow Cistercian monks preached the crusade throughout Europe, officiating at the taking of crusader vows and urging with personal letters those who hesitated ("Letter of Bernard of Clairvaux," *CR*). Leading the Second Crusade were two monarchs: King Louis VII of France (r. 1137–80) and King Conrad III of Germany (r. 1138–52). Louis was accompanied by his wife, Queen Eleanor of Aquitaine (1122–1204), and Conrad by his nephew, the future emperor Frederick Barbarossa (r. 1155–90). Not all made it to the Holy Land. Flemish and English forces took the cross, but in choosing the sea route they were lured into a campaign against the Moors by the king of Portugal. Afterwards some settled in the region while the rest continued their journey. Saxon crusaders, looking to conflicts closer to home, had asked and were granted permission to transfer their vows to fight against the pagan Wends of northern Europe, a venture that became the first of the Baltic Crusades.

Conrad arrived at Constantinople in September 1147, but he received minimum help from Emperor Manuel I (r. 1143–80). Byzantium had troubles of its own, not least of which was a treaty with the neighboring Turkish sultan, made to check the advances of Roger II of Sicily (r. 1130–54). Without waiting for Louis, Conrad led his army into Anatolia where his force divided, a small section of the army taking the coastal route within Byzantine-held lands, while the bulk of the force followed the way of the first crusaders into enemy territory. Near Dorylaeum, this latter force was met by the Turks and suffered a crushing defeat, with nearly the whole of the army destroyed. The survivors, who included Conrad, retreated to Nicaea and awaited the French crusaders.

Louis, meanwhile, had stalled, as he had had to send messages back home asking for additional funds. His army then pillaged and plundered their way to Constantinople, where the king and queen were briefly entertained by the emperor before crossing the Bosporus. Louis met up with Conrad in Nicaea, and together they marched down the safer coastal route. Conrad fell ill on the journey, however, and was sent to Constantinople to recover. On the march south, Louis's army was subject to raids and attacks from the Turks. To hasten the journey, Louis and other high-ranking crusaders boarded ships in January 1148, leaving the greater part of the army to continue on foot. The plan was to meet in Antioch, but the abandoned army was waylaid by Turks, with very few surviving to complete the journey.

Raymond, prince of Antioch (ca 1115–49), had counseled Louis to attack Aleppo. Its ruler, Zengi,· had recently been murdered by one of his servants, leaving the territory in the hands of his son, Nur al-Din (r. 1146–74). Louis, however, did not trust Raymond, and a heated disagreement sprang up between them. Matters were not helped by his wife Eleanor's support of Raymond (who was her uncle) or by her threat to end their marriage should Louis not take Raymond's advice. There were subsequent rumors of an affair between Eleanor and her uncle, but no proof of adultery came to light (Bennett 2001, 22–23).

BOX 1.4   *Women on Crusade*

The inclusion of women on crusades was generally discouraged by the Church. Crusading was a penitential act, and the Church felt that women would distract crusaders from their holy vow. Nevertheless, women served various crusading roles both at home and on campaign. Even before the First Crusade, Mathilda, Countess of Tuscany (1046–1115), had supported a designated group of clergy to develop a theology of holy war for Pope Gregory VII (Riley-Smith, 2014, 29-30; Hay 2008, 15).

Women were known to accompany their crusader husbands, sometimes taking their children with them. Many, especially those of higher rank, took the cross alongside their husbands and were thus considered equal, at least in terms of their penitential status. As for military leadership, this was clearly a male prerogative, although there is evidence of elite women taking part. Ida of Austria and Alice of Blois, for example, each led their respective territory's crusaders to the Holy Land.

In a letter to the archbishop of Canterbury, Pope Innocent III stated that women of wealth were allowed to lead crusaders to the Holy Land at their own expense. While this almost certainly was not meant to include battle situations, it does show that women could take an active role in the gathering and directing of troops (Rousseau 2001, 38–39). Elite women could also play a political part while in the Holy Land, as evidenced by the negotiations with Saladin conducted by Queen Sibylla of Jerusalem and those of Queen Marguerite for the release of her husband, King Louis IX (Friedman 2001, 128). Day-to-day administrative and diplomatic duties were, in addition, carried out by queens and noblewomen of the Crusader States.

Women of property who remained at home also had crusade responsibilities. Evidence shows that many actively participated in the recruitment of soldiers and the raising of funds. Crusading was very much a family-led affair, and marriage alliances could create and spread traditions of taking the cross from one family to the other via its women. Churchmen and secular rulers sought to legislate for the protection of a crusader's family and their holdings. Unfortunately, in the absence of their husbands, some women found themselves facing legal or military action that could result in the loss of their lands and titles. Loss of life was also a real danger: "William Trussel's wife was murdered six weeks after he left on crusade in 1190 and ... Peter Duffield's wife was strangled while he was on the Fifth Crusade ..." (Riley-Smith 1995, 72). Single women of the Church also had a domestic role to play, with nuns regularly offering prayers for the Crusades. We also know that advice was sought from the abbess Hildegard of Bingen by Count Philip of Flanders prior to his journey to the Holy Land, and that Saint Birgitta of Sweden wrote arguments supporting the fourteenth-century Baltic Crusades (Hodgson 2006, 1289).

Women of the lower ranks were generally taken on crusades as cooks, water bearers, nurses, servants, and washerwomen (a job that included the periodic delousing of the army). Prostitutes also made up a portion of any female crusade contingent. As for actual warfare, there are accounts of women on the battlefields ferrying much-needed water and supplies. In some instances they were paid for these duties out of the spoils of the campaign (Caspi-Reisfeld 2001, 96). There are also stories of women taking a more direct role in combat, often in siege warfare (Hallam 2000, 142, 183). Both Christian and Muslim sources tell of women warriors in battle at the siege of Jerusalem in 1099, and later during the Third Crusade. In a passage entitled "Frankish Women of Peace and War," Saladin's secretary, Imad ad-Din, recorded:

> Another person to arrive by sea was a noblewoman who was very wealthy. She was a queen in her own land and arrived accompanied by five hundred knights ... she paying all their expenses.... They rode out when she rode out, charged when she charged, flung themselves into the fray at her side, their ranks unwavering as long as she stood firm. (Gabrieli 1984, 206–7)

One of the most interesting accounts of a woman crusader is that of Margaret of Beverly, who assisted in the defense of Jerusalem in 1187—a battle in which she was wounded and later captured ("Thomas of Froidmont: The Adventures of Margaret of Beverly, A Woman Crusader," CR).

Generally, the sources are more critical than favorable when detailing the lives of women on crusade. Yet whether welcomed or vilified, these women had an important part to play in the crusading movement.

Louis met up with Conrad in Jerusalem, and together they worked through the spring of 1148 to regroup and reinforce their armies. It was decided to attack Damascus, then an ally of the kingdom of Jerusalem. With the zeal of new crusaders, they dismissed the standing treaty and set out with hopes for a quick conquest. The siege of Damascus, however, was a catastrophe. Unable to construct siege machines, under constant fire, and with word of reinforcements on the march from Aleppo and Mosul, the crusaders felt they had no choice but to retreat. The humiliating march back was accompanied by relentless Turkish assaults, which further reduced what was left of the army. Once back in Europe, blame was attributed to several factors, including the Byzantines, the treachery of Jerusalem's King Baldwin, and, according to Bernard of Clairvaux, the sins of European Christians ("Analyses of the Second Crusade," CR). From start to finish, the Second Crusade was an utter failure for the west. It did, however, achieve the unification of previously fragmented

Muslim states. Under Nur al-Din, the fight against the crusaders also took on a more religious tone. Prior to this, the concept of *jihad*, or holy war, had rarely been used. Now it became a rallying cry and a means by which Nur al-Din could support his claim to leadership. Within the Muslim-held regions there also emerged an Islamic counterpart to penitential war, with Paradise offered to those who died in battle against the Franks.

The fortunes of the Crusading states varied widely during this period. The kingdom of Jerusalem, in particular, was often undermined by dynastic instability and the shortage of fighting men. Yet Nur al-Din initially held back a full attack on the Crusader States, concentrating instead on the acquisition of Shi'a Egypt, a territory that was not only wealthy but also strategically necessary if there was to be any hope of ousting the Franks. In 1164, Nur al-Din sent his Kurdish general, Shirkuh, to invade the region. Traveling with the general was his young nephew, Salah al-Din, or Saladin as he became known in the west. Not long after their arrival, the Fatimid vizier was assassinated and Shirkuh ruled in his stead. Now both Egypt and Syria were under Sunni control. Unfortunately, Shirkuh, overweight and hard-living, died of a heart attack just two months after gaining his prize. His nephew Saladin (r. 1169–93) succeeded him, quickly consolidating his position, reorganizing Egypt's defenses and bringing the government firmly under the rule of his family, the Ayyubid dynasty.

The Crusader States looked on with horror at these events. In 1169, King Amalric of Jerusalem (r. 1163–74), with Byzantine naval support, failed in his final attempt to take Egypt, and each blamed the other for the loss. Appeals were made to the pope for a new crusade, but European kings were too busy with domestic politics to come to his aid. Amalric died in 1174, leaving his 13-year-old son, Baldwin IV (r. 1174–85) to succeed. The succession of a minor was dangerous enough in the medieval period, but Baldwin had contracted leprosy, an illness that would lead to an unstable rule and divisive plotting by those with a claim to the throne. Baldwin died in March of 1185, and his nephew and heir, the nine-year-old Baldwin V, died the following year. Hostilities then broke out between two rival claimants, Baldwin V's mother, Sibylla (r. 1186–90), and her sister Isabella (r. 1190–1205).

This, of course, was of great benefit to Saladin, whose good fortune was augmented by the death of Nur al-Din. Despite having no dynastic claim to Nur al-Din's realm, Saladin came to be recognized as the rightful ruler of Syria and Egypt. His biographers recorded how he experienced a religious epiphany at this point in his life and how, by this, he was accorded the mantle of leader of *jihad* against the Franks ("Baha ad-Din's *Life of Saladin*," *CR*). Yet Saladin's ambitions were not unopposed: there were legitimate heirs to contend with, as well as dangers from Shi'a Muslims. One of the best known of these was the Nizaris or Assassins, a Shi'a group that carried out political assassinations, most often against Sunni leaders.

If Saladin needed an excuse for launching an attack against the crusaders, this was provided by Reynald of Châtillon (ca 1125–87). Reynald was a rash and brutal man. In spite of the treaty with Saladin, he made a habit of raiding Muslim caravans that passed too close to his territory, and one of those was said to have been a pilgrimage band on their way to Mecca. He was ordered by King Guy (r. 1186–94; husband of Queen Sibylla) to cease these activities and reimburse Saladin, but Reynald refused, saying he was not subject to the rule of Jerusalem. Saladin responded with an invasion across Galilee. The military orders raised a force of 450 in response and met up with the Muslim army of 7,000 at the springs of Cresson in May 1187. Only four knights survived the battle. Through the rest of May and June, Saladin gathered a force of around 30,000 from the north and south. The crusaders could have waited behind the walls of their castles and cities for Saladin to run out of supplies and disperse, but they chose instead to meet the Muslims with their own force of what is estimated to be an army of 16,000 to 20,000. This included the armies of King Guy of Jerusalem, Count Raymond of Tripoli, and Lord Reynald of Châtillon, in addition to those of the military orders and lesser lords.

Details of the battle of Hattin are provided in Chapter Three. Suffice it to say here that it was a decisive defeat for the crusaders ("Imad ad-Din on the Battle of Hattin," CR). The crusaders' sense of loss was compounded by the capture of the True Cross, a relic that had been brought from Jerusalem to aid the battle. Of those that survived, the 200 or so Templars and Hospitallers were executed and the surviving infantry were enslaved. Saladin's secretary Imad ad-Din records that after the battle Saladin offered Guy a cooling drink in hospitality, but he did not allow him to pass the cup to Reynald. With the memory of Reynald's raids no doubt still in his mind, Saladin unsheathed his sword and personally executed the lord of Transjordan ("Islamic Accounts of the Treatment of Prisoners," CR).

The battle of Hattin robbed the Crusader States of their best soldiers. One by one, the Christian-held coastal towns and cities fell to Saladin's forces. Finally, after less than a week's siege, Saladin entered Jerusalem. He chose 2 October for his entry, the anniversary of the Prophet Muhammad's Night Journey. In negotiations with Queen Sibylla and her advisors, Saladin offered the Christians of the city safe passage to the coast if they could pay their ransom. Many were ransomed, some were pardoned, and the rest were enslaved. Saladin removed the cross that had been placed on the Dome of the Rock and reinstated the al-Aqsa mosque. The Church of the Holy Sepulcher was not defaced, but its western clergy were replaced with Syrian priests.

The Third Crusade

The outcome of Hattin and the subsequent loss of Jerusalem profoundly stunned the Christian west. It is said that Pope Urban III (r. 1185–87) died upon hearing the news. His successor, Gregory VIII (r. 1187), issued a papal bull, *Audita Tremendi*, calling on new crusaders to take up the cross ("Letters on the Fall of Jerusalem," *CR*). This was the beginning of the Third Crusade. Of the major players, Richard (the "Lionheart"), duke of Aquitaine, was the first to join in November of 1187. By January, Richard had been joined by his father, King Henry II (r. 1154–89), and King Philip of France (r. 1180–1223). Frederick Barbarossa, emperor of Germany, completed this prestigious company in March of the same year.

Many historians see the Third Crusade as the height of the movement in terms of ideology, organization, and strategy. Pope Gregory VIII equated the success or failure of crusading with the spiritual standing of Christian Europe as a whole. Western Christians were encouraged to identify with and feel responsible for the movement. On the practical side, these later crusades were more carefully planned, preached, and coordinated, with dedicated financial backing from Church and state taxes. Tactically, future crusades favored sea routes and, at times, destinations other than Jerusalem.

To pay for the Third Crusade, Henry II imposed a new tax across England, the Saladin Tithe. This 10-per-cent income tax on non-crusaders was also taken up by Philip of France, although with less success ("Taxations and Regulations for the Third Crusade," *CR*). Henry, however, died in the summer of 1189, and his eldest son, the duke of Aquitaine, succeeded him as Richard I (r. 1189–99). The participation of three of the most powerful kings of Europe was a major boost to the crusade, but it also created difficulties. These were the representatives of kingdoms that, until recently, had been at war with one another. Trust and camaraderie were in short supply, and each knew that they could not afford to remain in the Holy Land even if they were successful.

Frederick Barbarossa was the first to set out in May of 1189, taking an overland trek and arriving in Asia Minor in February 1190. The army made good progress under Frederick's experienced leadership, but this came to an abrupt halt on 10 June when the emperor drowned while crossing the river Saleph. With the death of their leader, much of the army simply turned for home. Of those that continued, few survived the journey to the Holy Land. King Philip arrived at Acre in April 1191. Richard did not appear until June, having stopped off first to conquer Cyprus (which had been under Greek rule). Under their combined efforts, Acre surrendered on 12 July. After a division of spoils, Philip, ill and with troubles at home, left the crusade.

Negotiations followed the surrender of Acre. Saladin agreed to provide a ransom for the Muslim garrison and to return the True Cross that had been captured at the battle of Hattin. As was the custom, hostages (thought to be around 2,700) were given to Richard to ensure the deal. The deadline for payment, however, was delayed and Richard, impatient to move onto Jaffa, ordered their execution in sight of Saladin's forces (see "Islamic Accounts of the Treatment of Prisoners" and "Accounts of the Third Crusade," *CR*). Richard then marched on to Jaffa with his force of 15,000. Once there, the crusaders could either set up a base from which to attack Jerusalem or simply use the city as a stop en route to Ascalon, where they could cut off Muslim supplies from Egypt.

The 80-mile march was, in any case, a master class in military logistics. With the sea to their right, the crusaders were accompanied by Richard's fleet, which supplied arms and food. Arriving in Jaffa, there was disagreement over whether to attack Ascalon or Jerusalem. Meanwhile, Saladin began to dismantle both Ascalon's walls and all fortifications between Jaffa and Jerusalem. He also destroyed the wells and cisterns around Jerusalem. As Richard's forces marched toward Jerusalem, it became increasingly clear that without fortified bases and reliable sources of water, it would be difficult to advance, much less stage a successful siege. Despite proceeding to within a day's march of Jerusalem, Richard knew that even if he was able to take the city, he could not stay to hold it. Word from home confirmed that Philip was busy appropriating Richard's lands and that his own brother John (r. 1199–1216) was a willing ally to the French king's aims. The army was ordered to retreat in January 1192, much to the disgust of the rank-and-file crusaders who felt that Jerusalem had been denied them at the eleventh hour. Richard had also fallen ill during this period—another reason, perhaps, for his willingness to consider alternative schemes.

In the end, the Third Crusade was determined by diplomacy rather than warfare (see the "Case Study" in Chapter Four). In early September 1192, a three-year truce, known as the Treaty of Jaffa, was finally settled. The agreement allowed the crusaders the coastal territory between Jaffa and Tyre. They and western pilgrims were also granted access to the Church of the Holy Sepulcher and other Christian sites within the region. While some crusaders made their way to Jerusalem soon after the signing of the treaty, Richard chose to abstain from the pilgrimage, reportedly saying that he "could not consent to receive by the courtesy of the infidels that which he could not obtain by the gift of God" ("Accounts of the Third Crusade," *CR*). Richard finally sailed for home in October 1192, and Saladin's field army was soon disbanded. Saladin himself fell gravely ill at the beginning of the new year and died in early March 1193.

The implications of the Third Crusade were wide-ranging and complex. While failure to recapture Jerusalem was an obvious disappointment, the crusaders were able to secure vital coastal territory, thus maintaining the kingdom of Jerusalem (albeit a realm that lacked its titled city). The Third Crusade also altered the religious tone, organization, and financing of such ventures, ushering in a greater use of diplomacy and treaties alongside military conflict—a situation that would come to characterize Christian–Muslim relations in the Levant for the remainder of Ayyubid rule.

As for Saladin, constant campaigning against the crusaders had exhausted his military and financial resources. Moreover, the strains of war had revealed weaknesses in his command and family relations. At his death, Saladin's territories were divided among his Ayyubid relations. Without even a recognized first among equals, this sort of political system encouraged instability, as the more ambitious heirs sought to expand their lands and power. It also had the effect of watering down the notion of military *jihad*, as Ayyubid rulers were content to make alliances with both Christians and Muslims. Trade between Muslims and Christians also flourished under Ayyubid rule, and this, coupled with the more conciliatory atmosphere, instigated a new era of east–west relations (Christie 2014, 95).

Armed conflict was still a major feature of the period with each new arrival of zealous crusaders, yet these encounters would be moderated by a wider understanding of the "other," and an eye toward compromise as well as conquest.

A NEW CRUSADING VISION: AT HOME AND ABROAD

Pope Innocent III

The driving force behind the early-thirteenth-century crusades was Pope Innocent III (r. 1198–1216). One of the great administrative popes of the medieval period, Innocent took a direct interest in the planning and preaching of crusades. Under Innocent, crusades were to be a group effort. The landed classes were the obvious targets in raising crusading armies, but Innocent went further to instigate a means by which those deemed unfit for military service could still provide and pay for a substitute. This was the beginning of the indulgence. Penance involved the confession of sins followed by acts of suffering to cleanse the soul in preparation for heaven. Crusade indulgences, as developed by Innocent III, saw crusading itself as the penance, rather than the suffering associated with the experience (acts of merit, in effect, replacing the suffering). In the case of those who could not go on crusade, all or part of their time in purgatory could be lessened with the purchase of indulgences (with the strength of the indulgence dependent on the amount paid).

Clergy were called upon to offer full support to the crusade movement and to show solidarity in the bearing of its financial burdens as well as its spiritual obligations. To this end, Innocent established the first direct papal tax, which had the express goal of raising funds for the Crusades ("Letters of Innocent III," *CR*). Detailed instructions on the urgency of this collection were provided along with orders to supply "an empty trunk" in every church for the collection of alms in aid of crusading. The faithful were to be reminded each week at mass to contribute for the remission of their sins, while clergy were allowed to accept "the gift of alms for the performance of penance." Support for the Holy Land also extended to the merchant class, as seen in 1198 when Innocent wrote to the traders of Venice forbidding them under threat of excommunication to "have anything to do with the Saracens either directly or indirectly." They were also to contribute to the crusading cause lest they find themselves under "divine condemnation" ("Letters of Innocent III," *CR*). Such interference was typical of Innocent's manipulation of secular resources to bring about his spiritual aims.

At the same time, Innocent promoted crusades within the Iberian peninsula and eastern Europe. The definition of crusading was further widened to include perceived home-grown threats to Church and papacy (with some exhibiting strong political motivations). Outside Innocent's influence, the period also saw examples of popular crusading in the form of the Children's and Shepherds' Crusades.

The Fourth Crusade

Soon after assuming the papal throne in 1198, Innocent called a crusade to retake Jerusalem. This is known to us as the Fourth Crusade of 1204. Yet despite careful organization and clear incentives, neither sufficient funds nor crusaders materialized. Historians may argue over the reasons for Innocent's failure to implement a successful crusade, but it is clear that he did not fully understand the contributions made by its secular participants. Crusading was, first and foremost, a family enterprise, and efforts by Innocent to direct diverse nobles, their households, and vassals on how, where, and when to embark simply did not work. The starting date of March 1199 came and went, with a second call having to be made at the end of the year.

Two nobles, Count Thibaut of Champagne (1179–1201) and his kinsman Louis, count of Blois (1172–1205), had taken the cross at a tournament in November 1199. Tournaments, with their emphasis on chivalry, might well have helped to promote the crusading cause. Both nobles came from a family with a long crusading history. They were joined in early 1200 by Count Baldwin of Flanders (1172–1205), and together they sent an envoy to Venice to negotiate transport for the crusade. The envoy included Geoffrey of Villehardouin (ca 1160–1213), who was to write an account of the crusade's preparations, deeds, and aftermath ("Accounts of the Fourth Crusade," *CR*). Without the ready funds afforded to kings, the crusade leaders needed to broker a loan. An agreement was signed with the Venetians for the construction of a fleet large enough to transport 33,500 crusaders as well as their horses and provisions. Even for the mercantile Venetians this was a massive order, and they were forced to put much of their trading activity on hold to complete it. All this was agreed without the knowledge of Innocent. No previous pope had played a role in logistical arrangements, and the crusaders saw no reason to consult Innocent on this occasion. The crusaders began to arrive in Venice in June 1201, but the final tally was only 13,000 men—over 20,000 short of the promised number. The lack of coordination between the secular leaders and Innocent must account, in part, for this ruinous outcome.

Popular accounts of the Fourth Crusade have tended to cast the Venetians as the villains of the affair—luring the gullible crusaders into a deal that they could not possibly meet with the ultimate aim of taking control of the venture. This judgment is, however, undeserved, as the Venetians had as much to lose as the crusaders (Byrom and Riley 2013, 124). But whatever the expectations and failings, Venice also needed to find a swift solution. That solution materialized in the person of the city's doge, Enrico Dandolo (r. 1193–1205). As the Venetian chief magistrate, Dandolo negotiated an agreement with the smaller crusading force. The debt would be suspended in exchange for the crusaders' help in taking the city of Zara, a long-standing enemy of Venice, located on the Dalmatian coast. The leaders felt they had no choice but to agree, although this was an attack on a Christian city whose ruler, King Emeric of Hungary, had himself fought as a crusader. Innocent sent letters threatening excommunication should they go ahead with the plan, but the letter was not shared beyond the crusade leaders. In protest, some crusaders abandoned the venture before it sailed in October 1201. The rest arrived at the walls of Zara on 11 November, and the city surrendered 14 days later. The spoils were then divided between the crusaders and the Venetians. Those crusaders who had refused to take part in the attack left for Europe with their followers in the spring of 1203. This included Simon of Montfort (1150–1218), who would later lead the Albigensian Crusade. The remainder stayed on in the hope that the eventual fulfillment of their crusading vow would diminish the pope's disapproval.

In the absence of any papal representative, the crusade became increasingly subject to political intrigue and financial obligations. The original plan to free Jerusalem via Egypt was consequently sidetracked, ending with the sack of Constantinople. How and why the crusaders allowed it to happen is still a matter of debate. However, as Zara's plunder proved insufficient to pay off their debt, it could well be that the crusaders looked to Constantinople as a possible solution. In Constantinople, Alexius Angelus had been deposed by his uncle, Alexius III.

Alexius Angelus promised the crusaders that if they would help him regain his rightful title he would pay off their Venetian debt. The crusaders made their way to Constantinople, placing Alexius Angelus on the throne with comparative ease in July 1203. The money, however, was not forthcoming, and the crusaders were still waiting in January 1204 when Alexius was deposed by a rival who took the name of Alexius V. Alexius Angelus was imprisoned and then murdered in early February. Under attack by this new ruler, and lacking supplies, the crusade leaders met and decided that the only way out was by taking the city itself. Constantinople had repelled invasions for 900 years, but on 12 April 1204, its walls were breached and the inhabitants subjected to a three-day sack of the city ("Documents on the Sack of Constantinople," *CR*).

The Fourth Crusade ended at Constantinople. Rather than moving on to Egypt and then Jerusalem, the crusade leaders instead founded the Latin Empire of Constantinople. Its first emperor, Count Baldwin of Flanders, was crowned in May 1204. East and west had finally been united, although not as Urban II and his successors had envisioned. Innocent had initially forbidden the taking of the city, and writing afterwards he lamented that the Byzantines now detested the Latins "more than dogs" ("Documents on the Sack of Constantinople: Letters of Innocent III," *CR*). The sack of the city severed relations between the eastern and western churches, creating bitter memories and divisions that survive even today. The Latin Kingdom itself would last only until 1261, leaving a much weakened Byzantium to struggle on until its final stand against the Ottoman Empire in 1453.

Crusading within Europe

Under Innocent's direction, the period also saw the rise of crusades within Europe itself. His first "political" crusade was leveled against Count Markward of Anweiler, a German imperial official who held Sicily and parts of southern Italy. Believing the papal territory and his own authority to be at risk, Innocent called a crusade against Markward, whom he referred to as "another Saladin," in 1199. The death of Markward in 1203 removed any need to continue the campaign, yet a precedent for political crusading had been set.

Innocent also instigated the first crusade against heretics, the Albigensian Crusade of 1208. The Albigensian heretics were named for the city of Albi in southern France; they were also called Cathars (their heresy Catharism). Heresy—that is, any belief or practice that deviated from accepted Christian doctrine—was considered a serious threat to the Church. It was also viewed by Innocent as a dangerous impediment to the eastern crusades, as the failure of previous ventures was thought to stem, in part, from Europe's spiritual shortcomings. Efforts were therefore made to bring heretics back into the Christian fold, with the aim of persuading them to denounce their beliefs. In southern France, within the region of Languedoc, specially trained preachers were employed to deal with the Albigensians. Those who did not recant could, however, be handed over to the secular authorities for execution.

The origin of Albigensian or Cathar belief is unclear, although it may have had its roots in the tenth-century Bogomil church found in certain regions of the Byzantine Empire. This was a dualist belief that held that there were two gods or divine forces—one of the spiritual world, believed to be good, and the other of the evil, material world. The aim of humankind was to break free from the material world and join with the spiritual god. What distinguished the religion as a heresy, rather than a pagan belief, was its link to Christianity. Although Christ was believed to be a god, Albigensians held that the Catholic Church had distorted his true nature as well as his teachings by claiming he was "made man." All this was more than enough to condemn them in the eyes of the Church ("Bernard of Gui's Manual for Inquisitors," *CR*).

At the time of the crusade there were less than 1,000 *perfecti* (Cathar religious leaders) in the region. Of these, many were women (69 per cent of those who can be identified), and overall, 35 per cent came from the noble class (Riley-Smith 2014, 190). Given their high profile, the Albigensians of Languedoc caught the attention of the pope and church officials. As early as 1199, Innocent had requested the aid of King Philip II of France, offering the possibility of confiscated lands and crusade indulgences (Hallam 2000, 229). Nothing came of this request, as Philip was embroiled in a dispute with King John of England. Moreover, little was done by those nearer to the problem. Count Raymond VI of Toulouse had, in fact, been excommunicated for not dealing with the heretics of his region. It is not known whether he was a believer himself, but he was a sympathizer, especially when it served his secular aims. Preaching campaigns were stepped up, including the efforts of Dominic of Calaruega (ca 1170–1221), the later founder of the Dominicans. The Dominicans (as well as the contemporary Franciscans) differed from monks in that they were not cloistered and thus could engage directly with the population through preaching. Known for their devotion to poverty, they represented church reform and were seen as a welcome contrast to the more wealthy clergy.

In January 1208, the papal legate, Peter of Castelnau, was murdered by one of Count Raymond's vassals. Raymond denied all involvement but did nothing to apprehend the perpetrator. Innocent was furious at the news and immediately called a crusade against the heretics, likening them to the Saracens (Sibly and Sibly 1998, 31). The crusade's European location allowed for wider participation, but the term of service was set at just 40 days—a decision that would result in the extension of the campaign over many years. Recruitment carried on into 1208, and although King Philip declined to join, many powerful French nobles heeded the call. Among these was Count Simon IV of Montfort. Last seen leaving the Fourth Crusade in protest over Zara's fall, he was recognized as the crusade's leader.

In an attempt to save his title and lands, Raymond enacted a public penance at the abbey of St. Gilles in June 1208. He also took the cross against the heretics, although at the time some questioned his sincerity. The city of Béziers was then besieged by the crusaders, and despite pleas by their Catholic bishop to give up its heretics, the inhabitants refused, seeing the conflict more in political than religious terms. The walls of Béziers were formidable, and a stalemate seemed likely until, on 22 July, these fortifications were breached. As the papal legate for the crusade, Arnold of Cîteaux (d. 1225), recorded: "Our forces spared neither rank nor sex nor age.... Thus did divine vengeance vent its wondrous rage" (Hallam 2000, 232). The walls of Béziers probably encircled fewer than 10,000 inhabitants, of whom heretics made up a small portion (between 2 and 7 per cent). The extent and brutality of the city's sack were such, however, that all settlements and fortifications between Béziers and Carcassonne were abandoned or surrendered to the crusaders as they continued their march.

The Albigensian Crusade continued on and off for the next 20 years. The required 40 days of service per year made it difficult, however, for Simon of Montfort and others to make good their gains. Law and order broke down in the scramble for lands, and cruelties were inflicted on heretic and Christian alike. In 1226 the new king of France, Louis VIII (r. 1223–26), led another crusade to the south of France, resulting in the Treaty of Paris (1229) and the submission of the nobles of southern France. The Albigensian heresy would continue up to the early fifteenth century, when it would finally be driven out, not by the sword, but by the workings of the Dominican-run Inquisition. The Inquisition's purpose was to investigate an individual's heretical beliefs and practices and, if possible, bring them back into the Church. Those who did not recant were to be handed over to the secular authorities for execution, as church law did not allow for this ultimate punishment. Heresy increased overall in the later years of the medieval period, with Innocent's formal crusade against the Albigensians serving as a model for the suppression of other prohibited religious sects. Such ventures, however, would involve the Church in the often grubby business of secular politics and pragmatic rather than compassionate policies.

The failure of the Fourth Crusade, and the heightened fervor brought about by the Albigensian, Iberian, and Baltic campaigns, served to create, in some regions of Europe, popular responses to crusade rhetoric. The spread of Innocent's message that crusading was everyone's concern might also have encouraged periodic outbursts of popular piety. Amid this background of sharpened religious awareness, Innocent planned his second overseas venture, the Fifth Crusade.

BOX 1.5   *The Children's and Shepherds' Crusades*

The popular crusading movements of the thirteenth and early four-teenth centuries differed from those of the earlier period in that their participants rarely managed to reach the Holy Land. The prevailing choice of travel by sea put crusading beyond the monetary reach of the common people (Riley-Smith 2014, 196). No longer able to tag along with organized, funded campaigns, those of the poorer classes struggled to express their piety through crusading, although efforts were made by some.

The so-called Children's Crusade of 1212 was such a mission. The event itself is poorly documented, with no first-hand narrations ("Accounts of the Children's Crusade," *CR*). Moreover, it became one of those historical episodes transformed by myth and legend. Accounts nearer in date to the event are sketchy, while many of those written later embellish the story, mythologizing its participants and their exploits. Even the well-known tale of the Pied Piper is thought to have some link to the memory of the Children's Crusade (Dickson 2015, 10–11, 141–43).

It is believed that the crusade was the result of a penitential proces-sion held in Chartres in May 1212. Pope Innocent had called for preach-ing and penitential processions throughout Christian Europe to support crusaders fighting in Spain. Stephen of Cloyes was a young shepherd boy thought to have been inspired by the Chartres procession. Returning home, he claimed that he had been accosted by Christ, who entrusted him with a letter for the king of France. Somehow Stephen persuaded thousands of followers to accompany him to St. Denis, outside of Paris, to deliver the letter. This crowd of 15,000 to 30,000 included children, but also youths and adults. The sources disagree on whether the letter was delivered when the marchers reached their destination, but many of the participants seem to have gone home soon afterward and we hear no more of Stephen. It can be argued that this was not a crusade, and certainly not a children's crusade. Nevertheless, it does demonstrate the intensity of the popular piety that animated the population during the period, as well as the power of Innocent's vision of a godly Europe in support of the Crusades.

Dickson (2008, 82–84) proposes that some moved on from St. Denis to Cologne, igniting the next youth-led movement. While a num-ber of historians have questioned the theory, the sources tell of a boy (or youth) called Nicholas of Cologne who, with thousands of followers, young and old, made his way to Italy with the aim of crossing the sea to the Holy Land. Once in Italy the group split up, each seeking out a port from which they could embark. Transport, however, was not forthcoming (nor did the sea part, allowing them to walk, as some accounts claim was their expectation). Many had no choice but to turn back, and they had a difficult journey home. Later accounts tell how some were offered sea passage but were deceived and sold into slavery upon reaching Muslim-held lands. There are also accounts that assert that many never attempted the journey home but chose instead to settle where they could in Italy and other regions. Again, one has to be careful, as many of these stories were written well after the event and include details that cannot be verified.

Another popular thirteenth-century religious movement was the Shepherds' Crusade of 1251. This event was the direct result of the defeat of King Louis IX's (r. 1226–70) Egyptian crusade. With Louis imprisoned in Egypt and the crusade in ruins, there arose a crowd of shepherds and other humble folk from the north of France who expressed a desire to join their defeated king in the Holy Land ("Matthew Paris on the Shepherds' Crusade," CR). Their leader, known as the Master of Hungary, carried with him a letter purporting to be from the Virgin Mary endorsing the crusade. The shepherds made a penitential march to Paris, handing out crosses and offering indulgences. There they were met by the king's mother, Blanche of Castile (1188–1252), and offered support and supplies.

At this point, the movement became more radical and violent, with a strong anti-clerical and anti-Jewish agenda. They attacked and murdered scholars, clerics, and townspeople of Orléans. Queen Blanche, when she heard of the riot and destruction, called for the group to be "excommunicated, seized and destroyed." Arriving in Bourges, they attacked the Jewish synagogue and its members, but the master himself was killed by one of the townsmen and the crusaders dispersed. Attacks and rioting continued, however, throughout the region. The crusade marched as far south as Bordeaux, where, unable to gain admittance to the city, they were threatened with annihilation by the sixth earl of Leicester, Simon of Montfort (ca 1208–65, not to be confused with the Albigensian Crusade leader). The chronicler Matthew of Paris records that at this point they "became like sand without lime" and "dispersed in all directions" ("Matthew Paris on the Shepherds' Crusade," CR).

Popular crusade movements would continue throughout the medieval period. In 1309, the "Crusade of the Poor" saw thousands of people leave their homes. Only a small portion, however, managed to leave Europe, and these were sent to Rhodes to aid in the Hospitallers' consolidation of their new headquarters. A second Shepherds' Crusade, more violent than the first, emerged in the spring of 1320. The movement followed the Great Famine of 1315–17 and was the result of preaching for a new crusade to the Holy Land. The stated destination was the Holy Land, but the movement quickly degenerated into anti-Jewish and anti-clerical riots. As the movement traveled south, John XXII (an Avignon pope, r. 1316–34), understandably felt the need for immediate action. He excommunicated the participants in June. Many were subsequently killed in battle or simply starved, while others who were captured were sentenced to mass hangings. A smaller contingent escaped to Spain, where they carried on attacks against Jews until dispersed by the king of Aragon.

Similar to their fight against heretics, these wayward crusades compelled the Church and papacy to rely on secular authority to quell the resulting violence, drawing ecclesiastics further into the politics of the day. As for the movements themselves, their crusading goals were merged with, and at times eclipsed by, a wider protest against elites and outsiders (clergy, nobles, and Jews) who did not, in their opinion, adhere to the religious and political policies they espoused.

The Fifth Crusade

Pope Innocent called for a Fifth Crusade in his emotive encyclical *Quia maior*. This included the assurance that those unable to take the cross could gain full penance by providing for a crusader to go in their place. Partial penance was also extended to those who provided funds ("Decrees of the Fourth Lateran Council," *CR*). Innocent was not to see the results of his careful preparations, however, as he died suddenly of a fever in July 1216, but his successor, Honorius III (r. 1216–27) was eager to continue the work. Honorius dispatched preachers, but for once the response from France was sparse. The Albigensian Crusade, which offered penance for only 40 days' service, met the ends of many French nobles, while interactions involving internal and external enemies kept others fully occupied. The call was answered for the most part by Germany, with Hungary, Italy, and the Netherlands also making a contribution. King Andrew of Hungary (r. 1205–35) was the first to set out with his army in 1217, but he did not remain long or accomplish much in the Holy Land, returning home in January 1218. Crusaders from the Netherlands, Germany, and Italy sailed into Acre over the spring, and by the end of May the full force had sailed south and was gathered at the mouth of the Nile. The city of Damietta, their first target, was well defended, and the siege dragged on for a full year before the city fell.

In the summer of 1219, the camp was visited by Francis of Assisi (1181–1226), the founder of the Franciscans. Although a supporter of the Crusades, Francis preached a "spiritual" crusade, believing that conversion of the Muslims would result in a swifter and more lasting result. In 1219, he arrived at the camp of the Fifth Crusaders with the aim of converting the Egyptian sultan, al-Kamil (r. 1218–38). Francis's conversion efforts, however, were politely refused by the sultan, who then sent him on his way unharmed.

Over the course of the siege, warfare and disease ate away at the crusading forces, yet there was also a steady stream of replacements from Europe. Al-Kamil sued for peace in 1219, offering the entire kingdom of Jerusalem, with the exception of two Transjordan fortifications, in exchange for the evacuation of the crusaders from Egypt. King John of Jerusalem (r. 1210–25) pushed for the acceptance of the offer, but he was overruled by the Templars, Hospitallers, and Cardinal Pelagius (d. 1224).

What made both sides offer and reject such an all-encompassing settlement was the fear, on the part of al-Kamil, and the hope, on the part of the crusaders, of the forces of Frederick II (1194–1250), ruler of Germany. Frederick had taken the crusader vow upon his succession to the German throne in 1212. The grandson of Frederick Barbarossa, he had spent his youth in southern Italy in the learned and multicultural environment of the Sicilian court. Nicknamed *Stupor mundi*—the "Wonder of the World"—Frederick was well versed in both arts and sciences and was fluent in Arabic. Pope Innocent had died believing that Frederick would honor his crusading vow and not seek to rule both Sicily and the German Empire together. Frederick, however, had other ideas and made it clear that he would not commit himself or his army to the crusade until he was guaranteed the imperial title by the new pope, Honorius III. Neither, however, was willing to compromise.

Back in Egypt, al-Kamil upped his offer of the kingdom of Jerusalem by proposing to rebuild its dismantled walls, return all prisoners, and hand over the True Cross, which had been lost at the Battle of Hattin. Again, the offer was rejected, as those in control felt that if they could conqueror Egypt, then Jerusalem would follow. Within a week, on 5 November 1219, Damietta fell to the crusaders. The scene that greeted them as they entered the city, however, explained its capitulation: "Not only were the streets full of the dead, but in the houses, in the bedrooms, and on the beds lay the corpses" ("Oliver of Paderborn on the Fifth Crusade," *CR*). Famine and disease had decimated all but 17 per cent of the city's population. Divisions between Cardinal Pelagius and King John then deepened, and the crusade ground to a halt. Some historians speculate that had the crusaders pushed on to Cairo, they might have succeeded in taking Egypt. Instead, they waited for over a year and a half for Frederick's forces to arrive, while al-Kamil worked steadily to reinforce his position in the Nile Delta.

In November 1220, Pope Honorius anointed Frederick II as emperor. The first of Frederick's crusaders arrived in Egypt in May 1221, but without Fredrick himself. Rather than wait, Pelagius decided to attack al-Kamil's fortifications at Mansourah. King John warned them of the folly of the plan, but he was threatened with excommunication by Pelagius if he did not support it. The crusaders camped opposite the site on 24 July, but their position was subject to flooding. As July turned to August, the river began to rise. Muslim forces then blocked and flooded the Christian camp, forcing them to surrender. While al-Kamil was advised by some to kill his Christian captives, the sultan thought it better to facilitate their retreat. The crusade leaders were treated with civility, and food supplies were provided to the army. The agreement posed by al-Kamil was that all crusaders would leave Egypt in exchange for an eight-year truce. Thus the Fifth Crusade ended in what could only be seen as a shameful defeat, and one without even the consolation of the True Cross, which, although offered, had never been in al-Kamil's possession.

The Crusade of Frederick II

Blame for the crusade's outcome was swift and fell on two individuals. As leader of the enterprise, Pelagius was criticized for rejecting a settlement that would have seen Jerusalem back in Christian hands. Fury was also directed at Frederick II who, six years after his initial crusading vow, had yet to take one step toward the Holy Land. Frederick's wife Constance had died in 1222, and in November of 1225, with the pope's support, he married Yolande of Jerusalem (1211–28), the daughter of King John. Afterward, Frederick proclaimed himself king of Jerusalem, much to the anger of his new father-in-law. Frederick's marriage and title redirected the crusade focus from Egypt to Jerusalem. More Germans made their way to the Holy Land, both as pilgrims and crusaders. The period also saw the growth in lands and influence of the Teutonic Knights, a German military order that had been founded in 1190 and militarized in 1198. Frederick's crusade sailed without him in the summer of that year as the emperor had fallen ill. Pope Gregory IX (r. 1227–41) lost patience and excommunicated him on 29 September. The emperor's claim to Jerusalem was further threatened by the death of his wife in childbirth in April 1228. She had given birth to a son, Conrad (1228–54), who now by right was the king of Jerusalem, leaving Frederick as regent. The emperor, however, had no intention of taking the title of mere regent and maintained his claim to the crown. When Frederick finally did sail for the Holy Land, in June 1228, he did so as an excommunicated and unsupported crusader with only a tenuous claim to the Latin Kingdom of Jerusalem.

There were difficulties also for the sultan of Egypt, al-Kamil. After the victory at Mansourah, relations between the sultan and his brothers broke down, forcing him to seek other alliances, including one with Frederick II. Egypt was still under threat, this time from both the west and Ayyubid rivals. In 1226, al-Kamil sent an envoy, Fakhr-ad-Din, to Sicily to offer the same settlement he had placed before the leaders of the Fifth Crusade. This time the terms were accepted: "Frederick would get his little crusade and a kingdom in Jerusalem: al Kamil would get peace from the Franks and, he believed, a powerful regional ally" (Cobb 2014, 210). Yet by the time Frederick arrived in Acre (September 1228), the alliance had lost some of its original shine. Al-Kamil's brother had died, leaving him in a stronger position. Frederick was forced to renegotiate the treaty, this time with less favorable results, although Jerusalem would still be handed over to the Christians. Many crusaders, including the Templars and Hospitallers, refused to acknowledge Frederick as their leader, and his arrival in Jerusalem on 17 March 1229 was met with a subdued welcome. After a quick self-coronation in the Church of the Holy Sepulcher, Frederick left Jerusalem the next day and returned to Acre ("Frederick II on His Taking of Jerusalem and Sibt ibn al-Jawzi's Recording of the Event," *CR*). There he faced an angry reception. The Templars and Hospitallers were especially aggrieved at Frederick's actions, refusing to bow to his authority ("Responses to Frederick II's Crusade," *CR*).

News came soon afterward that Frederick's father-in-law had invaded his lands in Sicily, requiring his immediate return home. The emperor quietly slipped out of Acre on 1 May. Yet even as he was waiting to board his ship, butchers from the local market mocked him, pelting him with offal. Behind him Frederick left an undefended Jerusalem in the hands of squabbling Christian factions. In the remaining years of his life, he would be absolved, and then excommunicated again by Gregory IX. A crusade was called against Frederick in 1239 and repeated in 1244 by the pope's successor, Innocent IV (r. 1243–54). Neither proclamation came to fruition before Frederick's death in 1250, but each served to normalize the calling of internal political crusades alongside those to the Holy Land.

Skirmishes between competing Christian factions continued in the Levant up to 1239, when the treaty of Jerusalem expired and the city was again placed under Muslim control. From 1240 to 1241, two campaigns, known collectively as "The Barons' Crusade," achieved, via alliances and treaties, the return of Jerusalem and other holdings in Galilee. These gains were facilitated by the confusion and conflict that followed the death of al-Kamil in 1238 and the ensuing struggle of succession among his heirs—a situation that allowed the crusaders to play one side against the other to gain their objectives.

This game of alliances, however, did not end well. In 1240, the crusaders had made a pact with Damascus against the Egyptian ruler al-Salih (r. 1240–49), who countered this partnership by recruiting the Khwarazmians. This brutal Turkish mercenary force of around 10,000 had originated in central Asia but later settled in Anatolia and Mesopotamia. In the summer of 1244 they spilled into the region surrounding Jerusalem, raiding and looting. With no defensive walls, Jerusalem was an easy target, and in July of that year the city was sacked and its inhabitants massacred. In October 1244, the crusaders and their Syrian Muslim allies came face to face with the forces of al-Salih and his Khwarazmian mercenaries at the site of La Forbie, near Gaza. The battle demonstrates the political reality of the time and region, for while some may have felt unease in fighting alongside those of a different faith, such alliances were not only common but also necessary to achieve each faction's aims. Unfortunately for the crusaders and their Muslim allies, the battle was a total defeat, with casualties similar in scale to those suffered at the Battle of Hattin. The surviving crusaders limped back to the coastal towns, sending their pleas to Europe for aid, lest they lose their last foothold in the Holy Land.

CRUSADES ACROSS THE BORDERS

Leaving the east for the moment, we turn to two crusading theaters on the borders of medieval western Europe. These were the Iberian *Reconquista* (reconquest) and the northern crusades against the pagans of the Wendish and Baltic regions.

The Reconquista

At first glance, there are many facets of the Iberian *Reconquista* that resemble the more traditional eastern crusades. These were campaigns supported by the papacy, often meriting penitential rewards, that were fought against Muslim forces with the aim of taking their territory. They differed, of course, in that there was no Holy Land to gain, but rather a strong belief among Europeans that Islamic Spain had once been Christian and should be Christian again. The peninsula had fallen to Muslim forces in 711, and a thriving society had developed over the centuries that included Christians and Jews (*dhimmis*). As "People of the Book," they were allowed to live and work within the Muslim region. Before the eleventh century, elite non-Muslims could rise to positions of authority and wealth, and persecutions were rare (Catlos 2014, 8; "Moorish Laws" and "Christian Laws," *CR*).

Alliances could be fluid during this period, with so many Islamic *taifas*, or sub-states, and a range of Christian rulers looking to expand their holdings. The legendary "El Cid" (Rodrigo Díaz de Vivar, ca 1043–99) was hailed as a model Christian warrior in later narratives, although in truth he fought for both sides before creating his own independent kingdom ("Chronicles of the Cid," *CR*). The initial success of such warriors, and tales of the treasures and lands to be gained, attracted others, including those beyond the Pyrenees. By the 1170s the participants' efforts were being equated to a penitential act by the Church. Later, Urban II would repeat this offer at the same time as he was conferring it on crusaders heading to the Holy Land.

When the strategic city of Toledo fell to King Alfonso VI (r. 1065–1109) in 1085, the event united many of the Muslim-held *taifas*, and a call for aid was made to the north African Almoravids. Not only did this fierce Berber force defeat Alfonso's army in October but their ruler, Ibn Tashfin, also went on to bring the dissident *taifas* under his rule. The year 1147 saw the arrival of the Almohads, a reformist faction from the southern region of Morocco. By 1172 they were the undisputed Islamic force in the peninsula, and they gained a decisive victory over King Alfonso VIII of Castile (r. 1158–1214) in 1195. Yet allegiances in this volatile region could still be defined as changeable. There are examples of Christian nobles fighting for the Almohads and Muslims fighting within the forces of Christian rulers. Crusade rhetoric continued nevertheless, with Pope Innocent III offering indulgences for those willing to take the cross to Spain.

In 1212, the combined armies of Castile, Aragon, and Navarre defeated the Almohads ("Alfonso VIII's Report on Las Navas de Tolosa," *CR*). By 1250 only Granada remained, but it would be over 200 years before Islamic Spain was finally conquered by Queen Isabella I of Castile (r. 1474–1504) and King Ferdinand II of Aragon (r. 1479–1516). Under their leadership, Granada surrendered on 2 January 1492. The fall of this last Islamic capital was followed by the expulsion of Jews and Muslims from the realm ("Expulsion of the Jews from Spain" and "Abu Abdilla Mohammed on the Expulsion of the Muslims," *CR*). The crusade was then carried on from the Iberian peninsula into and across north Africa, reaching as far as Tripoli in 1510. Documents from the period show that the reconquest of the Holy Land was considered a real possibility. The fall of Constantinople to the Ottomans in 1453 had shaken the Christian west, and many feared they would spread across north Africa and into Europe. Tripoli, however, remained the extent of Spain's eastward crusade, although we have evidence that at least one individual looked westward for Jerusalem's gain. Christopher Columbus (1451–1506), writing in 1492, believed that the gold and spices recovered from the passage to the east (via the west) would enable the recovery of Jerusalem. He might also have hoped to engage the Mongol Khan, mistakenly believed by Europeans to be receptive to Christianity, in the fight against the Ottomans (Delaney 2012, 39–40). His vision was not, however, realized.

Despite obvious parallels, the Iberian Christian–Muslim conflict never gained the same status as the eastern crusades. Historians have speculated why, with some suggesting that these were, in essence, secular campaigns of a kind that would have taken place with or without papal support. That many were clothed with crusading rhetoric and accorded papal privileges perhaps reflects more their role in church and secular propaganda than any manifestation of crusading purpose or zeal. An exception to this argument is the final campaign of Ferdinand and Isabella. Here was a campaign that had foreign participation and an uncompromising crusading agenda, one that resulted in the expulsion of Muslims and Jews and an ultimate, if unrealized, goal of recapturing Jerusalem.

The Wendish and Baltic Crusades

The northern crusades have been described as a massive land seizure in the guise of a conversion mission. Taking place outside the borders of Christendom and involving pagans rather than Muslims, these were not campaigns against those who directly threatened the papacy or the Church. The regions had, for the most, no Christian past, and therefore nothing to provide a sense of recovery (except for very recent Christian settlements and past tributes paid to Christian lords) (Christiansen 1997, 51–3). Their crusade status can be traced back to Bernard of Clairvaux's preaching of the Second Crusade. In March 1147, the abbot was approached by German nobles who asked if they could direct their crusading zeal against the pagan Wends rather than the Muslims of the Holy Land. After consultation with Pope Eugenius III it was agreed, with remission of sins as part of the package. Yet unlike the eastern crusades, conversion was the declared aim of the enterprise. Forced conversions were counter to church law, but Bernard's policy that "they shall be converted or wiped out" was nevertheless accepted by the pope ("Proclamations of Northern European Crusades," CR).

The Wends were located east of the Elbe River adjoining the territory of the Saxons and Danes (who were the first northern crusaders). The Abotrite Wends had recently made raids on bordering Christian lands. Revenge for these attacks and a desire for more land galvanized the crusaders, who launched a strike on the Wendish town of Dobin. The leader of the Wendish Abotrites was Nyklot (d. 1160), and Dobin was his political base. The campaign dragged on, with both Danes and Saxons accusing each other of lackluster fighting and Bernard's call for conversion yielding to the more secular aims of the crusaders ("Helmold's *Chronicle of the Slavs*," CR). Dobin was finally taken, and the army went on to acquire other settlements, destroying pagan sites and idols along the way. Nyklot submitted to the crusaders with the promise of baptizing his followers and returning Danish prisoners. He himself remained pagan, and indeed, despite the baptisms, pagan sites and temples also remained. The Wendish Crusade carried on up to 1185, with sporadic conversions and a steady siphoning of pagan territory into crusader hands.

The first of the Baltic Crusades was called in 1198 at the instigation of Pope Innocent III. Campaigns against the pagan territories of Prussia, Estonia, and Livonia were fought alongside conversion efforts in the twelfth century, with first partial and then full penitential status (Phillips 2010, 215). The arrival of the Teutonic Knights in the 1230s altered the political face of the Baltic Crusades. Formed in the Levant as a counterpart to the French Templars and Hospitallers, this Germanic military order had the full backing of the papacy. Their transfer to the Baltic region, and in particular Prussia, provided them with the opportunity to expand their authority and holdings. Here they had the support of the German emperor and were even able to take over the home-grown military order, the Sword Brothers, in 1237.

Their power was further strengthened in 1245 when Pope Innocent IV granted the order the right to recruit crusaders as and when needed, rather than wait for a papal declaration. Such a decree enabled the Teutonic Knights to wage a perpetual crusade against the Baltic pagans, with full control of the recruitment and planning of the campaigns, including the granting of indulgences. Lands acquired by the order were allowed to stay in their possession—a unique situation. Under their direction, a system of conquest, conversion, and German colonization was implemented. Prussia, their strongest center of operations, became, in effect, a thriving outpost of German culture. This was often accomplished by brutal means, however, with many Prussians condemned to serfdom and forced labor.

The fourteenth century witnessed a series of crusades called by the order against the pagans of Lithuania. The crusaders' loss of the Holy Land in 1291 meant that many in Europe now traveled to the Baltic to exercise their crusading skills and win spiritual glory. The Teutonic Knights ran these crusades almost as adventure holidays, offering, alongside battle, hunting expeditions, feasts, and even prizes. The Crusades lost a fair degree of their attraction, however, with the conversion of the Lithuanians in 1386. In 1525, the Prussian lands of the Teutonic Knights became a secular German principality. Conversion of a new sort was responsible for this final change, as the order's master, Albert of Brandenburg (1490–1545), became a Lutheran. The order's Livonian members held out for another 37 years, but invasions and defeats at the hands of the Russians weakened them over this period. Their pleas for papal aid went unheard, as Pope Pius IV (r. 1559–65) felt the need to keep the Russians on side against the Ottoman threat. The decision of its final master to become a secular duke occurred in 1562. By this point, the Baltic region had been effectively

Christianized and Germanized. The Teutonic Knights had therefore outlived their purpose to convert and settle.

THE TWILIGHT OF THE CRUSADES

The final phase of the medieval crusades ran from 1244 until the end of the fifteenth century. It was a period that witnessed the rise of the Mamluk Sultanate, the invasions of the Mongols, the final expulsion of crusaders from the Holy Land, and the fall of Constantinople to the Ottoman Turks.

The First Crusade of Louis IX

The year 1244 marks the disastrous battle of La Forbie and King Louis IX's decision to take the cross. Louis, the son of Louis VIII of France and Blanche of Castile, was known to be especially devout. He left for his first crusade in 1248, but unlike Frederick II, the delay between his vow and departure was due to the venture's meticulous planning and provisioning. Indeed, this was perhaps the best-prepared crusade the west had ever seen. The route and strategy were similar to that of the Fifth Crusade. The crusaders would sail to Egypt, with the aim of destroying the Muslim power base, before moving on to Jerusalem. The crusaders, around 15,000 in total, captured Damietta in May 1249. They then proceeded to march on the Muslim fortress of Mansourah, just as their predecessors had done in the Fifth Crusade. The site was defended by the Ayyubid sultan's Mamluk force. The Arab term *Mamluk* refers to one who is a slave. The practice of procuring young slaves from the borders of Islamic territories dated back to the ninth century. Male slaves were schooled in Arabic and religion and trained as soldiers. Granted their freedom on reaching adulthood, Mamluks continued to serve their former owners and could rise to positions of great power and influence. In November 1249, the Ayyubid sultan al-Salih died in the camp adjoining Mansourah. This was initially kept quiet while his widow sent for the heir. Unfortunately, this took three months, by which time cracks were beginning to show between the Ayyubids and their Mamluk army.

Up to the taking of Damietta, things had gone well for Louis and his campaign, but in moving into the Nile Delta they faced a challenging terrain. Weeks were taken up trying to construct a causeway across the Tanis River, with the king eventually opting to cross a ford further downstream. The army forded the river on horseback on the morning of 8 February 1250, where they met the Egyptian army. The result was a stalemate that left them trapped between the river and Mansourah. Jean of Joinville (1224–1317), a knight in the king's service, recorded: "When the king saw that he and his people could only remain

there to die, he ordered and arranged that they should strike their camp ..."
("Joinville's *Life of St Louis*," CR).

Exhausted, starving, and ill, the crusaders turned back for Damietta. Many were surrounded and killed as they tried to make their way. Joinville himself was captured, as was the king, who was suffering from dysentery and unable to proceed on foot. Of those taken prisoner, lower-ranking crusaders were executed or enslaved, while those of higher rank were held for ransom. Louis's wife, Queen Margaret (1221–95), was in Damietta, having given birth to a son, John Tristan, just three days after hearing of her husband's capture. The city fell soon afterward, and the queen sailed to Acre to await her husband's fate. With the queen's help, Louis was able to settle his ransom and left for the Holy Land in May. He would spend the next four years there reinforcing crusader defenses and, as most of his surviving crusaders were still held captive, negotiating their release (which was completed by 1252). Before leaving the Levant in 1254, he established a garrison of knights, archers, and lesser soldiers funded out of his own treasury, which served the region until his death in 1270 (Goldsmith 2015, 164).

The Rise of the Mamluk Sultanate and the Mongol Invasions

Despite the victory, there were tensions in the Egyptian camp. On 2 May, days before King Louis's departure, the new sultan was murdered by a band of senior Mamluks. Years of unrest followed, ending with the clear establishment of the Mamluk dynasty in both Egypt and Syria. Their dynastic rule would last up to 1517, but its success looked far from certain in 1259. The crusaders of the Levant still offered resistance, but the real threat came from the east in the form of the Mongols. The Mongols were a warrior society whose vast empire stretched from the Black Sea to the eastern shores of China. They had already conquered both Muslim and Christian territories as of 1260, and then they turned on Palestine.

BOX 1.6   *The Mongols and the Legend of Prester John*

Mongols (or Tartars, as they were called by Europeans) were nomadic peoples from the region of Asia where Russia, China, Mongolia, and Kazakhstan meet today. Nomadic pastoralists herding sheep and horses, they formed a militaristic society headed by warrior chiefs. Mongol religion was polytheistic, with both greater and lesser gods, but they were also amenable to merging their beliefs with other religions, including Buddhism, Islam, and Christianity.

The rise of the Mongol Empire is usually dated to 1206 when Chingiz (or Genghis) Khan (d. 1227) came to power. Mongol warriors were expert horsemen, which accounts for the swiftness of the army's movements and their agility in battle. They were also skilled in siege warfare (Nicolle 2007, 284–85), and few cities were able to hold out against them. The Mongols' passion for conquest was fueled by their belief that they were destined to rule the world. They had a reputation of being fearless and brutal in battle, and this often meant that their victims capitulated out of terror and without a fight. Willing to ransom those who surrendered, the Mongols were known to massacre any individual or group that offered resistance ("Ibn al-Athir on the Mongol Invasion," *CR*).

Many Christians of the period mistakenly equated the Mongol khan with the legendary figure of Prester John. Tales of a Christian king ruling a wealthy eastern empire grew as contacts with peoples such as the Mongols increased. The legend might have had its origin in the Nestorians, a Christian sect of Syria that sent out missionaries as far as China between the ninth and thirteenth centuries ("John Mandeville on Prester John," *CR*). There were known Nestorian converts among the Mongols, including some within the khan's own family. Yet even when it became clear that the khan was not Prester John, Christian leaders still felt he might have a role to play in the fight against Muslims. In 1245, Pope Innocent IV sent a letter and missionaries to Guyuk, the Mongol khan. In it he encouraged the khan to "acknowledge Jesus Christ" and "worship his glorious name by practicing the Christian religion." To the khan, the pope's Christendom represented only a tiny fraction of his envisioned empire, and he replied, "... come at once to serve and wait upon us!" ("Letters between Pope Innocent IV and Guyuk Khan," *CR*).

Although short-lived in comparison to other realms, the Mongols created one of the largest empires ever seen. While the violence of their conquests cannot be denied, their occupation sparked an exchange of ideas as well as goods, establishing lasting east–west relationships (Rossabi 2012, 124).

Louis IX had written to the Mongol leader while in the Holy Land, seeking an alliance against the Muslims. The khan saw no reason, however, to parley, much less make a pact, with such a minor ruler. The Mongols had taken the lands of the Seljuk Turks as well as the Christian regions of Armenia and Georgia. They swept into Syria, sacking Baghdad in February 1258 and claiming they had slaughtered 200,000 in the fall of the city. Muslim Aleppo and Damascus followed, spreading panic throughout the rest of the region. In March, however, the Mongol leader, Hulegu (1218–65), suddenly withdrew the majority of his forces. The Great Khan Möngke (r. 1251–59) had died in 1259, and tradition required that the chieftains gather to elect his successor. Some historians also attribute Hulegu's withdrawal to the fact that the Middle East did not adequately support the grazing of the Mongol livestock on which the army depended.

Kitbuqa (d. 1260), the leader of the remnant force of around 10,000, sent a message to Egypt, demanding the surrender of the Mamluk sultan Qutuz (d. 1260). The envoys who carried the message to the sultan were cut in half and their heads displayed on Cairo's gate. With the future of the Mamluk sultanate on the line, Qutuz marched his army north. Other Muslim forces joined in the advance, but the crusaders remained neutral, although they did allowed Qutuz safe conduct across their lands and even offered provisions. The battle took place on 3 September at the site of 'Ayn Jalut, in Galilee. Baybars, a rival Mamluk leader, drew the Mongols into an ambush, and Qutuz's forces sprang the trap. Kitbuqa was slain and the Mongols were dispersed. This was a significant turn of events, for it halted the Mongols and placed the Mamluks firmly in control of Islamic lands. Qutuz, however, did not live to see the results of his victory, as he was assassinated in late October. Baybars was among the murderers and afterwards claimed succession. In addition to securing his position as the undisputed sultan of Syria and Egypt, Baybars's primary goal was to drive the crusaders out of the region. His aims were political, but *jihad* also had a part to play in the fulfillment of his goal. As with Saladin, *jihad* served to unite disparate Muslim forces and provide legitimacy to his rule.

The crusaders, for their part, were in a state of turmoil. Disputes over territory and a lack of firm leadership eroded their combined strength. Baybars (r. 1260–77) showed himself to be a cunning diplomat and political strategist. Between 1260 and 1265, he made alliances with various Christian factions. Constantinople returned to Byzantine hands in 1261, and here too Baybars sought a commercial treaty with its emperor, Michael VIII (r. 1259–82). Although there were intermittent raids into crusader territories, Baybars was not able to turn his full attention to the region until 1265, when he captured several crusader fortifications including Crac des Chevaliers. His grand plan was to expel the crusaders from the coast and then to destroy their fortifications and cities, thus obliterating any hope of the west regaining a foothold in the region. Jaffa fell in 1268 along with Antioch. Both suffered brutal sackings, but Antioch in particular as Baybars had ordered the city's gates to be locked and all its inhabitants massacred. The greatest prize was Acre, but there was no attack on the city. This might have been because of Acre's economic role and Baybars's need to maintain its infrastructure (Riley-Smith 2014, 268–69).

The Second Crusade of Louis IX

Back in Europe, the news of the Mongol incursions and Baybars's conquests spurred on calls for a new crusade. Since his return from the Holy Land in 1254, Louis IX had become more religious in his lifestyle and activities. He took the cross in 1267, even though Joinville and other nobles had argued against the venture. Louis, however, was unmoved. As with the earlier campaign, this one was carefully planned and well funded. Crusaders from France, England, and Aragon joined in alongside three of the king's sons and his brother, Charles of Anjou (1227–85). England sent Lord Edward (the future king Edward I, r. 1272–1307), while King James I of Aragon (r. 1213–76) led the Spanish contingent, although storms at sea meant that only a small Spanish force ever reached Acre, the rest, including the king, having turned back.

Louis IX left with his army in the summer of 1270. His plan was to aim for Tunis on the north African coast. Rumors that the city's emir would convert might have influenced his strategy, as Louis was a great supporter of both the Dominicans and Franciscans (who promoted the conversion of Muslims, Mongols, and eastern Christians). However, Louis was sailing toward another defeat. The emir of Tunis had no intention of converting and stayed safely within his walls. Camped in the ruins of ancient Carthage, in the heat of the north African summer, the army was suddenly struck down by what appears to have been dysentery or typhus. Louis fell ill and died on 25 August. The crusaders left Tunisia on 11 November following Charles's negotiations with the emir for tribute and trading rights.

King Louis IX's bones were carried back to France and interred at the abbey of St. Denis (his heart had been buried with his crusaders in Tunisia). Even before his arrival, there had been stories of miracles associated with his remains, and these continued once he was laid to rest. In 1297 he was canonized. Saint Louis was neither the first nor the last canonized crusader, but as a king his example was held up for others to follow.

Lord Edward, who had sailed on to Acre, had only a small force of around 1,000. Once there, he was frustrated by the lack of cooperation between crusader factions and the absence of a coherent policy against the Mamluks. He was also perplexed by the free trade between Muslims and the northern Italian merchants, a trade that seemed to carry on, without regulation or censure, in the midst of the most violent conflict. Edward and his brother Edmund (1245–96) engaged in some fighting, but their only real gain was the negotiation of a 10-year truce with Egypt concluded in April of 1272. In late September he sailed for home and was crowned king of England the following year.

The Last Years of the Crusader States

Baybars died in 1277, and his heirs soon became embroiled in internal power struggles. In the end, however, they lost out to another Mamluk upstart, Qalawun (r. 1279–90). Skirmishes with rival emirs and Mongol factions kept Qalawun busy, but he also continued the *jihad* against the crusaders. By the 1280s, the only primary crusader cities left were Tripoli and Acre. Within their walls, crusaders fought among themselves to decide who should rule these diminishing realms. Tripoli fell to Qalawun in April 1289. Acre alone now stood as the final remnant of what had once been the Latin Kingdom of Jerusalem. Aware that this was a well-defended city, Qalawun made a peace pact with its inhabitants and then turned his attention to building up arms and forces sufficient to destroy this last crusader foothold.

Qalawun died in the midst of these preparations, but his son al-Ashraf Khalil (r. 1290–93) renewed the *jihad*. By April 1291 al-Ashraf was ready to begin the siege of Acre. Hospitallers and Templars had recruited and organized for the city's defense, but on 18 May the defenses were breached and Acre fell (Rodriguez 2015, 110; "Ludolph von Suchem on the Fall of Acre and Its Aftermath," *CR*). The Templars were able to hold out for a time in one of the towers, but they were overcome and the entire city was plundered and leveled. Ludolph, writing some 50 years after its fall, lamented, "Thus Acre has remained empty and deserted even to this day." The lesser settlements were then systematically abandoned or captured.

Jerusalem and its territory would remain in Muslim hands for the next 600 years. The Crusades to the Holy Land were indeed over, but Europe was not aware of this and would continue to call and plan for them well beyond the medieval period.

Crusading in the Fourteenth Century

The loss of the Holy Land was devastating news for Christian Europe. Any attempt to retake the region would now involve a full-scale invasion and one without the benefit of coastal towns and fortifications. Soon shock and disbelief gave way to anger and censure. The military orders bore the brunt of the blame, followed by the nobles of the Levant. Yet this did not extinguish enthusiasm for crusading itself. The fourteenth century was, after all, the period that saw the Crusade of the Poor in 1309 and the Second Shepherds' Crusade of 1320. The papacy and the rulers of Europe were equally sincere in their desire to reestablish Christian rule in Jerusalem.

This was not, however, the age of Innocent III or King Louis IX. Fourteenth-century popes struggled to unite and command warring secular rulers, while the papacy itself was confronted with numerous religious and political challenges to its authority. The Avignon Papacy (1309–78) which saw the popes relocated to France, and the subsequent Great Western or Papal Schism (1378–1417), when there were two, and at times three, rival popes, weakened both the papacy and the Church. The beginning of the Hundred Years' War in the 1330s further distanced European kings and nobles from the crusading cause. The period also suffered natural disasters, including the Great Famine of 1315–17 and the arrival of the Black Death (1347–48). It was during this time that the so-called lesser crusade (*passagium particulare*) grew to be the norm, while the traditional crusade (*passagium generale*), with its emphasis on penitential pilgrimage, the recovery of Jerusalem, and the overthrow of Muslim rule became a longed-for, but unobtainable, ideal.

BOX 1.7   *The Fate of the Military Orders after 1291*

The Templars, Hospitallers, and Teutonic Knights had played an important role in the military defense of the Levant. They had also contributed to the care and protection of Christians within the region, running hospitals and looking after pilgrims and the poor. Yet in the final years of crusader rule, they often found themselves in the middle of commercial disputes between Italian merchants or mediating the power plays of secular rulers (both resident and foreign). When Acre fell, the military orders shouldered much of the blame. As their *raison d'être* had been to defend the Holy Land, it was obvious to those in Europe that they had failed. Furthermore, they were accused of serving their own needs and growing rich off the donations of their patrons. Although exiled from the Holy Land, the military orders did not give up on crusading. The masters of the Templars and Hospitallers met with Pope Clement V (r. 1305–14) in 1306 to discuss tactics for a new crusade. While in Cyprus both Templars and Hospitallers began to build warships to patrol and protect the eastern Mediterranean.

None of this activity, however, helped their reputation in Europe. Indispensible within the Latin States, the military orders came to be seen as arrogant, suspiciously wealthy, and of no real value to European society. And there was some truth to these accusations. The orders owed no allegiance to kings or nobles; their loyalty could not be commandeered, and they refused to provide military aid against fellow Christians. Their perceived military uselessness would later prompt the rise of secular knightly orders, such as the Hungarian Order of St. George (1325), England's Order of the Garter (ca 1348), and France's Order of the Star (1351). For secular leaders at the beginning of the fourteenth century, the presence of an unhelpful, independent, and wealthy military force began to rankle.

Of the three orders, it was the Templars who suffered the most dramatic and violent end. They were perhaps the wealthiest of the three, with thousands of properties throughout Europe. They also engaged in banking and money-lending activities both in the east and in Europe. One in their debt was King Philip IV of France (r. 1285–1314), who had borrowed heavily to pay for his wars against England and others.

On 13 October 1306, without warning, hundreds of Templar Knights were arrested throughout France. They were charged with a range of offenses including sacrilege, witchcraft, and homosexual acts. Interrogated and tortured, many knights, including the grand master, James of Molay (ca 1243–1314), confessed to these misdeeds. Arrests spread to Italy and England, while in France Philip took steps to seize Templar property and goods. As with any military order, the Templars were under the protection of the papacy, but Clement V offered them no defense or refuge in their moment of need. Clement was the first of the "Avignon popes," heralding a period when the papacy ruled not from Rome but from southern France. As such he was under pressure from the French crown ("Order for the Arrest of the Templars and Papal Bull Suppressing the Templars," CR). He nevertheless reduced the king's gains by ceding the Templars' property to the Hospitallers (although Philip was allowed to receive a large sum for incurred expenses).

While there may have been some irregularities or unusual rites within a small number of Templar groups, the accusations were clearly exaggerated and then later embellished by torture. Between 1307 and 1314, some knights were found guilty and executed. Their grand master Molay was condemned as a heretic and burned in 1314, professing to the end his own innocence and that of his order.

By 1309 the Teutonic Knights of the Levant had relocated north to the Baltic Crusades. Whether they were influenced by the fate of the Templars is unknown, but there they stayed. Over time, their influence and holdings in western Europe diminished and then disappeared.

The Hospitallers first settled in Cyprus, but they increasingly found themselves marginalized by its king, Henry II (r. 1285–1324) (Morton 2013, 131). Seeking a safe retreat outside the reach of secular rulers, they launched an attack in 1306 against the island of Rhodes, held in fief by the Byzantine emperor. The arrest of the Templars might have spurred their efforts, and Rhodes was theirs by 1309. Within this island sanctuary the Hospitallers could carry on their activities unchecked. They built and repaired fortifications, developed the main commercial harbor, and constructed warships to guard the eastern Mediterranean (Billings 2010, 216). The Hospitallers remained in Rhodes until 1522, when they were ousted by the Ottomans. They then relocated to the island of Malta, where they continued until the order was driven out by Napoleon Bonaparte in 1798. The order was revived in 1834 and continues to this day, primarily as a medical charity but also retaining a limited military role.

Both the Teutonic Knights and the Hospitallers were saved by the fact that they had realms they could call their own. What the fate of the military orders demonstrates is that fourteenth-century secular rulers were no longer willing to tolerate independent, church-linked military institutions, nor was the papacy able or willing to defend them.

The lesser crusades varied widely in their aims and success. The majority took place within Europe and were directed against heretics and rival secular powers. There is no doubt that the Church lost prestige through these campaigns, and popes were often criticized for diverting troops and revenues from more obvious crusading causes. They were, moreover, costly and undermined the goodwill and support of secular kings and nobles. Anti-clerical feeling among the populace, such as that witnessed in the Shepherds' Crusades, was also fueled by the Church's perceived neglect of traditional crusading ideals.

External crusading did not disappear altogether, but it was changing to fit the political and military state of affairs. New campaigns against Muslims took to the seas, as did the warships of the military orders and the fleets of northern Italian merchants. Crusading naval leagues were created between various Christian factions, with each providing ships to patrol the Mediterranean. Yet throughout the first half of the fourteenth century, although nobles and kings took the cross, many crusades simply stuttered and failed. One exception to these half-formed crusades was that of King Peter I (r. 1358–69) of Cyprus. Aided by the Hospitallers and their fleet, Peter's force was able to take and plunder the Egyptian city of Alexandria, but the crusaders were forced to retreat to Cyprus and the mission never attained the promised status of a *passagium generale*. Other lesser crusades followed in its wake, but none came near the Holy Land.

By the 1370s, Europe was facing the Ottoman Turks (Riley-Smith 1991, 146–47). The Ottomans had settled into northwestern Anatolia in the thirteenth century and were now threatening not only Mamluk- and Mongol-held lands but also Christian Europe. Much of the Balkans fell to them in 1389, as did Bulgaria in 1393. In July 1396, crusaders met up in Buda under King Sigismund of Hungary (1387–1437) to address the issue. With him were troops from Spain, Italy, Poland, and Bohemia. While this force of around 10,000 marched south toward the Bulgarian city of Nicopolis, Hospitaller, Genoese, and Venetian ships were sailing along the Danube to meet them, bringing the force up to around 15,000. Their optimistic aims were to defeat the Ottomans, move on to Constantinople, and then to Jerusalem. Leading the army of 15,000 Ottomans was Sultan Bayezid (r. 1389–1402), "The Thunderbolt." The battle ended in defeat for the crusaders, largely due to their own mistakes according to Johann Schiltberger, a 16-year-old German page who was captured at the battle and enslaved for many years ("Johann Schiltberger on the Nicopolis Crusade," CR). Historians differ on the significance of Nicopolis. Traditionally it has been seen as the last crusade, but others have questioned that interpretation, arguing that it did not diminish the west's dream of recovering Jerusalem.

Late-medieval Balkan history presents a complex web of fluctuating political and religious alliances, the details of which are still fiercely debated. Some Christian states were required to pay tribute and provided troops to the Ottomans. As such a state, Christian Serbia supplied horsemen to the Ottoman force at Nicopolis (Fine 1994, 608–10). Christians also fought alongside Muslims in 1402 at the battle of Ankara, and at the siege of Constantinople in 1453. *Jihad* and crusading rhetoric were still very much in evidence during the period, but the conquests of the Ottomans and the alliances and treaties between Christian and Ottoman leaders were driven primarily by secular aims.

After Nicopolis, the advance of the Ottomans into Hungary looked certain. They were, however, temporarily checked by the threat of a combined Turkish–Mongol force led by a warrior known as Timur or Tamerlane (r. 1370–1405). Timur was of Turkish origin but had risen to power serving under the Mongol rulers. With his army, Timur had already conquered territory in Persia, southern Russia, Afghanistan, and India. He arrived in Syria in 1400, where he sacked Aleppo, Damascus, and Baghdad. Moving into Anatolia, the khan defeated Bayezid's Ottoman forces at the battle of Ankara in 1402. Bayezid himself was captured and later killed. At this point, however, Timur, left for Samarkand and died the following year as he was preparing to invade China. His empire was divided between his sons, but sibling rivalry ended any western advance. The Ottomans also became embroiled in dynastic disputes during this period, which lasted until the rise of Murad II (r. 1421–44 and 1446–51).

Crusading in the Fifteenth Century

Europe emerged from the Great Papal Schism in 1417. There was now a single pope, Martin V (r. 1417–31), but the reputation of the papacy and Church had suffered. Anti-clerical feeling and heretical views were on the rise. In 1415, a Czech reformer, John Hus (ca 1372–1415), had been burned at the stake for heresy, and his followers, known as Hussites, were perceived to be enough of a threat to merit a crusade. The Hussites, based in Bohemia, called for church reforms, including a rejection of the sale of indulgences and the right to preach. The first Hussite Crusade of 1420 was a failure, however, with several desertions and defeats. Subsequent campaigns were launched over the next 10 years, with repeated losses. In the end, the Hussites were brought under control by the Bohemian nobility, but conflict between Catholic and reform (later Protestant) groups would continue into the early modern period.

Europe's attention was once again directed toward the Ottomans in 1443 when Pope Eugenius IV (r. 1431–47) called for a crusade in defense of the Byzantine Empire. In the second year of his sultanate (1422), Murad II had attempted to lay siege to Constantinople. The walls stood firm, but this unsettled the emperor, John VIII (r. 1421–48), to the extent that he considered submitting the eastern Church to the rule of the papacy in exchange for aid from that quarter. In 1437, John met with Pope Eugenius at the Council of Florence, and an agreement was signed in 1439, formally acknowledging the unification of the churches under the authority of the papacy. The long-awaited goal of the crusading popes had finally been realized. It would not, however, be accepted by the Byzantines themselves.

Preparations for a crusade to save Byzantium began in January 1443, but the call went mostly unheeded in western Europe due to the Hundred Years' War and other domestic conflicts. In eastern Europe, where the Ottoman threat was closest, King Ladislas III of Hungary (r. 1434–44) and John Hunyadi (d. 1456), lord of Transylvania, gathered crusaders from their own realms as well as Poland, Bohemia, Moldavia, Wallachia, and Serbia. The crusaders were initially successful against the Ottomans in Serbia, and in June 1444 they and a naval fleet funded by the pope, Burgundy, Venice, and Byzantium lay siege to the coastal city of Varna. Murad and his army made their way to Varna, where, on 10 November, they shattered the crusader force, killing King Ladislas and forcing Hunyadi to flee. With the defeat at Varna, many of the Balkan rulers opted for the more realistic strategy of diplomacy, even if that required subjugation and tribute. Hunyadi, now regent to the Hungarian king, went on the offensive in 1448 with his final papal-supported crusade. He was defeated at Kosovo but continued to defend Hungary, dying in 1456, days after crushing the Ottoman forces at the Battle of Belgrade.

Murad II died in 1451 and was succeeded by his son, Mehmed II, also known as "Mehmed the Conqueror" (r. 1451–81). Following in his father's footsteps, he began almost at once to plan the fall of Constantinople, and by April 1452 the city was surrounded and the siege began. The emperor, Constantine XI (r. 1449–53), was given the chance to surrender but chose instead to rely on the city's defenses. They had served the inhabitants well in 1422, but with few to defend the walls and an almost constant barrage of cannon fire, the great city fell on 29 May 1453. The emperor was killed in the final battle along with many others. Constantinople was then sacked and the survivors enslaved or ransomed ("Kritovoulos on the Fall of Constantinople," CR).

A great city had indeed been taken, but Constantinople's days had been numbered for some time. Byzantium was not the grand empire of Alexius I but rather the smallest remnant of a divided, near-bankrupt realm. Mehmed II rebuilt the city, allowing eastern and western Christians as well as Jews to live and work within its walls. The Orthodox patriarch of the city was also reinstated and trade once more flourished. Not an insignificant number of local Christians had helped the Ottomans in their conquest of Constantinople (now Istanbul), and many benefited from the peace that followed in the wake of this new regime.

Reaction in the west was varied. While all bemoaned Byzantium's loss, few were prepared to do anything to secure its recovery. For the papacy and Church it was a more deeply felt loss, as the longed-for prize of Christian unity had been snatched from their grasp. Some historians have argued that Constantinople replaced Jerusalem as the primary goal of later papal crusades (Billings 2010, 235). The papacy twice initiated plans for a crusade in the years following Constantinople's fall, but neither was successful.

Crusading was not wholly discarded in the latter half of the fifteenth century. As we have seen, the campaigns in the Iberian peninsula continued against Muslim territories with an eye to expanding their reach across north Africa and to the Holy Land. Naval leagues also continued to operate. As the century drew to a close, the Ottomans continued to push their boundaries and further crusades were called. Little, however, was accomplished.

THE END OF MEDIEVAL CRUSADING

The sixteenth century completed the transformation of medieval crusading, forever altering and then terminating the movement. The medieval west had come a long way from the ideal of an armed penitential pilgrimage called by the pope with a mandate to recover the Holy Land. Jerusalem, although still a powerful image, was out of reach, overshadowed by the advances of the Ottoman Empire. Penitential indulgences sold for crusading missions were widely misused and subsequently held up as examples of church corruption. In the face of the Reformation, the authority of the papacy and, by association, papal crusades lost their meaning for the new Protestant population. For those who remained within the Catholic fold, the crusading ideal continued to circulate even if the Crusades themselves could not be achieved.

The Protestant/Catholic division was some way off when the Ottoman Turks took possession of Venetian territory in Greece at the beginning of the 1500s. Successive popes worked to organize and launch a crusade in response, but it was not until news of the Ottoman conquests of Syria and Egypt (1516–17) that secular rulers took serious notice. The papacy played on this heightened tension, sending out church officials to discuss terms by which the rulers of Europe could cease their warring and join a crusade. By 1518, many kingdoms had agreed to a five-year truce. The famous Field of the Cloth of Gold, held in June of 1520 between England's Henry VIII (r. 1509–47) and Francis I of France (r. 1515–47), was staged to highlight this crusading ceasefire. All came to naught, however, with the death in that same year of the Ottoman sultan Selim I (r. 1512–20). Unaware of the determination and military prowess of his successor, Suleiman I (r. 1520–66), the crusade was allowed to fade into the background of European politics.

With the Reformation beginning to take hold, news came of the fall of Belgrade in 1521 and the Hospitallers' loss of Rhodes in 1522. The year 1529 saw Suleiman on the doorstep of Europe with an unsuccessful siege of Vienna. Land and naval encounters continued throughout the century, some successful, others not. Yet, as is often the case, relations between Muslims and Christians were not solely defined by conflict. Treaties, truces, and trade existed alongside the skirmishes and battles. As the century drew to a close, crusade rhetoric and ritual became the customary window-dressing for wars of border, commerce, and sea defense. While still in the guise of a crusade, national interests and protection of one's *patria* would replace the ideal of a united Christendom fighting for a revered holy land.

CHAPTER TWO

THERE AND BACK AGAIN: THE LOGISTICS OF CRUSADING AND LIFE AS A CRUSADER IN THE LEVANT

Crusades were complex, expensive, and dangerous expeditions. Preparing to go on crusade required a great deal of planning, both for the trip itself and to secure possessions and family left behind. Urban II knew this from the start, advising would-be crusaders to "... rent their lands and collect money for their expenses," and also condemning "all those who dared to molest the wives, children and possessions" of those undertaking the journey ("Urban II's Call for a Crusade," *CR*). This chapter will consider the logistics of crusading, including preparation, finance, transport, and provisions. Instances of military life in the Levant, including desertion, captivity, and treatment of the dead, will also be explored, before concluding with a reflection on the experience of some crusaders on their journeys home and their post-crusade lives.

PREPARATION AND FINANCE

After taking the cross by choice or, more likely, through the traditions and obligations of family and vassalage, preparations began for departure. These could take months or even years, depending on the domestic agendas of the crusade's leaders and the difficulties of organizing large military forces. Divisions of crusader armies were defined by the senior lord, and this was generally how they were also organized, funded, provisioned, and transported. The independent crusader was a rarity (although crusader bands could be quite small). For the lower classes, it was essential to belong to a lord's company. Examples of the very poor taking the cross on their own demonstrate that the majority never made it out of Europe (for example, the Children's or Shepherds' Crusades). Serfs, who were bound to the land and a lord, were not allowed to undertake a crusade without their lord's permission. Few serfs had the funds to start, much less complete, such a journey. A fair number tried, putting their trust in God and charity, but the majority turned back well before they had progressed very far. Even those with military skills, such as archers, were known to abandon their vow if they could not gain the support of a lord. The change from overland to more expensive sea routes in the late twelfth century further diminished the number of participants from the lower classes.

Non-nobles made up a sizable portion of any crusade retinue. Foot soldiers with their array of weaponry were joined by blacksmiths, cooks, grooms, washerwomen, engineers, carpenters, sailors, barber-surgeons, physicians, chaplains, scribes, administrators, and a host of other workers deemed necessary for the venture. They would have been in the noble's care or pay, although others such as merchants or artisans could operate independently. For the upper classes, crusades were incredibly expensive, with the cost averaging four times the income of even the lowliest knight (Riley-Smith 2008b, 112). Efforts to raise the needed revenue ranged from individual loans, mortgages, and sales of property to Europe-wide tax schemes. We have seen in Chapter One how taxes such as the Saladin Tithe helped to support the Third Crusade. The Church also supported the collection of specific crusade taxes, adding to the income from church collection chests and taxation on monastic and other ecclesiastical institutions. A portion of a king's or lord's own revenue could be given over to a crusade, and large loans were arranged when other sources of funding fell short.

Jewish communities were also plundered for crusading funds. In the reign of Louis IX, the General Council of Lyon called for the profits made by Jewish money-lenders to be confiscated for holy war. This was one of many anti-Jewish decrees and policies that the king himself used to raise money for his campaign. Synagogues were despoiled and Christian debts to Jews were written off (with a portion of the debt transferred to the Crown). These actions culminated, on the eve of Louis's first crusade, with the expulsion of all Jewish money-lenders from his realm, after which their property was confiscated for the king's treasury (Jordan 1979, 85). Variations of these anti-Semitic fundraising measures were practiced throughout the crusade era, from the highest to the lowest levels of church and secular government.

Every knight and noble had their own personal expenses to fund, as well as that of their household and retainers. Property was their main asset and served as the primary means of raising funds. The property of crusaders enjoyed certain privileges and protection guaranteed by the secular authorities and the Church. By the late twelfth century, there were also exemptions from a selection of taxes. The selling or mortgaging of lands to religious establishments was seen as a safer means of obtaining income, although these were often veiled as exchanges of "gifts" or "donations." While some crusaders would bankrupt their families in their efforts to equip themselves for a crusade, many were also realistic about their chances of seeing home again and settled their estates accordingly ("Personal Arrangements," *CR*).

BOX 2.1   *Crusade Charters*

We can learn something about how crusaders prepared for their departure through medieval charters (Constable 2002, 129–53). A charter is a legal document, usually drawn up by the clergy, recording the transfer of property, tax rights, or other privileges. There are thousands of crusade charters in existence, and these have helped scholars to identify hitherto unknown crusading individuals or families. Many describe mortgages or sales of property, as well as loans and gifts (although the former were at times disguised as the latter). They also demonstrate the crusader's desire to set his house and conscience in order by laying out inheritance details, settling property disputes with religious institutions, or requesting prayers from these institutions for the crusader and his kin.

Below is a crusader charter from 1270. In reading through it, note the information it provides on the crusader, his funding for the crusade, and the settlement of his estate.

* * *

To all who will see or hear this present document, I, Eustace, lord of Trazegnies [Wallonia] and heir of Roeulx, and Agnes, his wife, send greeting in God and wish knowledge of the truth. Because the memory of human beings is short and soon fails, it is right and reasonable to place

---

in writing that which can change with time and persons. We, therefore, make known to all those who are and who will be that the church of Floreffe, by its great good will, because we, the aforementioned Eustace, are to go across the sea to the Holy Land, having shown us honorable courtesy by making us a fitting gift of one hundred pounds to support our journey, we, for our part, in response to their good will and the great kindness they have done us, wish likewise to show them courtesy. And so we, both ourselves and our wife Agnes, in the fullness of our life and good sense, have given, donated, granted and quit-claimed [given up any right to] all the rights that we or our heirs had or could have had in the taxable lands that are between the Pieton and the Chaussée [possibly the tributary Piéton and main rural road]. We wish and grant that these lands and the rights that they will bring or could bring should be under and return to the uses and customs of their court of the Chapel from now henceforward, save only our rightful advowson [the right to present a candidate to a benefice or church office]. We also wish and grant that the abbot and the aforesaid church have the peaceful enjoyment and possession of their court of the Chaussée about which we fought with them and said that it extended further than it should toward the road of the Chaussée. We also end the quarrel concerning the trees which were and are outside the court near the road and say and recognize that neither we nor our heirs can or should ever claim anything by any right except that we retain in that area our advowson, as we have done for the rest.

Concerning the trees, the ditch and the seat of the court, which we contested with respect to the road of the Chaussée, we end all quarrels and claims, save the aforesaid advowson. We further wish and grant that all the wealth that comes to the aforesaid church of Floreffe from John Dyron, our vassal, and Liegard, his wife, whether in arable lands or other things, remain to it as a perpetual inheritance. The aforesaid church may grant them to whomever it wishes whether lay or in orders.

To these aforesaid arrangements the following were witnesses: Walter, abbot of Floreffe; Gérard, abbot of Leffe; John of Rayome, bailiff of Trazegnies; John of Tuing, bailiff of Morlanwies ...; Walter of Leibrecht, provost of Floreffe; Walter de Leez, master of Herlaimont; Godfrey of Trazegnies; John of Nivellers; John of Dinant; Lambert of Liè; John of Huy, a brother of Floreffe, and many other good men. And so that these arrangements may remain firm when we have legitimate heirs begotten of our flesh, we have sealed this document with our seal.

> This ordinance is made and confirmed in the year of the Incarnation
> of our Lord 1270, on the day of the Holy Trinity.
>
> (Slack and Feiss 2001, 194–98)

While knights and lesser ranks had their own personal expenses and provisions to arrange, budgeting on a grander scale was carried out by the crusade's leaders. We are fortunate to have surviving extracts from the crusade accounts of King Louis IX. These cover the first three years of his time in the Holy Land (the period from 1250 to 1253). They do not, however, include expenditures for the campaign in Egypt (1248–50) or for Louis's final year in the Levant. Estimates of the total cost of the crusade for the French king are equal to five times the annual royal revenue, an enormous sum, but one that the king did not hesitate to shoulder. The document itself dates from the reign of Philip VI (1328–50), who had the original copied as he himself was planning a crusade (Tyerman 2015, 195). As such, it lends some credibility to the account, as Philip would have wanted as accurate a rendering as possible.

In the translated account below, note that 12 pence (d.) equal one shilling (s.), and 20 shillings equal one pound or livre ($\pounds$). This was an account rather than a budget, but even so, it highlights the expenses incurred by Louis IX, including unexpected payments (e.g., the king's ransom). The account shows expenses for each of the three years and a summarized account for the three-year period.

> These are the expenses of the king Saint Louis and of the queen when they were overseas, and for war and ships, the king's ransom, building operations [the campaign including the building and repair of defenses], and ransoming captives, and other items appearing below, for 2,120 days, which is three years and 25 days; that is, from the octave of Ascension 1250 to the octave of Ascension 1253. ...

	$\pounds$	s.	d.
Cost of food, with provisions and wages for the members of the household	28,990	15	8
Cloaks for knights and clerks	331	5	0
Robes and furs for the king	228	15	2
Harness and robes for [knights and clerks]	9,367	4	2
Gifts of robes and of money	1,410	15	8
Alms	1,689	16	8
Household crossbowmen and sergeants-at-arms	3,507	12	6

	£	s.	d.
For 136 war-horses, riding-horses, and mules, and 15 camels purchased for the household	3,032	10	3
Total household expenses for the time aforesaid:	48,558	15	1
Expenditures for war and ships for the time aforesaid:			
Pay of knights on wages	50,195	5	9
Gifts and promises to knights serving for a year without wages	23,213	14	8
Mounted crossbowmen and sergeants	17,170	0	6
Replacements and [new] horses	22,383	5	10
Crossbowmen and sergeants on foot	30,164	12	4
Carpenters, miners [sappers], and other workers	2,010	15	9
Customary expenditure, including £3,914 5s. 2d. to ransom captives	72,907	3	6
Loans made against wages	2,096	6	4
[Other] money paid out	400	59	6
Payments for ships	20,258	16	6
Total for war and ships for the time aforesaid:	240,800	60	8
Total of the household expenditures, war, and ships, for the time aforesaid:	289,361	15	9
Item, paid in this period to ransom the king	167,100	58	8
Similar expenditures for the household, war, and ships from the octave of Ascension 1251 to the octave of Ascension 1252, for 351 days, in the Holy Land:			
Cost of food	31,595	11	10
Robes and furs for the king	104	12	9
Cloaks for knights and clerks	312	10	0
Harness and robes for the same [knights and clerks]	12,910	8	11
Gifts of robes and of money	771	10	0
Alms	1,515	3	9
Household crossbowmen and sergeants-at-arms	4,494	6	6
105 war-horses, riding-horses, and mules purchased for the household	1,916	18	11
Total expenditures of the household for the king and queen for the time aforesaid:	53, 621	2	8
Expenses for war and for ships for the time aforesaid:			
Pay of knights on wages	57,093	17	10
Gifts and promises to knights serving without wages	23,253	18	4

	£	s.	d.
Mounted crossbowmen and sergeants	22,242	13	6
Replacements for 264 horses	6,789	17	0
Crossbowmen and sergeants on foot	29,575	0	6
Carpenters, artillerymen, and other workers	689	12	3
Customary expenses, including £41,366 14s. 9d. for workers in various places overseas, and £967 13s. 9d. to ransom captives	66,793	19	6
Payments for ships	5,725	15	0
Total for war and ships for the time aforesaid:	212,164	13	11
Total expenses of the household of the king and queen, and of war and ships, for the time aforesaid:	265,758	16	7

Similar expenses for the household, for war and ships, from the octave of
Ascension 1252 to the octave of Ascension 1253, which time was 385
days, that is, one year and 20 days:

	£	s.	d.
Total expenditures for the king's household:	60,678	10	10
Total for war and ships:	270,547	15	5
Total of the last two sums:	331,226	6	3
Total of the above days: 2,120 days, that is, three years and 25 days.			
Total wages of knights serving for the said 3 years and 25 days:	177,938	15	7

[It should be noted that, as appears from the above accounts, each of the said
knights received daily wages of just 7s. 6d., and so the number of knights
each day comes to 424, so that the wages came to £157 17s. 6d. per day.]

Total of gifts and payments made to knights serving without wages for the entire time aforesaid:	65,189	8	6

[These gifts and payments, if apportioned as are the customary wages of the
knights above, that is 7s. 6d. per day for each knight, would be enough
for 155 knights each day, for the entire time aforesaid, costing, per day,
£58 4s. 1d. or thereabouts.]

Total for the said knights, calculated at the customary wage as above:	243,128	4	0

[Thus the king could have in his company each day, for the entire time
aforesaid, 529 knights, [costing] about £217 19 d. per day.]
[Three year costings]

Total of the household expenses for all three years and 25 days above, for both the king and the queen:	162,858	8	7

[That is, per day, about £145 8s. 2d.]

	£	s.	d.
Total for the king's ransom:	167,102	18	8
Total for war for the aforesaid time:	594,600	4	10
[That is, per day, £530 17s. 10d.]			
Total for ships for this entire time:	32,026	2	8
Total for building operations overseas for this entire time:	95,839	2	6
Total for ransoming captives. [*this appears lower than perhaps expected]	1,050*	0	0
Total of all these expenditures for the three years and 25 days aforesaid; that is, for the household expenses of the king and queen, for the king's ransom, for war, ships, building operations, and for the ransoming of captives:	1,053,476	17	3

("Financial Accounts," *CR*)

There are some discrepancies in the figures, as well as inconsistencies in the recording of expenditure items. The account should also been seen in light of the time period and political context of Louis and his crusade. Even so, it provides useful information on the types of expenditures taken on by a crusading king and the relative cost of seeing through the venture. In analyzing the account, the following questions should be considered:

What was the range of positions and duties within Louis IX's crusader army as indicated by the document?

What were the various arrangements for the payment and maintenance of the crusaders under Louis IX's charge?

What does the document tell us about transport and provisions?

What entries are specific to Louis IX's campaign, and what would have been applicable to any crusade?

The financial burden of crusading was balanced against the hope for some degree of recompense via booty and plunder. There was also, for some, the prospect of gaining cities, lands, and their associated revenues. But the rewards of battle depended on success. Failure could be costly, and many crusaders, although perhaps feeling rich in spiritual rewards, returned home to forfeited lands and empty coffers.

TRANSPORT AND PROVISIONS

Generally, the cost of transporting crusaders was the responsibility of the crusade leaders. Prior to the Third Crusade, most crusaders traveled overland to reach their destinations. While some provisions could be transported in this manner, supplies also had to be available along the way. In the First Crusade, negotiations were held with the king of Hungary to ensure that markets would be open to the army. There is also evidence of prior planning for the arrival and supply of crusading forces once they reached Constantinople. A breakdown of discipline could result in plundering and reprisals, but when dealing with allies, the general rule was to avoid situations that might lead to the pillaging of cities and their surrounding regions.

Departure dates and routes were coordinated between the crusade leaders and the pope. Lesser clerics worked to get the message out with preaching tours, and muster points were designated for the gathering of armies. There were instances of delay and diversion, as seen with Louis VII, who halted in Hungary while waiting for more funds, and the English and Flemish forces, which stopped off in Lisbon to aid the Iberian crusades. The change from overland to sea routes came with the loss of key ports to Saladin in the late twelfth century. Richard I and Philip Augustus both opted for a sea passage. This decision had to accommodate the transport of horses and, during this period, we can see developments in ship construction and facilities to carry and unload large numbers of these essential animals. An average vessel could carry between 30 and 40 horses, although some larger ships were said to take between 80 and 100. As for passengers, Richard I's ships carried between 80 and 160, while later crusading vessels could transport nearly 500. Overall, western ships outclassed those of the Islamic and Byzantine fleets. Spurred by trade and crusading, and with a ready supply of wood, the west came to dominate the Mediterranean in the later centuries of the medieval period.

Arms and armor aside, ships also had to carry food and drink for men and horses. The amount required was not left to chance, and there is evidence of careful calculations on what each individual and animal would need while at sea and on land. Provisioning under Richard I demonstrates a high degree of planning and management, as demonstrated in the English Pipe Rolls (annual financial records of the Crown). These accounts note purchases ranging from 60,000 horseshoes and nails, to vast quantities of beans, cheese, and pork (Asbridge 2012, 386). There are noted gaps in the Pipe Roll entries, but as with the accounts of Louis IX, they supply evidence of the scale and complexity of provisioning a crusader army.

LIFE AND DEATH IN THE LEVANT

Settlement and Occupations

Those crusaders attached to a noble's household would have been accommodated as they were in Europe, either within the lord's own dwellings or in provided accommodation and fiefdoms. The settlement of Jerusalem after its fall in 1099 was a little more haphazard, if Fulcher of Chartres (1058–1127), a cleric and historian of the period, is to be believed:

> After this great slaughter they [the crusaders] entered the houses of the citizens, seizing whatever they found there. This was done in such a way that whoever first entered a house, whether he was rich or poor, was not challenged by any other Frank. He was to occupy or own the house or palace and whatever he found in it as if it were entirely his own. (1969, 29)

Many of the elite of the Latin States resided in cities and coastal ports, although there is archaeological evidence to support a wider rural settlement and participation in rural life than previously acknowledged (Boas 1999, 60). For many years historians have debated whether the society created by the Latin States reflected peaceful coexistence or an uncompromising "clash of civilizations." The current consensus is that there was both conflict and coexistence within the region. The degree of integration varied, but there is no doubt that the crusaders who remained in the Holy Land were, to some extent, influenced by eastern culture. Fulcher of Chartres observed the following of his fellow Franks:

> For we who were occidentals have now become orientals. He who was a Roman or a Frank has in this land been made into a Galilean or Palestinian. He who was of Rheims or Chartres has now become a citizen of Tyre or Antioch.... Some have taken wives not only of their own people but Syrians or Armenians or even Saracens who have obtained the grace of baptism.... People use the eloquence and idioms of diverse languages in conversing back and forth. Words of different languages have become common property known to each nationality, and mutual faith unites those who are ignorant of their descent. ("Fulcher of Chartres's *History*, CR)

Fulcher's words were directed toward potential European crusaders and may, therefore, paint a rosier picture with regard to issues such as language. Nevertheless, evidence from the period has shown that there was more than a little truth to the cleric's assertions.

BOX 2.2   *Muslims under Latin Rule, 1099–1291*

Significant numbers of Muslims are known to have remained in the Holy Land following the fall of Jerusalem in 1099, but the paucity of sources makes it difficult to understand the conditions of their life (especially those of the lower classes) (Catlos 2014, 130; Kedar 1990, 137–43). The ethnic and religious make-up of this region was diverse, and there were areas, such as the territories surrounding Antioch and Edessa, where Muslims were in the minority. Initially, Muslims and Jews were forbidden to live in Jerusalem and there was considerable violence as crusaders went about establishing the Latin States. Time, however, saw the reduction of crusader numbers and a more conciliatory attitude toward non-western inhabitants. This was due in part to the Franks' need for stable agricultural, trade, and artisan communities.

Muslims, and indeed all non-Franks, were subject to rents and taxes. These were collected locally by an official (a *rays*) who was appointed by the Frankish lord. Such officials were supported by translators and scribes, and evidence suggests that some were Muslims. In law, Muslims and other non-Franks had access to their own civil courts. For more serious crimes they were tried in a 'Burgess' court, where Muslims were permitted to take oaths on the Qur'an. Justice was not, however, assured as Muslims did not serve on juries. Evidence also indicates that punishment of Muslims was harsher than for other ethnic or religious groups (Asbridge 2012, 180–81).

Muslims of the peasant class were generally treated as serfs with little opportunity to own, sell, or bequeath their holdings. Muslims above this class could, however, prosper, acquiring wealth from their lands and/or commercial enterprises. With regard to religion, there was no great effort made to convert Muslims to Christianity. There also appears to have been minimal interference in the religious practices of the Muslim population. Muslim pilgrims were recorded traveling to and between Islamic holy sites and, as before the Latin conquest, there were examples of Muslims and Christians sharing the same place of worship (Catlos 2014, 147–51).

Integration was more likely in the urban centers, where people of business, administrators, travelers, and pilgrims met daily. The twelfth-century aristocrat Usama ibn Munqidh (1095–1188) offers several anecdotal tales on Frankish–Muslim relations within the Latin States (most of which take place within cities). Historians caution that these stories were meant to entertain rather than provide an historical record, but although colorful, they do provide detail on attitudes toward the "other" during this period in the Latin States (see Cobb 2008, 147; "Memoirs of Usamah Ibn Munqidh," *CR*).

In the nearly 200 years of Latin rule, borders fluctuated, rebellions erupted, and violence was visited on numerous villages and cities. Muslim non-combatants found themselves caught in the middle of such conflicts and were in the front line of any reprisals. That so many Muslims chose to remain in the Levant is perhaps testament to the overall volatility of the age and region, where oppression could come from any state, be it Latin, eastern Christian, or Muslim. It was also their home, and in a period of shifting borders this was perhaps the one reality that did not change.

In times of peace, crusaders were occupied in several duties and pastimes. There were household and occupational tasks to be performed by the servants, craftsmen, and lower ranks of the army. Knights, especially those without estates, were called upon to garrison the city walls, citadels, and palaces and to offer protection to their lords. Higher-ranked crusaders could be found administering their property, serving on advisory councils, and undertaking judicial duties. More peaceful times also offered opportunities for traditional pilgrim activities or leisure. Amusements included chess, dice, and the comforts of the public baths and taverns. Prostitution was found in all cities and offered by camp followers in the field. Lordly pastimes such as hunting, feasting or martial displays were also part of the elite crusader's calendar.

Frankish women of the Latin States enjoyed greater freedoms than their European counterparts. Such women held a higher percentage of inherited wealth and were able to take on a more public role due to the general shortage of men and the high death rate of crusaders. The fiefs of both husbands and fathers could be inherited by a widow or daughter and passed on to the husband of a first or, in the case of a widow, subsequent marriage. Widows had greater choice as to whom they married, especially if they had inherited a fief that owed no service. They were also generally allowed a year and a day of mourning before being asked to marry again and could not be forced into marriage after the age of 60. Guardianship was another means by which women of the Levant could rule and maintain control over the family lands. These conditions allowed women greater power and control over their lives, although it must be remembered that this was amid the larger background of a violent society where women generally had little say regarding military or political decisions (Schein 2001, 140–47).

In times of conflict, crusaders on the march in the Holy Land required clear supply lines and army provisions, which were carried by baggage trains. Life in the field offered a range of accommodation. Depictions of crusader camps show

ILLUSTRATION 2.1   Baggage cart showing arms and armor, food, and cooking pots (ca 1250). From the *Morgan Bible* (also called the *Maciejousky* or *Crusader's Bible*, 1240), Pierpont Morgan Library MS M. 638.

tents, some with elaborate furnishings and fittings (see Illustrations 2.1 and 3.9). Those of the lower ranks might have had little or no shelter against the elements, and given the harshness of life for foot soldiers, it is perhaps not surprising that these conditions could result in desertion.

Desertion

Desertion was common during the Crusades, and did not limit itself to the lower ranks. Early medieval laws stipulated that desertion should be punishable by death. Richard I, before his attack on the Sicilian city of Messina, decreed: "Let the law be enforced without remission; let the footman who flies full speed [deserts], lose his foot, the knight be deprived of his girdle [a belt symbolizing the status of knighthood]." We do not know if any crusader suffered these punishments, although many were shamed for their actions. The high status of some of these deserters, or perhaps the sheer numbers involved, might have dampened such conventions. The first siege of Antioch demonstrates how hunger and disease drove hundreds (some say thousands) to abandon their posts. Not all, of course, managed to return home to Europe. In the case of Antioch, some took refuge in the newly formed crusader state of Edessa (as some later deserters from the siege of Jerusalem would settle in Antioch). Many may have tried to return home but were unable to afford the sea passage or undertake the long and dangerous overland journey.

Desertions of the lower ranks at Antioch began with the siege and intensified once they had gained the city (when they were themselves besieged by Turkish forces). So desperate were the troops to leave that the crusade leaders barred and set guards on the gates to prevent exit. Even so, many managed to escape, some via rope ladders (earning the derogatory name of "rope danglers"). Those who escaped but fell into enemy hands were said to have been summarily dispatched. There were quite a few high-profile deserters at the siege of Antioch, the best known being Count Stephen of Blois. Stephen had been given a position of authority in the campaign, but illness and despair led him and his entourage to desert a day before the city fell. Higher-ranked deserters could offer a way home for their subordinates, and many escaped on Stephen's coat-tails. Peter the Hermit had also deserted but was caught and brought back. Although humiliated and made to pledge his support, he was not punished in any way. After the fall of Jerusalem in 1099, Pope Urban's successor, Paschal II, threatened excommunication to those who had deserted during the First Crusade—a decree that played some part in the return of Stephen of Blois and others to the Holy Land in the later 1101 "wave" of crusaders.

A leadership crisis could also trigger desertion, as shown by the disintegration of Frederick Barbarossa's forces after his unexpected death. The Fourth Crusade offers an instance of desertion on the grounds of principle when Simon of Montfort refused to take part in the attack on the Christian city of Zara. Whatever the cause, such scenes of desertion were repeated throughout the crusading period. Although each should be examined within the context of individual events, most were due to a combination of poor leadership, political uncertainties, and the harsh conditions of crusader warfare.

Massacre and Captivity

An ever-present danger of crusader life in the Levant was, of course, war-related violence. Massacre and captivity usually occurred in the aftermath of battle or in the fall of cities and fortifications. It was not, however, a risk for soldiers alone, as non-combatants (men, women, and children) were also regarded as targets or spoils of war. Women more often than men appear to have been the victims of captivity, and both Christian and Muslim forces are recorded as having fled the enemy while leaving their women behind (Friedman 2001, 122–23). Women captives were routinely raped, with rape itself being used as a weapon of war and a means of humiliating the enemy. If freed, women captives were often looked upon with suspicion or derision. King Baldwin of Jerusalem cast off his wife and forced her into a nunnery because she had been captured and raped by pirates on a sea journey to Jaffa. In another instance, a noble did the same to his own wife upon her return after two years of captivity, believing that "[s]he had not satisfactorily preserved the sanctity of the marriage couch as a noble matron should" (Friedman 2001, 133).

Many captives were massacred, either in the heat of battle or as a gesture of revenge or contempt. Saladin's command to execute all those of the military orders perhaps stemmed from their reputation as the most disciplined and danger-ous of crusader forces (and the fact that neither Hospitallers nor Templars gener-ally paid ransom for their captive members). Reasons for marking the poor for slaughter, rather than the elite, was that the latter offered the possibility of a ransom.

The ransoming of captives, which could take weeks, months, or even years, was a regular practice for both Franks and Muslims. Reynald of Châtillon was held captive by the forces of Nur al-Din for 16 years, although most were held for shorter periods. It was also a costly business. Louis IX's accounts (see above) record a staggering amount dedicated to ransoming the king and his soldiers. Lower-ranked soldiers and the civilian poor might be spared in the hope of a general exchange of prisoners, but they would not have been able to raise suf-ficient funds for their release. Those spared slaughter but unable to pay a ransom were at times released out of charity or political expediency. On the fall of Jerusalem in 1187, for example, Saladin demanded that the captive men pay 10 dinars, women 5 and children 1, within a 40-day period. Thousands who could not pay were taken into slavery, although some of the poorest were pardoned and escorted to the coast. During this period the European Trinitarian Order was founded to raise money for the ransoming of prisoners in the Holy Land. Muslims too saw the ransoming of prisoners as an expression of alms-giving.

Slavery

Thousands of Muslims and Christians were sold into slavery as a result of these conflicts. Slave trading and ownership were well established in the Islamic world, and those taken or born into slavery performed a range of services from the most menial to positions of high authority. We know the fate of some captive Christians, such as Johann Schiltberger, who was enslaved after the battle of Nicopolis and escaped some 30 years later. The story of Margaret of Beverly also details the trials of being taken into slavery (see box 1.4), including hard labor and frequent beatings before she was able to escape and tell of her experiences. Most, however, simply disappeared and were never heard from again. By church law Christians were not allowed to enslave other Christians; the enslavement of non-Christians, however, was accepted, and there are many recorded cases of Christian forces participating in the enslavement of captives. The fall of Caesarea to King Baldwin in 1101 saw most of its male inhabitants slaughtered and its emir ransomed, but the city's non-Christian women and children were forced into slavery. The leaders of the Fifth Crusade demanded ransom for 300 of the

Muslim survivors of the siege of Damietta, while others "were sold for a great price" ("Oliver of Paderborn on the Fifth Crusade," *CR*). Many of the Muslim slaves in the Levant worked on agricultural estates or in the various urban industries and trades. The military orders were known to employ slave labor on their agricultural estates, and slaves were used to man the oars of the Hospitaller ships of the later medieval period. A relatively small number of non-Christian slaves were traded in Europe, although this type of servitude was much reduced by the end of the medieval period.

Burial

Those crusaders who died while on campaign were usually buried according to their rank. In the aftermath of a battle or siege, this could be a simple mass grave. Burial so far from home might not have been viewed as a tragedy. This was, after all the Holy Land. Many crusaders expressed a strong wish, in case of death, to be buried in the Levant, with burial in Jerusalem being particularly desired. In some cases the crusader's body was separated from his or her heart, with one or the other interred in the Holy Land. In Jerusalem, crusaders of high status, including the first eight Latin kings, were buried in the Church of the Holy Sepulcher. Others of the elite class were interred in the Tomb of the Virgin Mary or various other holy sites scattered within or outside the city walls. The Templars are thought to have had a burial ground on the Temple Mount, as this was their headquarters. The site's status was enhanced by the belief that it lay on the route taken by Jesus on his entry into the city.

The poor were buried in charnel houses or pits located outside the walls. The Akeldama Charnel House, to the southeast of the city, served both the poor and those who died while in the care of the Hospitallers. The medieval pilgrim John of Würzburg (d. 1170) recorded that as many as 50 a day were taken from the hospital first to a local church, where mass was said, and then on to the charnel house. Bodies were lowered through holes in the roof of the structure as there were no doors or window openings. A fifteenth-century description concludes, "It is a dwelling for the dead alone, and I believe that since the hour it was finished no living man has entered this chamber" (Boas 2001, 180–81, 185–87).

Returning Home

The majority of those who survived their armed pilgrimage chose to return home. The return journey could be just as dangerous and expensive as the initial trip, and by this point many might have been suffering from injuries or ill health. The homecomings themselves varied depending on the duration of the crusader's absence and the state of his family and financial circumstances. A fair number came home out of pocket, although some had fared well. As with any soldier returning from the stress and horror of war, there were adjustments to be made. Nearly all, however, must have acknowledged the benefit to their souls as crusader vows had now been fulfilled. There are numerous accounts of crusaders offering relics, bought or plundered in the Holy Land, to their local churches or monastic institutions, while some crusaders, their best years behind them, took up monastic retirement.

Other factors could affect a crusader's reception, as shown in the case of Anselm, a son of the lord of Ardres. Anselm had gone to the Holy Land as a crusader, but while there he was captured by Muslims and converted to Islam. Although he escaped and was able to return home, he did not hide the fact that he had been an apostate. The source relates that this caused him to be hated by his Christian relatives, so much so that he left once more for the Holy Land and never returned. There is also recorded an instance of identity theft in which a man claimed to be the crusader Baldwin of Ardres, who had been away on armed pilgrimage for some 30 years. In this disguise he fooled most of the family and servants, and it was only when he absconded with "a great treasure" that the deceit was revealed ("Accounts of Crusader Homecomings," *CR*).

It was not only crusaders who faced difficulties returning to their former life. Women who had been captured or enslaved were shamed for any sexual abuse they endured. Viewed as damaged by their experience, they were often considered not fit for marriage, with convent life the only respectable conclusion to their lives. Margaret of Beverly's plight is a case in point, for although her account does not say she was raped while in servitude, her contemporaries would certainly have suspected that she had been. On her return home to her family, her brother, who was by this time a monk, believed her only option was to become a nun ("Thomas of Froidmont: The Adventures of Margaret of Beverly, A Woman Crusader," *CR*).

Among the casualties of crusading were also the missing: those that were never accounted for and who never returned home. Whether taken into slavery or buried anonymously in an unknown grave, these lost crusaders must have created deep sadness and serious legal and political uncertainties for their families back in Europe (Paul 2012, 134–70). Count Baldwin of Hainault, for example, went missing in 1198 after his company was attacked by a Turkish force in Anatolia. Baldwin had been part of an assembly sent to request aid from the Byzantine emperor after the fall of Antioch. Eight years later his widow, Ida of Louvain, made a pilgrimage to the Holy Land, during which she also organized a search for her husband. Whether her journey eased the difficulties of sorting out the count's estate we do not know. The thousands of crusade charters do, however, stand as witness to the risks and sacrifices made by crusaders for the pope's holy wars.

CHAPTER THREE

HOLY WARFARE: COMBAT IN THE CRUSADING AGE

Crusading meant war. Endowed with penitential privileges and framed as a holy pilgrimage, at the heart of every crusade was the practical machinery of medieval warfare. In this chapter we will explore the military aspects of crusading. Using manuscript and material evidence, we will consider Muslim, Byzantine, and western armies of the Middle East, their arms and armor, strategy, and the consequences of illness and injury. The Baltic and Iberian peninsula have not been included in this chapter, but useful summaries on crusading warfare in these regions can be found in Ekdahl (2006) and Nicolle (2006a).

GENERAL ORGANIZATION AND RECRUITMENT

European crusading armies were manned by the fighting subjects of the land-holding elite. Kings, lords, and knights all called upon family and vassals to take up arms. The upper ranks were generally mounted warriors, while the remainder of the army served as foot soldiers. Among these were spearmen, archers, and crossbowmen, as well as those wielding axes, clubs, and other implements of close-quarter combat. The social division between *milites* (mounted) and *pedites* (foot) soldiers was not always as expected, and there were instances of higher ranked infantry and lower ranked cavalry. Mercenaries also played a role in the composition of crusader armies, offering both mounted and foot soldiers of varying ranks. Yet whatever the hierarchy, the reality of many armies brought together as a single crusading force often resulted in a tangle of obligations and loyalties.

The military orders—Hospitallers, Templars, Teutonic Knights, and other, lesser groups—formed a unique fighting force that combined the monastic vows of poverty, chastity, and obedience with combat. Traditionally, churchmen were not allowed to participate in warfare or even to carry arms, the orders originally having been founded as places of rest and care for pilgrims and the poor. Over time, however, they added a military role to their mission, serving as a perfect outlet for crusaders to exercise their piety and military prowess. More organized than their secular equivalents, each military order was governed by a "rule" similar to that drawn up for monastic communities (see "The Rule of the Templars" and "The Rule of the Teutonic Knights," CR). Allegiance was offered solely to the papacy, giving them independence from secular crusade leaders. Each order was commanded by a grand master, with marshals in charge of military matters. "Brother knights" formed the upper tier of the order and were normally of knightly or noble birth, while "Brother sergeants" were of a lower social standing. Knights of the military orders wore distinctive habits, which indicated the order by their colors and symbols (Morton 2013, xvii–xviii). Within the Latin east they lived together in urban houses and rural fortifications. In addition to their military duties, they contributed to the care and protection of Christians within the region, looking particularly after pilgrims and the poor and providing them with refuge and hospital treatment.

Islamic forces were drawn up by dynastic rulers who co-opted their subordinate family members and retainers. These were supplemented with a system of slave soldiers, or Mamluks. Mamluks could rise to positions of great power, as in Egypt where they were able to create their own dynasty at the time of Louis IX's first crusade. Islamic armies were an ethnic mixture that included Turks, Arabs, Greeks, Armenians, as well as those from Russia, the Balkans, and even western Europe. Mercenaries were employed in times of need, and local volunteers were recruited under the banner of *jihad*, primarily from urban environments. Lesser emirs provided regional forces for a sultan, but there was also the option of granting a territory's taxes in place of military service (called *iqta*; Christie 2014, xxxii). On the whole, Islamic forces were more sophisticated in their structure and administration than their crusader counterparts. Foot soldiers were also an important component of any force, especially in situations of siege warfare, although the use of cavalry depended on the region in which they were deployed (pasture being scarce in territories such as Egypt). The ruling sultan always had his own bodyguard unit, which at times constituted a sizable percentage of the overall army (Nicolle 2006b, 1255–57).

The Naziris or Assassins were a small, independent Isma'ili Shi'a force that arose in response to the tensions between the Shi'a and Sunni sects. The nickname "assassins" is a westernized rendering of *hashīshiyya*, an Arabic word referring to the use of hashish. This, however, was probably a derogatory term, as drug-taking was linked to the lower classes. The Naziris engaged in political assassinations, in particular against Sunni leaders, although other Muslims and Christians could be targeted. They settled into the region of northwest Syria and from their bases carried out a series of assassinations in the twelfth and thirteenth centuries. Their influence was considerable, given their size. Crusaders were known to make alliances with the sect, and in the twelfth century the Naziris paid tribute to both the Hospitallers and Templars before coming under the rule of the sultan Baybars. The Mamluks employed them against the Mongols and other enemies, although the movement later declined, dying out in the fourteenth century.

The role of the Byzantine army in the fortunes of the crusading regions should not be overlooked. Military forces were maintained by centrally organized taxation. Although commanded by the emperor, recruitment was based on a "theme" system, that is, regional units led by the local elite. The system did, at times, invite rebellion, as some regional leaders fought to establish their own territories. From the twelfth century, soldiers could be paid in land, a system that later became hereditary. Emperors also had to supplement regional forces with their own recruitment of mercenaries (whose diverse ranks did, at times, include western Europeans). Palace officials included eunuchs, who could be found in prominent administrative and military posts. They were recruited from a wide range of backgrounds—from foreign slaves to elite families willing to castrate kin to place them in high office.

Another specialist Byzantine force was the Varangian Guard. Originating in the tenth century, these mercenaries were primarily composed of Scandinavian warriors who had traveled down the Russian rivers (having earlier mixed with the Slavic populations). In the 1170s their leaders were joined (or, as some historians believe, displaced) by Anglo-Saxons who had lost out to William the Conqueror in 1066. At what point the Varangians evolved from a field army to an imperial guard is debated, but by the time of the First Crusade the force numbered somewhere between 1,000 and 3,000 men-at-arms. A contingent of the Varangian force served in Constantinople as the emperor's personal bodyguard and a security force for the city. Other units were regularly sent out, or rode out with the emperor on campaign. Still others were employed as part of the Byzantine navy to deal with piracy. Many Scandinavians saw the Varangians as a military training ground, its most famous trainee being Harald Sigurdson, "Hardrada," who later went on to become the king of Norway (r. 1046–66).

ARMS AND ARMOR

Manuscript illuminations offer a window into the world of crusading warfare. It is important to remember, however, that many illuminations were created long after the incident being depicted, and far from where events occurred. Illuminations can also be quite stylized, showing, for example, ceremonial arms and armor rather than what was usual in battle. There are also instances where the depiction of the enemy has been simplified or made grotesque, out of ignorance or perhaps to emphasize the superiority of the illustrator's side. With these caveats in mind, manuscript evidence can still be a useful tool in understanding, if not always the exact nature of crusading warfare, then at least how it was perceived and presented to the illustrator's respective audience.

Manuscript evidence can often be verified by checking it against written sources and material remains. While not a new field, the archaeology of crusade sites has grown since the beginning of the millennium, especially in relation to issues of warfare, injury, and disease (see, for example, Mitchell 2004). There is more work to be done, and sadly at the time of writing, many sites are under threat: the UNESCO World Heritage site Crac des Chevaliers, for example, came under fire and was damaged in 2013, while many other sites remain inaccessible.

The following section presents manuscript and material evidence on arms and armor. Readers are encouraged to look closely at the provided visual evidence to determine the extent to which such materials aid our understanding of crusader warfare. In each case, consider not only what we might learn from the illustrations or objects but also what questions they raise.

Illustrations 3.1 and 3.2 depict a drawing of a crusader from the first half of the thirteenth century and arms and armor dating to ca 1190. The manuscript

ILLUSTRATION 3.1   Kneeling crusader from the Westminster Psalter (ca 1250), British Library (MS Royal 2A XXII fol. 220).

ILLUSTRATION 3.2 Arms and armor of Baron Adhemar of Beynac, ca 1190 (?), displayed in the Castle of Beynac, France (photo by Stephen Bowden).

illumination in Illustration 3.1 shows the crusader kneeling in an attitude of prayer. The symbol of the cross covers both his surcote (tunic) and the banner attached to his lance. The banner served as an emblem of identity for a lord or commander and a rallying point in battle. Lances were generally the weapon of mounted warriors, while spears and javelins (the latter for throwing) were more often carried by infantry. A straight sword is held by a belt. The crusader's helmet and shield are not pictured, although the head is protected by a mail "coif." It is not clear whether this is part of the overall mail hauberk (coat) or a separate hood (as was becoming the fashion in the thirteenth century). The hauberk itself is split at the bottom to allow for it to be worn on horseback. Thickly padded garments would have been worn beneath the armor, offering further protection. The illustration shows the legs and feet protected by mail, with the horseman's spurs attached to the foot armor. Mail armor was employed up to the fourteenth century, when scale and plate armor came into use.

The photograph in Illustration 3.2 shows an array of arms and armor said to have belonged to Baron Adhemar (ca 1120–94). Adhemar was known to have accompanied Louis VII on the Second Crusade, although the armor appears to be dated to 1190 (the time of the Third Crusade). The collection shows straight swords, as pictured in the manuscript, but also includes helmets that were intended to cover the entire face (called "great helms"). These came into use in the twelfth century alongside the earlier cap helmets that covered only the head (some with nose guards, as depicted in the Bayeux Tapestry). The size of the two small shields indicates that they were probably used for mounted combat. Two crossbows are also displayed. Originating in the ninth century, crossbows were deadly weapons whose quarrels (bolts) could pierce mail armor. Crossbowmen could be mounted or serve as foot soldiers. and many are shown in manuscript illuminations wearing armor. Archers with longbows, who were usually on foot, wore little if any armor. The longbow was generally a long-range, quick-fire weapon that, when launched *en masse*, could send a shower of arrows down on an enemy. The crossbow took longer to arm and had a shorter range, but the speed and penetration of its bolt were much greater. The ax, pictured behind the sword and shields, was a more ancient weapon and was used by mounted knights and foot soldiers.

Illustrations 3.1 and 3.2 are both representative of the type of protection and weapons worn and wielded by upper-class knights and nobles. There are fewer manuscript depictions of foot soldiers, as illustrations were typically created for the landed class. Even soldiers shown fighting on foot are often dismounted knights rather than infantry. As for the equipment of the more humble crusader, most would have had to make do with less effective weaponry and armor made primarily of leather, felt, or some other type of padded cloth (France 1999, 26–28).

For the most part, Muslim forces fought with similar arms to those of the crusaders. The straight sword was preferred to the scimitar or curved saber, although many western illuminations depict Muslim soldiers with the latter (perhaps to distinguish them from crusaders). Large daggers and axes were also used. The mace, a weapon often associated with the west, was in fact eastern in origin. Maces with flanged terminals were common for the period and were carried by both infantry and cavalry. Maces could be used by infantry to bring down mounted soldiers and their horses, but they were equally deadly as a cavalry weapon against enemy horsemen or those on foot.

Both infantry and cavalry included archers and crossbowmen. Mounted archers could harry an enemy, firing rapidly and moving quickly. Javelins (for throwing) and lances or spears (for thrusting, often under the momentum of a charge) were also an effective weapon whether on horseback or foot. Illustration 3.3 shows both bows and spears/javelins being used. This is a twelfth-century depiction of a battle that took place in Edessa in 1031 between Byzantine and Turkish forces. Here we can also see round shields, which were commonly used by Islamic soldiers.

Comparing western and eastern armor, we find similarities and differences in preferences and design. Some visual and written sources (as with Illustration 3.3) show Muslims wearing only turbans. This is often seen in western depictions of Muslim soldiers, but it is known that fitted iron helmets were often worn underneath (Nicolle 2007, 191). Other helmet designs included a one-piece bulb-shaped headpiece and a segmented helmet with protection for the sides and back.

Although it appears in Illustration 3.3 that the majority of the Muslim forces have no body armor, mail shirts were often worn under their outergarments. Leather or padded cloth armor was also used. The Muslim soldier heading the line of javelin holders in Illustration 3.3 seems to be wearing lamellar body armor, which was made of rectangular metal or leather plates that were perforated and laced together to form overlapping horizontal rows. In later periods,

ILLUSTRATION 3.3   Twelfth-century Byzantine manuscript showing Islamic forces (Seljuk Turks) attacking Byzantine garrison at Edessa in 1031 (Synopsis historiarum of John Scylitzes, Biblioteca Nacional, Madrid Matritiensis Vitr. 26–2).

a combination of mail and plate armor would be used, although the European style of full-plate armor was never adopted.

Arms and armor dating from the crusade period are also found in Byzantine manuscripts. The scenes themselves, however, are often those of biblical or past historical events. Byzantine art generally presents "a high degree of stylization and archaism" and for these reasons must be used with care (Bartusis 1997, 325). Byzantine forces were known to wear lamellar armor as well as mail. Cap helmets were worn, some with attachments of mail, leather or fabric to protect the sides and back of the neck. Helmets that covered the entire face were probably worn by heavy cavalry. The *chapel de fer*, or "war hat," is a later design (ca thirteenth century), with a conical headpiece and wide brim that could be worn over a mail hood (Illustration 3.6 shows one of the sappers wearing such a helmet). Kite-like shields made of wood, leather, and iron were common, and both mounted warriors and infantry used a variety of swords, lances/spears, maces, axes, bows, and crossbows. Again, many of these elements can be seen in Illustration 3.3.

A brief word should be offered on chemical/incendiary weapons, including the role of gunpowder. Such weapons had been known to the Byzantine and Islamic forces since before the crusading period. Mineral oil was a necessary component of these devices, although the exact chemical composition of many is not known. The use of "Greek" or liquid fire, or *naft*, was perhaps the most alarming. This was a mixture of naphtha and sulfur, with lime, resin, or other combustible material. Liquid bitumen was also used and was particularly effective as it could be put out only with sand. Liquid fire was kept in clay or metal containers called "siphons" and could be thrown with pumps from the prows of ships, as shown in Illustration 3.4.

Other, less complicated incendiary devices were also used. Flame-tipped javelins and crossbow bolts are recorded, along with the medieval version of the

ILLUSTRATION 3.4   Byzantine manuscript, the Madrid Skylitzes, showing Byzantine ship attacking with Greek fire (Codex Skylitzes Matritensis, Bibliteca Nacional de Madrid, Vitr. 26–2, Bild-Nr. 77, f 34 v. b).

grenade. Various forms of liquid fire could be poured into small glass or clay receptacles (see Illustration 3.5), which then could be thrown by hand from a city wall or hurled from siege machines.

The incendiary grenade was particularly useful against the crusaders' wooden fortifications and siege equipment. Its general use declined, however, as crusaders learned not to use as much wood in their constructions or not to leave it exposed to attack. Fireproof material was devised as early as the twelfth century for clothing, horses, and structures (Nicolle 2007, 242–44, 247).

Gunpowder, a Chinese invention, arrived in the Middle East as early as the mid-twelfth century. Its development is debated, in part because the term *naft* was used for both liquid fire and gunpowder. Cannons appeared around the

ILLUSTRATION 3.5   Twelfth-century Islamic clay incendiary grenade (12 cm in height) (Sévres National Ceramics Museum, Aj 1).

mid-thirteenth century, although initially their range and firepower were not much better than stone-throwing siege engines. The dangers of carrying and loading gunpowder were considerable, and the cannons themselves were known to jam and explode. Indeed, it was not until the mid-fourteenth century that the full potential of this weapon was realized, and we can see its effect in the 1453 siege of Constantinople. In this instance, Sultan Mehmet II had gathered an array of cannons for the siege, the largest being 27 feet long and requiring 60 oxen to pull. Their fire-power was formidable, with 200- to 1,200-pound cannonballs reaching a range of a mile at their farthest point. The defenders of Constantinople fought back with their own cannons, but these were smaller versions and lacked the range of the Ottoman artillery. The Byzantines also quickly ran short of gunpowder, while we know that the Ottomans were well supplied (as the largest of their cannons used 1,000 pounds of gunpowder a day).

The changeover from medieval to modern arms had its beginnings in the late crusade period, but it was too late to make a significant contribution to the crusade movement as a whole.

STRATEGY AND TACTICS

Manuals on military strategy (the grand plan) and tactics (individual maneuvers) are found in both western and eastern writings. In the west, there was a great reliance on the late-fourth-century work *De re militari* (*On military matters*) (Milner 1997). Written by the Roman bureaucrat Vegetius, this manual was copied and incorporated into military guides throughout the medieval period (Nicholson 2003, 7). More contemporary advice was provided by several sources. The rules of the military orders, for example, included instruction on tactics: "... and when they [Templar knights] are armed and they go in a squadron they should place their squires with lances in front of them, and those with horses behind them, in such a way that the marshal or the one who is in his place commands" ("The Rule of the Templars," *CR*). Specific strategies and tactics for crusading increased beginning in the thirteenth century as the conditions in the Holy Land and the tactics of the Muslim forces became better known.

Byzantine manuals of warfare date to periods well before the Crusades (Dennis, 2001, 2009 and 2010). The *Strategikon* of Emperor Maurice (r. 582–602) and the *Tatika* of Leo VI (r. 886–912) were in circulation, as well as later works such as *Skirmishing* and *Campaign Organization and Tactics*, which date from the late tenth century. The latter works covered warfare in the mountains along the Syrian frontier and the Balkans. The Islamic east also had its treatises on war, which increased in number during the crusader period. Often they would be written for and presented to a particular sultan, although Hillenbrand cautions against assuming that they all reflect "actual military practice" (2000, 435). One of these was written by

Murda al-Tarsusi for Saladin. It was drawn up with crusader warfare in mind, although we do not know the extent to which it was used by the sultan. Other treaties of the Ayyubid and Mamluk dynasties followed, including those devoted to *furusiyya* (horsemanship) and *futuwwa* (Islamic chivalry) (Hillenbrand 2000, 435–39).

WARFARE

The following sections will consider the three main ways in which wars were planned and fought in the crusader period: siege warfare, open or field battle, and naval engagements.

Siege Warfare

Small raids and skirmishes aside, by far the most common military engagement during the Crusades was the siege. The Middle East was a fortified landscape with walled cities and strategically located strongholds. Laying claim to any territory required taking possession of its defended sites. The advantage of a siege, however, usually rested with those on the inside. The besieged needed enough defenders to "man" the walls and enough provisions to wait it out, but at least they were on home ground. Antioch's walls, for example, stretched for seven and a half miles, making it difficult to defend but a challenge to "starve out." Coastal cities also favored the defenders, as they were often able to get supplies in by sea.

Besiegers, on the other hand, found themselves committing weeks or months to the effort, often in unfamiliar and unsupported circumstances. Those within the walls may have risked starvation, but those on the outside also faced serious shortages of food and water. At times, the situation was exacerbated by the defenders' scorched-earth policies. Wells were poisoned outside the walls of Jerusalem in the siege of 1099, and the area around Acre was stripped of food and supplies by Saladin's forces to weaken Richard I's siege. There was also the real danger of the sudden arrival of enemy reinforcements. Such an army could cut off much-needed supplies. Indeed, this was one of Richard I's reasons for abandoning his plans to besiege Jerusalem. Worse yet, reinforcements might attack, pinning the besieging army down within range of two opposing forces. Finally, natural impediments, such as weather and disease, often took their toll on besieging armies. Excessive rain, drought, and the harsh summer and winter conditions of the region could devastate the health of an army. A fever swept through the besieging crusader camps outside Acre in 1190, killing as many as 200 a day, and in 1250, thousands of crusaders fell ill outside the Mamluk fortress of Mansourah.

Given these difficulties, waiting for a city or fortification to surrender was not always an option. Efforts had to be made to speed up the process by getting over or bringing down its walls. Siege equipment was essential to crusader warfare, although the crusaders faced a steep learning curve when they first arrived in the east. As noted above, they soon found that wooden siege equipment needed protection against incendiary devices. There was also the constant challenge of finding wood to create their machines (scorched-earth policies often included denuding an area of suitable trees). There is a bewildering range of terminology for these machines, much of it vague or contradictory. We are, however, fortunate to have several manuscript illuminations showing the machines in action. Although somewhat stylized, they do provide a vital visual source for siege warfare.

Perhaps the best known of siege weaponry are the stone-throwing machines. Although tension-based engines were in existence at the time, it was the counterweight trebuchet (or mangonel) that we see most often in crusade manuscripts. Initially, these were operated manually, the swing beam being tilted by the weight of several men.

Illustration 3.6 shows a manual trebuchet. One man holds the sling with a stone, while on the other end we can see three rings from which ropes are suspended for a group of soldiers to pull (the soldiers holding these, however, are obscured by the knights on horseback). By the mid-twelfth century a new trebuchet was in use, one that employed a counterweight of boxed stones or sand (see Illustration 3.7). This type of counterweight trebuchet required fewer people to operate and was more precise in its aim. It was also, however, heavier and thus more difficult to move. Both the manual and box trebuchets hurled

ILLUSTRATION 3.6   A siege scene with manual trebuchet. Note the sappers at work by the walls and the defenders beheading prisoners and displaying a head to the besiegers. From the *Morgan Bible* (also called the *Maciejousky* or *Crusader's Bible*, 1240), Pierpont Morgan Library MS M. 638.

ILLUSTRATION 3.7   The siege of Antioch from a manuscript of William of Tyre's history, showing a counterweight trebuchet (Historia Rerum in Partibus Transmarinis Gestarum, MS 828. Thirteenth century, Bibliothèque Municipale, Lyon).

stones and incendiary devices, but these were not the only payload. Rotting animal parts were sometimes thrown over a wall to encourage the spread of disease. Psychological warfare was practiced during the First Crusade when the heads of captive Turks were projected into the city of Antioch. At the siege of Jerusalem, entire bodies were hurled over the walls.

In addition to trebuchets, sappers were engaged to undermine the walls. Towers were most often the target, with sappers digging beneath the foundations and then setting light to flammable material in the space created. This was dangerous work, as the structure could collapse on sappers and defenders alike. Sappers were also exposed to whatever could be fired or thrown at them from the walls. Battering rams offered another means by which walls and gates could be damaged, but as with the sappers, measures had to be employed to protect these who undertook this work. Illustration 3.8 depicts a moveable wooden shield under attack from stones and fire.

If unable to break through walls, siege towers and ladders allowed an attacking force to scale them. The First Crusade's capture of Jerusalem was brought about by the use of a siege tower (see Illustration 3.9), although there were often obstacles to overcome, such as rough terrain or ditches, and the most dangerous, fire. An extract from *De expugnatione Lyxbonensi* (*The Conquest of Lisbon*) describes how crusaders protected a siege tower during the Iberian crusade of 1147:

And when we had been at the siege for a fortnight, we began on both sides to build engines, the men of Cologne and the Flemings constructing a sow

ILLUSTRATION 3.8 **Sappers protected by moveable shield (sometimes called a "sow") (Les Grandes chroniques de France [between 1332 and 1350] British Library, Royal MS 16 G VI f. 74).**

[protective covering as seen in Illustration 3.8], a ram, and a movable tower, and we a movable tower 95 feet in height. At last our tower was completed and covered all around with woven mats of osiers [willow branches] and with ox hides in order that it might not be damaged by fire or by the impact of stones.... (adapted from David 2001, 143, 147)

In this instance the tower was attacked repeatedly, and despite soaking the hides in water, it eventually burned. Expensive and time-consuming to make, siege towers were generally a weapon of last resort reserved for the most prized objectives.

Open Battle

Open battles were generally avoided, as they were costly in terms of both arms and manpower. We have discussed general tactics, but this section will focus on one particular battle: Hattin (3–4 July 1187). Events leading up to Hattin, as well as the battle itself, can be traced on Map 3.1. It was fought between the forces of Saladin and crusader armies under the command of Count Raymond of Tripoli, King Guy of Jerusalem, Lord Reynald of Châtillon, and the military orders. Saladin's army numbered around 30,000, while the crusaders mustered between 16,000 and 20,000. Saladin's overall strategy was to lure the crusaders

ILLUSTRATION 3.9   Siege of Jerusalem, showing a siege tower, ladders, and counterweight trebuchet (1099) (William of Tyre, Histoire d'Outremer, French 13th century. Bibliothèque nationale, Paris, MS Fr. 9081).

into open battle, defeat them, and, with this victory, take back Jerusalem and its territories.

If open battle was such a risk, why was it one that Saladin was willing to take? Maintaining a field army in enemy territory was difficult at the best of times. Even his most trusted soldiers could not be in the field indefinitely, as they each had regions of their own to administer, or at least holdings that required their attention. If Saladin could not convince them that ultimate victory and booty lay in the near future, he would lose their support. Saladin's political position was also not as secure as he would have liked. His rule depended on the backing of other Muslim leaders. Any weakness or failure on his part would seriously undermine his standing as the leader of *jihad* (France 2015, 53–54).

The advantage lay with the crusaders. Yes, Saladin was in their territory, but they had only to wait safe within their castles and walled cities for the sultan's forces to run out of provisions and retreat. This had happened before with other, smaller encounters, and it seemed an obvious strategy. The crusaders knew what was at stake: if they committed the whole of their force to a pitched battle, there would be no one to defend the cities and castles. If they failed in the field, Outremer would fall. Yet a decision was made to gather as many crusader forces as possible at the castle of Saforie. Plans had been discussed earlier at Acre between the crusade leaders, but there appears to have been no decision as to what the force should do once brought together. This uncertainty may have stemmed from the tensions within the crusader camp. Years of infighting had eroded cooperation and mutual trust among the crusade leaders.

Saladin crossed into Palestine after his treaty with the crusaders expired in April 1187. He had destroyed the military order's force of 450 at the battle of Cresson on 1 May and carried out several smaller raids in the region. By 30 June, Saladin had established his army at the springs surrounding Kafr Sabt. Water was a vital component of a summer campaign, a factor Saladin was well aware of as he made his final plans. With the crusaders at Saforie, Saladin needed to provoke a response. He did so on 2 July by attacking the city of Tiberius on the shores of Lake Tiberius (also known as the Sea of Galilee). The city fell within a day and its defenders retreated to the settlement's citadel. Among these was the wife of Raymond of Tripoli, Countess Eschiva. Raymond, however, argued to stay put and negotiate for hostages. This would seem to have been a sensible option. The distance was less than 20 miles from Saforie to Tiberius, but in full armor, in the heat of summer, it would be asking too much for any army to achieve this in a day. King Guy agreed with Raymond at first, but he changed his mind overnight at the urging of Reynald of Châtillon and Gerard of Ridefort (c. 1141–89), the master of the Templars. With hindsight we know that this was a disastrous decision, although it is possible that the crusaders did not realize they were outnumbered. Contemporary sources say that Guy was shamed into action by those who had a grudge against him. As these men were also putting their lives on the line, however, there must have been some hope of success, even if it was tinged with spite. Whatever the true motivation, the crusader army set out from Saforie on 3 July.

Looking at Map 3.1, we can see the terrain from Saforie to Tiberius. Note the location of springs, and Saladin's encampment at Kafr Sabt. We know that Saladin had filled in some of the wells along the route, but there was sufficient water at the settlement of Hattin. Two routes to Tiberius are shown, one to the north and the other to the south. The crusaders would take the northern route, with Raymond of Tripoli's forces at the front, followed by King Guy and his army (including the relic of the Holy Cross), and finally a rearguard comprising the military orders, under the general command of Balian of Ibelin (ca 1140–93). Mounted warriors were to ride in the middle of these ranks, surrounded by foot soldiers who could protect the horses.

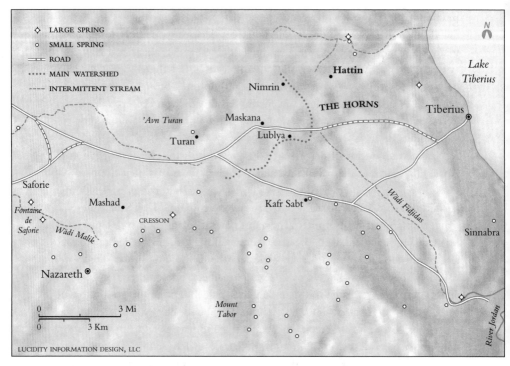

MAP 3.1   The Battle of Hattin (1187) (J. France [2015], Great Battles: Hattin [Oxford: Oxford University Press], p. 173). See also Nicolle (2011, 63).

The hope was to make Tiberius in a day, but failing this, the wells of Hattin, 12 miles away, could serve as a safe mid-point. From the moment they left the safety of Saforie, however, the crusader force was harassed by Saladin's mounted archers, a tactic designed to hinder and demoralize the army. The crusaders passed within a few miles of the springs of Turan but did not divert. This has always been judged a reckless decision, although Malcolm Billings (2010) has argued that the springs would not have provided nearly enough water for the army. This assertion is based on data from the Israel Hydrological Service, which holds that today's limited flow from the springs (180 liters an hour) is close to what it would have been in 1187. To put this into perspective, Turan provided 10 per cent of the water that was available to Saladin's forces at Kafr Sabt. Whether the crusade leaders were aware of the springs' limits, their diversion to Turan (or maintaining it as a fallback position) might not have significantly aided their cause (Billings 2010, 90).

Saladin's main force arrived that afternoon to offer a more concentrated attack. Divided into three units, the Muslims harassed the crusaders but did not commit to full battle. Perhaps this was because Saladin wished to wear his enemy down, luring them further into the territory and making retreat more difficult. Under constant fire, the crusaders continued on until they halted near the village of Maskana to make camp for the night. The site, however, provided little, if any water. During the night the remainder of Saladin's forces arrived and the crusader army was surrounded. Water and supplies had been ferried via a camel caravan from Lake Tiberius to the Islamic soldiers, and they were recorded as being in high spirits. During the early hours of 4 July, Saladin used another field tactic, that of bush fires. These were set to disturb the enemy's rest and intensify their thirst. Later in the day, others would be set to confuse, hinder, and constrain.

Before sunrise, the crusaders began their attempt to reach either the springs of Hattin or Lake Tiberius. The fighting was difficult for the exhausted and dehydrated crusader army. At one point, Raymond of Tripoli charged with his unit in the direction of Hattin. The Muslim line opened suddenly to let him through, but rather than pursuing him in a flanking maneuver, they let him pass, and then quickly closed ranks. Historians have debated the motives of both Raymond's and Saladin's forces. Raymond would later be accused of treachery, but it is likely that his charge was meant to break the Muslim line. Once through, however, and with the line reformed, he had no way of returning. Saladin's ranks had managed to sideline a formidable portion of the crusader force with minimal risk to its own troops. Raymond, realizing the situation, rode on to Tyre.

Meanwhile, the remaining crusaders' ranks were disintegrating. A contingent of infantry made for the Horns of Hattin, a volcanic formation of two low hills. Archaeological excavation has revealed that at the time these included the ruins of a defensive wall, as high as six feet in some places. They established themselves on the northernmost Horn, but there they halted, refusing to rejoin the cavalry fighting below. Lord Balian and others had managed to break through the lines and escape, but the bulk of the army, along with King Guy, Lord Reynald, and the master of the Templars, were increasingly restricted in their movement. Guy had ordered his tent to be erected on the southern Horn. He led two charges against Saladin's own unit, perhaps hoping to kill the sultan and thus win the victory. Both, however, were beaten back. It was during these final hours that the relic of the True Cross was captured, further weakening the crusaders' morale. Saladin's forces kept up their attack, and with the collapse of the king's tent, the battle was over. The remaining leaders slumped to the ground and offered no further resistance.

The Battle of Hattin demonstrates the strategies, tactics, and challenges of open warfare during the crusader period. The hazards of the Palestinian terrain and climate, as well as the importance of provisions and water supplies, were considerable (Lewis 2015, 460–89). Most of all, the battle illustrates the real perils of open warfare; after Hattin, there was no crusader field army, and before the year was out, Jerusalem and most of the Frankish cities and castles had fallen to Saladin.

Naval Engagements

For the first half of the medieval period, Byzantium had been the chief naval power in the Mediterranean, although it had been joined by Islamic fleets in the centuries leading up to the Crusades. The main purpose of the majority of these vessels, however, was shipping rather than battle, and the strength of such fleets varied over the period. The role of ships in crusader warfare began in earnest with the Third Crusade. Prior to that, vessels had been used, for the most part, to provide supplies, reinforcements, and transport. A thriving shipping trade had also been established by Italian merchants along the Levant's coastal cities.

The loss of most of these ports in 1187 and difficulties of overland travel necessitated the use of ships to transport crusaders to the Holy Land. Northern Italian merchants, having grown wealthy on east–west trade were also able and willing to combine their commercial interests with the aims of the crusaders. Clashes with Islamic fleets, as well as piracy (whether private or state-sponsored), intensified the need for defensive measures. As seen in Illustration 3.10, some ships were equipped with turrets or "castles" from which arrows, incendiary grenades, and other missiles could be hurled. Others were provided with battering rams and even small trebuchets.

The Third Crusade witnessed sea skirmishes between Saladin's navy and that of both Conrad of Montferrat (d. 1192) and Richard I. It was Richard's fleet that helped to ensure the success of his march from Acre to Jaffa, providing protection as well as supplies and arms. The Fourth Crusade relied on the provision of ships by the Venetians, and successive crusades to Egypt could not have occurred without a reliable flotilla. After the loss of the Levant in 1291, naval superiority become even more important, as Mamluks, and later Ottomans, fought with Christian leaders for control of the Mediterranean, its shores, and its islands. Trade and national interests, however, would come to replace traditional crusading objectives as the medieval period gave way to the early modern era. Even so, there is no doubt that the movement helped to spark development and innovation in maritime shipping and defense.

ILLUSTRATION 3.10   Crusader ship with "castle" tower: crusaders capture the island tower of chains at Damietta (1218) (Manuscript of Matthew Paris's Chronica Majora, ca 1255, Parker Library, Corpus Christi College, Cambridge).

BOX 3.1   *Crusader Castles*

Crac des Chevaliers is, for many, the archetypal crusader fortress. Yet crusader castles varied widely in their size, design, and purpose. After the fall of Jerusalem, efforts were made by the remaining crusaders to establish themselves in cities and rural areas. Two-thirds of these early fortresses were existing structures taken over from Islamic rulers. From this period up to the mid-twelfth century, the Latin States enjoyed an interlude of relative peace, allowing for the building of numerous fortifications. Most were small structures surrounded by a single wall and located away from frontier areas. Ellenblum, in his *Crusader Castles and Modern Histories*, has argued that the majority of early crusader fortifications served as administrative and agricultural centers rather than defensive constructions, thus suggesting a more integrated society (2009, 295–96). In the latter half of the twelfth century, as Muslim leaders began to organize and resist Frankish rule, castles were built in areas deemed to be under threat. These were generally larger structures with concentric fortifications.

The military orders were instrumental in the building and defense of castles and city walls. By the end of the twelfth century, many of the early castles that had proved too difficult or too expensive to defend were inherited by the military orders (Kennedy 2015, 49). In the early 1440s, for example, the Hospitallers were granted several castles bordering on the region of the new leader of *jihad*, Zengi.

ILLUSTRATION 3.11   **The Hospitaller castle of Crac des Chevaliers.**

This included Crac des Chevaliers, which they strengthened with a new outer wall four meters wide (to defend against tunneling) and round towers built into the wall with platforms large enough to support trebuchets. The inner wall was also redesigned with integrated towers. Both incorporated box machicolations—projections from the wall with holes in the floor to allow for the hurling of stones and other weapons. An aqueduct provided water (as can be seen in Illustration 3.11), but in times of siege, an outdoor water tank and nine underground cisterns could supply the castle for many months (Byrom and Riley 2013, 69).

The Templars also created and improved fortifications, many of which were only small forts for the protection of pilgrims, merchants, or villages. Mills, churches, and estates could also be fortified, depending on their location and perceived value. Many city defenses became the responsibility of the military orders, and these included walls, internal citadels, and important urban buildings (Morton 2013, 26).

MATTERS OF LIFE AND DEATH

The dangers of crusader warfare are readily apparent, given what we know of the arms and armor of the period. Add to this the hazards of travel, disease, climate, and the vagaries of medieval medicine and it is clear that this was not an occupation for the faint-hearted. Yet crusaders knew they were putting their lives in danger, and most chose to do so willingly. As members of the military class, risks to life and limb were already an accepted condition of their existence. Crusading, however, offered salvation for undertaking what was normally done for duty or worldly gain. Crusaders did not seek death but assumed that the perils of crusader life would be more than compensated for in the hereafter. With the development of *jihad*, Muslim soldiers also expected heavenly rewards for their military service.

This final section will consider the risks faced by Frankish, Byzantine, and Muslim soldiers in battle and everyday life in the medieval Middle East. Injury, illness, and medicine will be examined in turn, based on primary sources and archaeological evidence.

The exact number of crusaders who died on campaign to the east is not known. Historians have estimated that the death rate for knights of the First, Third, and Fifth crusades was somewhere around 25 to 35 per cent, with the cause of death divided equally between injury, disease, and malnutrition (Mitchell

2004, 176–77). This does not account for members of the lower ranks, who probably suffered and died in greater numbers due to inferior arms, poorer diet, substandard living conditions, and reduced access to medical care.

Injury

Excavation of crusader-period battlefields and burials has provided information on the types of injury sustained in combat and instances of survival from these wounds. Given the armor, battle stance, and the fact that most soldiers of the period were right-handed, most injuries appear on the left side of the head, the forearms, and the right leg. Arrows and crossbow bolts were the most common cause of injury, as these were fired in such great numbers. The lance, however, was also a deadly weapon, which, with sufficient momentum, could pierce armor.

Excavations at the Templar castle of Jacob's Ford (1179) reveal the wounds inflicted on crusaders by Saladin's army after the fall of the fortress. An archaeological report from 2006 provides details of five of the crusader skeletons excavated at the site: "Multiple sword and arrow wounds were noted, and arrowheads were still in situ at the time of their deaths. All the soldiers appear to have been stripped of their armor and then dumped together with corpses of horses that died in the battle" (Mitchell, Nagar, and Ellenblum 2006, 1). Primary written sources tell us that Saladin began the siege with an arrow barrage (confirmed by the hundreds of arrows found scattered at the site and embedded in the skeletal remains). This was followed by the sappers, who created a large tunnel underneath the walls. When the timbers within the tunnel were set alight, the walls fell and Saladin's troops surged through the gap. Half the garrison were taken captive for the slave markets, while the other half either died in battle or were executed. The Islamic sources say that Saladin carried away 1,000 coats of armor, although we do not know how many of the crusader force had armor. Those specifically marked for execution included the Frankish archers and what remained of the Templar force. In all, about 800 crusaders are believed to have perished at the site. It is not known, however, how many of Saladin's forces died during the siege.

Examination of the skeletal remains of one crusader shows that he had his forearm cut off at the elbow and suffered another blow that divided the front of his skull. Both wounds are thought to have been made by a sword in a face-to-face fight. The location of the arm wound is understandable as the style of mail sleeves for this period (if mail was worn) stopped at the elbow. We cannot know if the soldier was wearing a helmet. If so, the blow to the skull would have to have been particularly heavy to slice through the helmet and into the brain. There are some human remains at the site that do not display fatal wounds. Soft tissue wounds, however, would have left no trace in the skeletal record. These could include piercing or stabbing of the torso area or the opening of arterial regions such as the neck.

Illness and Malnutrition

Disease was another threat to the crusaders of the Middle East. Their Islamic opponents were more acclimatized to the region and thus had a definite physiological advantage as well as a better knowledge of how to prevent and treat such maladies. The cheek-by-jowl existence of crusaders, especially during periods of siege warfare, facilitated the spread of infectious diseases. Such epidemics could sweep through a camp, infecting hundreds. Unfortunately, there is not enough detail in most cases to determine the exact nature of the recorded illness. One of the most dreaded of the infectious diseases was leprosy. During the Crusades, a military order known as the Order of St. Lazarus was established for soldiers who had contracted the disease. It operated alongside civilian *leprosaria* (institutions caring for those with leprosy). *Leprosaria* were kept separate from other hospitals, and those with leprosy were usually excluded from mainstream society. An exception to this was King Baldwin IV of Jerusalem, who had contracted leprosy as a child but was crowned and ruled up to his death at the age of 24.

Non-infectious diseases also stalked the crusaders. Camp conditions often resulted in contaminated water, which led to illnesses such as dysentery. It was one of the main causes of sickness among the crusaders of Louis IX's first and second campaigns and had a marked impact on the outcome of both. The transfer of intestinal parasites by unsanitary conditions was also a regular occurrence (Mitchell 2015). Excavation of the latrines at the Hospitaller infirmary in Acre has revealed that its patients carried roundworm, whipworm, and fish tapeworm (Mitchell and Stern 2000).

Exposure to the extremes of temperature and humidity undermined the general health of the army. Heatstroke was certainly a factor with crusaders on the march or fighting in full armor. This was apparent at the Battle of Hattin but was a common factor on many campaigns, including the First Crusade's march across Anatolia in which hundreds, perhaps thousands, died from the heat and lack of water. Albert of Aachen records, "Then the day came ... when the great shortage of water became acute among the people. And therefore, overwhelmed by the anguish of thirst, as many as around five hundred people of both sexes gave up the ghost on the same day ..." (qtd. in Hallam 2000, 74). At the other end of the spectrum, the marshes of the Holy Land's coast and lakes, as well as Egypt's delta region, were breeding grounds for malaria.

Malnutrition and poor food hygiene were also responsible for illness and death among the crusaders. Food poisoning was an ever-present danger, while malnutrition could bring on scurvy and other diseases related to a poor diet. Starvation itself was perhaps the greatest hazard to an army on the march or in siege situations. The lack of provisions is a constant refrain in the sources of the period and again must have affected the lower ranks more so than the knights or nobility.

Medicine and Treatment

Those in the east and west both had faith in the ancient Greeks with regard to medicine and treatment. All believed that the body was composed of four "humors"—blood, yellow bile, black bile, and phlegm—and that one's health depended on their balance. Islamic scholars copied hundreds of these works, translating them into Arabic. Yet Muslim practitioners did not limit themselves to ancient medical learning. Added to the Greek texts were new observations and new drugs. Indeed, one of the primary differences between ancient and Islamic medical writing was the latter's greater emphasis on drugs rather than on alterations to diet or lifestyle. The identification and proposed treatment of diseases were also expanded, albeit within the framework of the four humors.

Although a subject of debate, it is generally believed that Islamic medical knowledge spread to Europe not through the eastern crusades but via the Iberian *Reconquista* and the west's conquest of previously Islamic islands such as Sicily and Sardinia. Access to Islamic medical works coincided with the west's economic growth and the subsequent rise of cathedral schools and scholarship. The first stage in the translation of these works into Latin occurred in the eleventh century, followed by a second stage in the twelfth.

Although physicians were known to have traveled with the crusaders, we do not have a great deal of information about them. The Islamic writer Usama ibn Munqidh criticized but also praised Latin doctors. Crusaders in turn were suspicious of non-Christian practitioners, yet as William of Tyre complained, "the Latin leaders, urged by their womenfolk, scorned Latin medicine and only trusted the Jews, Samaritans, Syrians and Saracens" (Krey 1943, 292). In the course of the Crusades, both eastern and western doctors would have been called upon to treat battle wounds and illnesses. It is important to remember that while opium and other drugs were known anesthetics, their use is not mentioned in non-medical sources. Emergency or field conditions might have prevented their use, and if so, many who received treatment could have died of shock. Cauterizing, that is burning the wound with a heated instrument to stop bleeding, is known to have been practiced for blade injuries. Stitches and bandages were also employed to bind the flesh. Those who survived the injury and treatment might still have succumbed to infection, and in those cases wine or vinegar could be used to clean and sterilize wounds. Persistent infection of limbs might require amputation. A manuscript from the eleventh-century Muslim author Albucasis notes how the patient's limb should be bound above and below the amputation line to ensure that only healthy, undamaged flesh is left after surgery. The stump would then be bandaged. As we saw in the case of the castle of Jacob's Ford, amputation could occur in the midst of battle, at which point time became the most important factor to stop the flow of blood and to prevent subsequent infection (Mitchell 2004, 152–53).

Treatment of injuries due to arrows, spears, javelins, and lances depended on whether the point was barbed or straight. A point without a barb, such as one found on a lance, could be used repeatedly if it did not catch on the victim's armor, clothing, or flesh. Points with barbs were more difficult to remove and potentially more damaging. If a barbed point achieved a deep penetration, but one that had not gone through the body part, the options were to push the arrow through, or wait until the flesh had decayed around the wound before pulling it out the way it had entered. Either way would have involved more damage, pain, and the risk of further infection. (See Illustration 3.12.)

The head was a popular target that quickly brought down an opponent and often resulted in his death. Helmets offered some protection but were not a guaranteed defense against blades, projectile points, or impact weapons such as maces or stones. Death could be instantaneous, but there are cases in which those injured lingered for days before succumbing. Detailed instructions on cranial surgery to remove bone fragments are recorded in the medical manuals of the period, although they make for gruesome reading:

> If the fracture of the skull is large, but the wound small in area, so that you cannot fully determine the extent of the fracture, introduce your fingers into

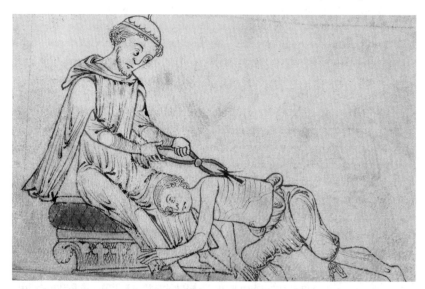

ILLUSTRATION 3.12   **Removal of arrow point from soldier's back. From Roger of Frugard (also known as Roger of Salerno), The Practice of Surgery (ca 1180) from a 13th-century manuscript, Trinity College Cambridge, 0.1.20.**

the wound and carefully probe it; for there is no better way to determine the nature of a skull fracture than by your sense of touch. After you have generally determined the extent of the fracture, cut the narrow wound with the razor in the form of a cross, and with a scraper—that is, an iron instrument—separate the flesh from the skull. And unless a large quantity of blood or something else should prevent it, bone or anything else that has to be taken out should be removed with forceps. (Roger of Frugard, qtd. in Wallis 2010, 183–84)

Crushing wounds originated from a variety of causes: falls, crowds, or blunt weapons, in addition to falling masonry or hurled stones. These could result in broken bones and internal injuries; but while the setting of bones was general knowledge, severe tissue and organ damage, or the crushing and blocking of arteries, was frequently fatal. The use of incendiary devices must also have resulted in injury for both Muslim and Christian soldiers. Treatment of burns included keeping the wound moist with ointments made from a range of substances such as vinegar, rose oil, egg, pork fat, and camphor, all mixed to varying recipes along with opium and herbs (Mitchell 2004, 167–68, 176).

Treatments of disease varied widely but included the use of herbal drugs and blood-letting, which was an accepted means of cleansing the body and restoring the balance of the humors. It was also performed as a preventative measure against illness. Not all treatments, however, were medical in nature. When large portions of a crusade army were struck down by disease, it was commonly believed to be a judgment of God. In such cases, atonement, rather than treatment, was required, with crusaders taking part in penitential prayers and processions. In more peaceful times, confession and penance would have been sought by individuals alongside the ministrations of physicians or less qualified practitioners.

BOX 3.2 *Hospitals*

Muslim hospitals, or *bīmāristāns*, were well established in the Middle East before the arrival of the crusaders. Indeed, the earliest date as far back as the ninth century. These benefited from the translation and expansion of Greek medical texts and the patronage of local emirs. In addition to offering medical care, *bīmāristāns* provided education and training. Historians have tended to view the Islamic hospital as a secular institution, citing its administration by physicians or state administrators rather than religious scholars. They also note the presence of non-Muslim practitioners in many of these institutions. Distinctions have also traditionally been drawn between Christian and Muslim hospitals, in that the latter were believed to focus primarily on the sick rather than on the infirm or merely poor. Ahmed Ragab has argued, however, that Islamic *bīmāristāns* were "charitable institutions aimed at serving the poor as part of a patron's charitable and pietistic endeavors" (2015, xii). Whatever the motivation behind these institutions, they provided a wide range of services and facilities.

In 1154, Nur al-Din founded a large hospital and medical school in Damascus. It was one of many public and religious buildings built by the sultan to enhance his political standing. The hospital of Cairo (completed in 1254) was one of the most impressive of the Islamic *bīmāristāns*, with separate wards for fevers, eye ailments, surgery, mental illness, and gastrointestinal complaints. The complex also housed a pharmacy, dispensary, lecture halls, a library, and a mosque. It was staffed by both men and women and had an out-patient clinic. There are also Abbasid records that confirm the existence of mobile hospitals that served the rural community.

In the west, hospitals were run by the monastic orders. Both monks and nuns provided rest for pilgrims and shelter for the poor, orphans, the elderly, and those with disabilities. Although the sick were also cared for, medical treatment was not normally a part of the service offered. Even as hospitals changed from monastic to secular administration beginning in the eleventh century, they still focused on care and continued to be religious in outlook and daily ritual.

In the Holy Land, western hospitals catered to the care of pilgrims and the local Christian population, especially the poor. The pace of medicalization in these institutions is debated, but medical practice was certainly in place by the later twelfth century. The Church of St. Mary in Jerusalem was linked to Benedictine monks and nuns, who had built two hospitals (one for women and one for men) in the eleventh century to look after pilgrims arriving in the city. Later another hospital was built with donations from Europe, and this was dedicated to Saint John. The Hospitallers of St. John, as they came to be known, were there when the first Latin Kingdom of Jerusalem was established. The order was shaped over the years by the conditions of the crusader occupation, however, and by 1130 it was a full-fledged military institution. Even so, it never lost its role as a provider of medical and protective care. The Hospitallers of Jerusalem took in all pilgrims, poor and sick, including

Jews and Muslims, and could accommodate up to 2,000 individuals. The Hospitallers also established an orphanage and an alms house for the poor. There was even a rudimentary ambulance service. It is estimated that at its height, the staff numbered over 600, including monks, nuns, lay physicians, nurses, servants, and volunteer pilgrims (Riley-Smith 2014, 96–97). Other military orders would also come to found hospitals, pilgrim sanctuaries, and specialized institutions such as *leprosaria*. These facilities spread to other crusader cities as well as rural settlements and fortifications. As time progressed, however, the military aspect of these orders would take precedence over their medical and caring duties.

CHAPTER FOUR

A CASE STUDY EXERCISE: SALADIN AND RICHARD I– NEGOTIATIONS FOR JERUSALEM

This chapter asks you to compare two primary sources. Both record negotiations on the fate of Jerusalem held between King Richard I of England (r. 1189–99) and the Ayyubid sultan Saladin (r. 1169–93). The reading and interpretation of primary sources is perhaps the most exciting aspect of historical research. New sources are, on occasion, discovered and translated, but even the best-known passages and authors merit reassessment. History and history books are not set in stone. As historians we are constantly testing and re-evaluating historical evidence. Such work can generate new ideas and perspectives that, in turn, shape our understanding of not just individual events, groups, and persons but also the period as a whole.

JERUSALEM

Jerusalem was at the heart of the traditional western crusades, but as we have seen, eastern Christians, Jews, and Muslims also felt (and still feel) a close bond to the city and its religious history. Byzantines played a significant role in the Christian life of

Jerusalem before the First Crusade. For much of Muslim rule they had been allowed to oversee the Church of the Holy Sepulcher and other sacred sites, a privilege that was lost under Latin control. Jews in far-flung regions longed for, and occasionally made pilgrimages to, the Holy City. Judah Halevi (ca 1075–1141), a Jewish physician and poet living in Spain, wrote of this yearning in his *Ode to Jerusalem*:

> Jerusalem! Don't you have some greeting to return to your last remaining flocks, your captive hearts, who send you messages of love?
>
> Here are greetings from the west and east, from north and south, from near and far, from every side; greetings also from a certain man, a captive of your love, who pours his tears like dew on Mount Hermón, and longs to shed them on your slopes. (Scheindlin 2008, 173–75)

Jerusalem was also extolled in Islamic poetry and highlighted in *fada'il*, or "merits." These were religious writings praising the Qur'an, *jihad*, pilgrimage, and holy cities. *Fada'il Quds/Merits of Jerusalem* literature had existed before the Crusades, but it grew after 1160 as Nur al-Din and his successors sought to promote the sacredness of the city as part of their *jihad* (Hillenbrand 2000, 162–65; Latiff 2011). The rise of Saladin and the victories of Damascus and Hattin altered the tone of the Jerusalem rhetoric from lamentation to hope. In his history of the fall of Jerusalem, Imād al-Din, an officer in the service of Saladin, quotes the sultan's praise of the city and promises of liberation. Jerusalem was, Saladin said,

> The place where the pious adore their God, the place that the great saints of the earth and angels of heaven visit. From there vast gatherings and leavings take place and crowd upon crowd of ambassadors of the pious friends of God go there. There is the Rock, whose eternal splendor has been preserved from any deterioration from which the Road of the Ascension (of the Prophet to Heaven) leaves the earth, above it the proud Dome rises like a crown, ... Jerusalem is the first of the two *qibla* [the direction of prayer, which was later changed to Mecca], the second of the two houses of God, and the third of the Sacred Zones.... (adapted from Gabrieli 1984, 151–53)

STALEMATE AND NEGOTIATIONS: THE EVIDENCE

Saladin recaptured Jerusalem in October 1187. The Third Crusade followed, but by October 1191, Richard and Saladin had reached a stalemate over its conclusion. It is important to remember, however, that both sides had vulnerabilities. For his part, Richard faced difficulties taking the city, as Saladin had begun destroying fortifications and wells on the route to and surrounding Jerusalem. Two attempts were made to reach the city in January and June 1192, but both were abandoned. Richard also knew that the longer he stayed in the east, the greater the chances were that he would lose territory at home to his rival, King Philip of France. Ill health in the summer of 1192 might also have contributed to his physical and mental ability to carry on the fight.

Saladin was also in need of a diplomatic solution. Ongoing warfare had taken a toll on his military and financial resources. Revenue-generating ports were lost (or never gained), and he did not have the funds to build up his navy to a standard that could counter the crusaders' fleets. There were also worrying signs that he was losing control over the Ayyubid dynasty as well as his army. Finally, his health was perhaps showing signs of wear before his death in March 1193.

Negotiations were held with Saladin's brother, al-'Adil, and others acting as go-betweens for the two rulers. Richard and Saladin never met face to face. Negotiation, treaties, and truces were as much a part of the Crusades as warfare, with 120 known treaties over the two centuries of Latin rule (Friedman 2015, 83–84). This treaty of the Third Crusade, however, formalized the diplomatic process to the extent that it would become a recognized means of resolution alongside military efforts.

Below are two documents detailing negotiations held between October 1191 and August 1192. Document 1 is taken from Baha' al-Din's biography of Saladin. Baha' al-Din (1145–1234) served the sultan as a *qadi* (magistrate). The two men became friends and he continued to support the dynasty after Saladin's death. Document 2 is the *Itinerary of the Pilgrims and Deeds of King Richard* (*Itinerarium peregrinorum et gesta regis Ricardi*), dated to sometime between the 1190s and 1220s. It was once thought to have been written by the Englishman Geoffrey de Vinsauf (*fl.* ca 1200) but is now believed to be a compilation of different works edited and amplified by Richard de Templo (*fl.* 1190–1229), a prior of Holy Trinity in London. While Richard de Templo is not believed to have accompanied the Third Crusade, it may be that some parts of the narrative are based on eye-witness accounts (Nicholson 2010, 6–7).

What is clear from the outset is that these are not comparable documents. The Islamic source, Document 1, offers a far more detailed and nuanced account of the events, while Document 2 deals with the negotiations in a cursory manner that is difficult to follow and interpret (Asbridge 2013, 277–78). The disparity of source material and the difficulties of extracting information from less than straightforward documents are, however, common challenges for the historian.

When reading these two primary sources, bear in mind the following issues:

The primary aims of each ruler and the difficulties they faced in achieving them.

The view of each toward Jerusalem and their reasons for wishing to rule the city.

The tone of the diplomatic dialogue and the tactics used by each side.
The internal tensions within each camp—Muslim and Christian.

The final result of the Third Crusade was a three-year truce between Saladin and Richard, known as the Treaty of Jaffa. By this agreement the crusaders were allowed to keep the coastal territory between Jaffa and Tyre. Saladin retained Jerusalem, but the crusaders and western pilgrims were granted access to the Church of the Holy Sepulcher as well as other Christian sites in the region.

Document 1: Baha' al-Din on Negotiations between Richard I and Saladin

On 26 Ramadān [587; i.e., 17 October 1191] al-Malik al-'Adil [Saladin's brother] was on duty with the outposts when the king of England asked him to send over a messenger. He sent his secretary and favorite Ibn an'Nahhāl, a fine young man. He met Richard at Yazūr, where the king had gone with a large detachment of infantry, which was now scattered over the plain. Richard had long private talks with him to discuss the peace, and Richard said, "I shall not break my word to my brother and my friend," meaning al-'Adil, and the secretary reported his words to al-Malik al-'Adil. He also sent a letter to the sultan [Saladin], through an'Nahhāl, which said in effect, "I am to salute you, and tell you that the Muslims and Franks are bleeding to death, the country is utterly ruined, and goods and lives have been sacrificed on both sides. The time has come to stop this. The points at issue are Jerusalem, the Cross [a piece of the True Cross captured by Saladin at Hattin], and the land. Jerusalem is for us an object of worship that we could not give up even if there were only one of us left. The land from here to beyond the Jordan must be consigned to us. The Cross, which is for you simply a piece of wood with no value, is, for us of enormous importance. If the sultan will deign to return it to us, we shall be able to make peace and to rest from this endless labor."

When the sultan read this message he called his councillors of state and consulted them about his reply. Then he wrote, "Jerusalem is ours as much as yours. Indeed, it is even more sacred to us than it is to you, for it is the place where our community will gather [on the Day of Judgment]. Do not imagine that we can renounce it or vacillate on this point. The land was also originally ours, whereas you have only just arrived and have taken it over only because of the weakness of the Muslims living there at the time. God will not allow you to rebuild a single stone as long as the war lasts. As for the Cross, its possession is a good card in our hand and it cannot be surrendered except in exchange for something of outstanding benefit to all Islam." This reply was sent to Richard by the hand of his own messenger.

On 22 Ramadān [20 October] al-Malik al-'Adil sent for me [Baha' al-Din], together with 'Alām ad'Din Sulaimān ibn Jandar, Sabiq ad-Din of Shaizar, 'Izz ad-Din ibn al-Muqaddam, and Husām ad-Din Bishara, and showed us the proposal that had been sent to the king of England by his messenger. He said that his plan was that he himself should marry the king's sister [Joanna of Sicily (1165–99)], whom Richard had brought with him from Sicily, where she had been the wife of the late king. Her brother had taken her along with him when he had left Sicily. She would live in Jerusalem, and her brother was to give her the whole of Palestine that was in his hands: Acre, Jaffa, Ascalon, and the rest, while the sultan was to give al-'Adil all the parts of Palestine belonging to him and make him their king, in addition to the lands and fees he already held. Saladin was also to hand over the True Cross to the Franks. Villages and forts belonging to the Templars were to remain in their hands, Muslim and Frankish prisoners were to be freed, and the king of England was to return home by sea. In this way the problem was to be resolved.

Such were the proposals brought by al-'Adil's messenger to the king of England. Al-'Adil thought them feasible, and so he sent for us, and sent us with a message to that effect to the sultan, charging me to speak and the others to listen. We were to present the project to the sultan, and if he approved and thought it to the advantage of Islam we were to bear witness that he had authorized and approved the treaty, and if he disapproved we were to bear witness that negotiations had reached this point, and that the sultan had decided not to confirm them. When we came before the sultan I expounded the matter to him and read him the message, in the presence of the men I have already named. Saladin immediately approved the terms, knowing quite well that the king of England would never agree to them and they were only a trick and a practical joke on his part. Three times I repeated to him the formula of consent and Saladin replied "Yes," calling on those present to bear witness. Now that we were sure of his views, we returned to al-'Adil and told him what had happened, and the others told him I had repeated to Saladin the declaration that took effect from the oath taken by him, and that Saladin had insisted on authorizing it. In this way he firmly accepted the proposed terms.

On 13 Shawwāl [3 November], the arrival was announced of the prince [Reginald, a vassal of the king of Jerusalem, who spoke Arabic and was on good terms with al-'Adil] of Sidon ambassador from the marquis of Tyre [Conrad of Montferrat (d. 1192), a claimant to the crown of Jerusalem]. Conversations had already been held between us on several occasions, the essence of which was that the marquis and his men were tired of the Franks, and of supporting them, and wanted to make a common cause with us against them. This arose from a quarrel that had been blowing up between the marquis and the Frankish kings, as a result of his marriage to the wife of king Guy's brother, a scandalous affair according to certain tenets of the faith. This led to a division of opinions, and the marquis, fearing for his life, took his wife and fled by night to Tyre. There he had begun to incline to the sultan, and made certain gestures of reconciliation toward him. The split between the marquis and the Franks was of advantage to the Muslims, for he was the strongest and most experienced of their generals, as well as a good governor. When the news of their ambassador's arrival reached the sultan he gave orders that he was to be treated with honor and respect. He had a tent erected for him, surrounded with an enclosure of cloth and containing as many cushions and carpets as are suitable when princes and kings meet. Saladin ordered that he should be shown to his quarters near the stores to rest, and then held a secret conference with him.

On 19 Shawwāi [9 November] the sultan gave an audience and summoned the prince of Sidon to hear his message and statement. He appeared with a whole group of companions—I was present at the audience—and Saladin treated him with great honor. He entered into conversation with him and had a sumptuous banquet served for them. After the meal he led them aside; their proposal was for the sultan to make peace with the marquis with whom various great Frankish lords had made common cause, among them the prince of Sidon himself and other distinguished persons. We have already stated his position. A condition of accepting his offer was that he [Conrad] should break openly with the Franks of Outremer, because of his great fear of them and because of the matter of his wife. The sultan appeared to be disposed to accept his proposal on certain conditions, by which he hoped to create discord among the Franks and to set them at loggerheads. Now after listening to him [Prince Reginald], the sultan promised to give him a reply later, and the ambassador retired for the day to the tent erected for him.

That night an ambassador came from the king of England: the son of Humphrey, one of the great Frankish leaders and kings (in his train was an old man who was said to be a hundred years old). The sultan sent for him and listened to what he had to say. His message was, "The king says, 'your friendship and affection are dear to me. I told you that I would give these regions and Palestine to your brother, and want you to be the judge between us in the division of the land. But we absolutely must have a foothold in Jerusalem. I want you to make a division that will not bring down on you the wrath of Muslims, or on me the wrath of the Franks.'"

The sultan replied immediately with fine promises and allowed the messenger to return at once. He was impressed by the message. He sent someone after the ambassador to check on the matter of prisoners, which was treated separately from the terms of the peace. "If there is peace," he said, "it will be a general peace, and if there is no peace the matter of prisoners will be of no account." The sultan's real object was to undermine the foundations of peace on those terms. When the audience was at an end and the Franks had gone, he turned to me and said, "When we have made peace with them, there will be nothing to prevent their attacking us treacherously. If I should die, the Muslims would no longer be able to muster an army like this, and the Franks would have the upper hand. It is better to carry on the Holy War until we have expelled them from Palestine, or death overtakes us." This was his opinion, and he only moved toward peace in response to external pressures.

On 21 Shawwāl [11 November], the sultan summoned his emirs and councillors and explained to them the terms of the agreement sought by the marquis, which for his part he was inclined to accept. The terms were that they should hand Sidon over to him in return for his military support against the Franks in open warfare. On the other hand, he was impressed by the terms proposed by the king [Richard]—that either he should have certain points on the coast and we the mountain region, or we should divide the total number of settlements in half. In both cases the Franks stipulated that their priests should have the churches and oratories of Jerusalem, and the king of England left us to decide between the alternatives. Saladin explained the situation to the emirs and asked them to reveal their hearts to him and tell him which plan, the king's or the marquis's, seemed preferable to them, and if the former, which of the two divisions mentioned above, proposed by the king of England. The councillors held that peace must be made with the king, since it was improbable that Franks and Muslims would live amiably side by side, and they had no security against treacherous attacks.

So the treaty [with the marquis] came to nothing and the peace negotiations continued, ambassadors coming and going to settle the terms. A basic condition was that the king should give his sister in marriage to al-'Adil who would, as her husband, acquire the whole of Palestine, Muslim and Frankish, the Frankish regions from the princess's brother, and the Muslim from al-'Adil's brother, the sultan. But the king's final message on this matter said, "The Christian people disapprove of my giving my sister in marriage without consulting the pope, the head and leader of Christianity. I have therefore sent a messenger who will be back in three months. If he authorizes this wedding, so much the better. If not, I will give you the hand of one of my nieces, for whom I shall not need papal consent." While all this was going on, the hostilities continued and took their inevitable course.

The prince of Sidon sometimes went riding with al-'Adil and they would go and inspect the Frankish positions. Every time the Franks saw him they would reiterate their offers of peace, for fear of an alliance between the Muslims and the marquis, and their strength of mind weakened. This continued until 25 Shawwāl.

Yusuf, one of the prince of Sidon's pages, came from the marquis to seek peace from the Muslims. One of the conditions imposed by the sultan was that the marquis should undertake to fight his compatriots and to detach himself from them. The Frankish territories that he himself took after the peace were to be his, those taken by us alone were to be ours, and of those taken by both together, he should have the city and we the Muslim prisoners and whatever else the place contained. He was to release all the Muslim prisoners in his domains and if the king of England should make him governor of the city by some agreement between them, peace between him and us should be based on the conditions laid down between us and the king of England, except for Ascalon and the regions beyond, which should not be subject to the treaty. The coastal region was to be his [the marquis's] and the region held by us, ours, and the area between was to be divided between us. The messenger left to carry these terms to the marquis [Conrad, however, was assassinated before the conclusion of the truce].

In Sha'ban 588 [late August 1192] al-'Adil came to Jaffa and was lodged in a tent outside the city, while the king was informed of his arrival. He was then sent for with the rest of the delegation, and presented the text of the treaty. The king, who was ill, said, "I have not the strength to read it now. But I agree to the peace, and here is my hand on it." The Muslim delegates conferred with Count Henry [of Champagne] and Ibn Barzah [the crusader, Balian of Ibelin] and submitted the document to them. They accepted the division of Lydda and Ramla, and everything else in the text. They agreed to take the oath on Wednesday morning, as they had already eaten that day, and it is not their custom to take an oath after they have broken their fast. Al-'Adil sent news to the sultan.

On Wednesday 22 Sha'bān [2 September] the whole Muslim delegation was conducted into the king's presence. They took his hand and meant to take the oath with him, but he excused himself, saying that kings do not take oaths, and the sultan was content with this declaration. So they took the oath at the hands of Count Henry, and his nephew, whom he [Richard] had made ruler of Palestine, and of Balian ibn Barzan [Balian of Ibelin], lord of Tiberias, with the agreement of the Templars, Hospitallers, and other Frankish leaders. In the course of that day they returned to the sultan's tent and joined him for the evening prayer, accompanied from the Frankish side by Humphrey's son, Ibn Barzan, and a group of generals. They were received with great honors and a tent worthy of them was erected. Al-'Adil presented his report to the sultan. Next day, 23 Sha'bān, the king's ambassador presented himself to the sultan, took his noble hand and undertook to keep the peace on the terms laid down. They proposed that oaths to this effect should be sworn by al-Malik al-'Adil, al-Makik al-Afdal, al-Malik az-Zahir, 'Ali ibn Ahmad al-Mash-tūb, Badr ad-Din Yildirīm, al-Malik al-Mansūr, and all the rulers whose territories bordered on those of the Franks, such as Ibn al-Muqaddam of Shaizar. The sultan for his part promised that he would send a messenger with them to all their neighbors to extract the oath from them. The king's ambassador also took the oath on behalf of the prince of Antioch and Tripoli, on condition that the Muslims did the same on behalf of the other Muslims. If not, the treaty was annulled. Then the sultan offered a proclamation to be issued to all military camps and markets stating that a general peace extended over the whole territory and that unrestricted coming and going was permitted between their land and ours. He also proclaimed that the route of the pilgrimage through Syria was open and expressed his intention of going on the pilgrimage himself, an idea that occurred to him when I was with him. He also sent a hundred sappers under the command of a great emir to break down the walls of Ascalon to enable the Franks to evacuate it. A Frankish delegation was to accompany them until the walls were down for fear that we should leave them standing.

It was a memorable day, one on which the two sides expressed unimaginable joy and happiness. But it is well known that the peace did not entirely please the sultan. In conversation with me he said, "I am afraid of making peace. I do not know what might happen to me, and the enemy would gain strength from my death because these lands are still in their hands. They would take the opportunity of attacking us and recovering the rest. You see how each of them is perched on his own hilltop," meaning their forts; and he concluded, "As soon as I am gone, the Muslims will be destroyed."

These were his words and it happened just as he said. Yet he felt that the peace was a good thing in that the army was tired and openly hostile [to a continuation of the war]. It was indeed a good thing as God in his prescience knew, for Saladin died soon afterward, and if he had died during a campaign Islam would have been in danger. Peace was therefore an act of divine providence and a fortunate occurrence for Islam.

(Gabrieli 1984, 225–34, reprinted in Rodriguez 2015, 71–76)

Document 2: The Itinerary of the Pilgrims and Deeds of King Richard (Itinerarium peregrinorum et gesta regis Ricardi)

Ch. XXV.—How the king was ill from his fatigue and exertions in the battle.

From the toil and exertion of the battle [a counter attack by Saladin's forces on Jaffa, 4–5 August], King Richard and several others, who had exerted themselves the most, fell ill, not only from the fatigue of the battle, but the smell of the ·corpses, which so corrupted the neighborhood, that they all nearly died.

Ch. XXVI.—Saladin sends word to the king, while he was sick, that he was coming to seize him. Richard sends to Caesarea for assistance from the French, who refuse to come.

In the meantime Saladin sent word to the king that he would come with his Turks and seize him, if he could only be sure that Richard would await his approach. The king replied instantly, that he would wait for him there, without stirring one foot from where he was, provided only that he had strength, to stand upright and to defend himself. Such was the king's courage, that it could not be overcome by any disasters. When the king, however, came to reflect on his actual situation, and the illness by which he was disabled, he thought it not expedient to be too secure when the serpent was in his neighborhood; he therefore sent Count Henry to Caesarea, with a message to the French, who had previously come thither, that they should join him and assist in defending the Holy Land, signifying also to them his present complaint, and the aforesaid message of Saladin. But the French refused to render him the least assistance; indeed, as far as they were concerned, he might have been destroyed by the multitude of the enemy, if he had not agreed to a truce which in some particulars was open to reprehension. So great was the multitude of the Turks that what chance could so small a body of men have had against them, even if they had not been sick? It was therefore agreed that Ascalon should be destroyed, rather than that so dangerous a hazard should be run; for if the enemy, meeting with no opposition, had seized the king lying ill upon his bed, Ascalon would of course have been taken possession of without resistance; but would Tyre or Acre have been safe?

Ch. XXVII.—How the king wished to return to Acre to be cured, but, on the people opposing it, he asked of Saladin a truce for three years, which was granted.

In the meantime the king began to be anxious about his health, and after long reflection he sent for his relation Count Henry [of Champagne (1166–97)], with the Templars and Hospitallers, to whom he explained the enfeebled state of his body, and protested that inconsequence of the vitiated atmosphere, and the bad state of the fortifications, he must immediately leave the place. He then appointed some of them to go and take charge of Ascalon, and to others to guard Joppa [Jaffa], while he went himself to Acre to be cured, as was now absolutely necessary for him. To this proposition they all with one heart and one voice made objection, saying, that they could not possibly guard Joppa or any other fortress after he was gone; and persisting in this refusal, they kept aloof, and no longer acted in concert with the king. Richard was vexed and embarrassed by this conduct, and it gave him the most bitter pain that none of them sympathized with his intentions or wishes. He then began to waver as to what he should do, but in all his deliberations he came only to the same conclusion, that there was none of them to sympathize with his misfortunes. Seeing then, that all left him, and that none took the slightest interest in the common cause, he ordered a proclamation to be made, that whoever wished to receive the king's pay should come together to give him their help. At once 2,000 footmen and 50 knights came forward. But the king's health now began to get so bad, that he despaired of its being re-established; wherefore, in his anxiety both for the others and for himself, he thought it best, of all the plans which suggested themselves, to ask a truce, rather than to leave the land a prey to devastation, as many others had done, by sailing home in numbers to their own country. Thus the king, perplexed and hesitating what he had best do, requested Saphadin [al-'Adil], the brother of Saladin, to mediate between them, and obtain the most honorable terms of truce in his power. Now Saphadin was a man of extraordinary liberality, who on many occasions paid great honor to the king for his singular virtues; and he now with great zeal procured for Richard a truce on the following conditions;

- That Ascalon, which had always been a cause of annoyance to Saladin's government, should be destroyed, and not rebuilt for the space of at least three years, beginning at the following festival of Easter; but at the end of that time, whoever could get possession of it might fortify it.
- That the Christians should be allowed to inhabit Joppa without let or molestation, together with all the adjoining country, both on the sea-coast and in the mountains.
- That peace should strictly be observed between the Christians and Saracens, each having free leave to come and go wherever they pleased.
- That pilgrims should have free access to the Holy Sepulcher, without any payment or pecuniary exaction whatever, and with leave to carry merchandise for sale through the whole land, and to practise commercial pursuits without opposition.

This treaty was presented in writing to King Richard, who gave it his approbation, for in his weak condition, and having so few troops about him, and that too within two miles of the enemy, he did not think it in his power to secure more favorable terms. Whoever entertains a different opinion concerning this treaty, I would have him know that he will expose himself to the charge of perversely deviating from the truth.

Ch. XXVIII.—How the king and Saladin corresponded amicably with one another by means of messengers.

When therefore the king, in his present emergency, had settled matters in the way described, he, in his magnanimity, which always aimed at something lowly and difficult, sent ambassadors to Saladin, announcing to him, in the presence of numerous of his chiefs, that he had only asked for a truce of three years for the purpose of revisiting his country, and collecting more men and money, wherewith to return and rescue all the land of Jerusalem from his domination, if indeed Saladin should have the courage to face him in the field. To this

Saladin replied, calling his own Holy Law and God Almighty to witness, that he entertained such an exalted opinion of King Richard's honor, magnanimity, and general excellence, that he would rather lose his dominions to him than to any other king he had ever seen, always supposing that he was obliged to lose his dominions at all. Alas! how blind are men, while they lay plans for many years to come, they know not what tomorrow may bring forth: the king's mind was looking forward into the future, and he hoped to recover the sepulcher of our Lord; but he did not.

'All human affairs hang by a slender thread' [Ovid, *Ex Ponto*, Book 4, no. 3, verse 35].

Ch. XXIX.—How the king went to Cayphas [modern-day Haifa] for his health.

The truce having been reduced to writing, and confirmed by oaths on both sides, the king went to Cayphas in the best manner he could, to take medicine and get himself cured.

(adapted from Bohn 1848, 328–31, reprinted in Rodriguez 2015, 76–78)

QUESTIONS

How generally should historians deal with gaps, inequalities, and inconsistencies found within sources for a particular event?

What are the primary differences between the two documents with regard to their usefulness on the treaty negotiations? As Document 2 is clearly the weaker source, should it be omitted altogether from any analysis of the event? Why or why not?

Which of the two documents would you consider to be the more reliable (rather than detailed or useful), and why?

By these accounts, what did each ruler want from the negotiations?

Compare how Saladin and Richard each viewed Jerusalem. What made it important to them, and how did they argue their case for it being a Muslim- or Christian-held city?

What rules of behavior were followed in this diplomatic exchange? In what ways, if any, were the meetings shaped by the codes of *futuwwa* and chivalry (see Glossary)?

Can you detect the use of diplomatic tactics? In negotiation, does either Richard or Saladin (or their representatives) betray the difficulties facing their side? Does either make any attempt to bluff, mislead, or intimidate?

Was the proposal to marry Richard's sister, Joanna of Sicily, to Saladin's brother, al-'Adil, a realistic solution to ruling Jerusalem and its territory?

What does the episode concerning the ambassador for the marquis of Tyre, Conrad of Montferrat, tell us about relationships between the crusade leaders? How did Saladin use this to his advantage?

Why is control of the coastal port of Ascalon a sticking point for both sides?

How did Saladin's and Richard's men feel about the negotiations and proposed solutions? How did their views on the outcome compare with that of their respective rulers?

How do Baha' al-Din and the author of the *Itinerary* each justify the decisions of Saladin and Richard not to resolve the conflict by warfare?

CHAPTER FIVE

THE CRUSADES AND MODERN MEMORY

It may seem strange that the Crusades should be linked to the twenty-first century and modern east–west relations. We are not talking here of "the long shadow of the Crusades." There is no such thing. The memory of the Crusades, as it developed from the Reformation up to our own century, offers a study in social and political change—a process that took the Crusades and fashioned them to suit the mandate and desires of each age. It is, therefore, important to keep a clear distance between medieval events and how these came to be interpreted and used in the centuries that followed, including our own. As Paul Cobb has cautioned, "The Crusades, understood from any perspective, cannot shed light on modern struggles and their motivations cannot be legitimately claimed as background or inspiration for contemporary conflicts. Medieval Muslims and Christians went to war for their own motives, not ours" (Cobb 2014, 278).

This final chapter presents a chronological narrative on crusade memory in post-medieval western and Islamic societies. There are gaps and exceptions to the narrative, and the evidence can be selective with respect to population groups and time periods. Nevertheless, the chapter aims to demonstrate how the Crusades were generally interpreted within the context of each respective period and how this might explain our current relationship with the movement and its perceived legacy.

THE REFORMATION (CA 1517–1649)

The Crusades began their fall from favor in the sixteenth century as a result of the Renaissance and the Reformation. The rediscovery of Europe's classical past, combined with the anti-papal sentiments of rising Protestant sects, set the tone for a more critical evaluation. An example of the Protestant view can be found in Thomas Fuller's 1639 work *The historie of the holy warre*. Fuller was a Church of England cleric and historian who laid the faults of the Crusades squarely on the shoulders of the papacy:

> Thus after an hundred ninety and foure yeares ended the Holy warre; for continuance the longest, for money spent the costliest, for bloudshed the cruellest, for pretenses the most pious, for the true intent the most politick the world ever saw.... Much also this warre increased the intrado of the Popes revenues. Some say, Purgatory-fire heateth his kitchin: they may adde, the Holy warre filled his pot, if not paid for all his second course. (Fuller 1639, 228, 250–51)

The book was prefaced by several supporting poems written by Fuller's friends and colleagues, one of whom quips:

On the Title of this book.

> How comes stern Warre to be accounted holy,
> By nature fierce, complexion melancholy?
> Ile tell you how: Sh'as ["she has"] been at Rome of late,
> And gain'd an indulgence to expiate
> Her massacres; and by the Popes command
> Sh'as bin a Pilgrime to the Holy land,
> Where freeing Christians by a sacred plot,
> She for her pains this Epithet hath got.

Fuller did, however, have some sympathy with sincere crusaders:

> Yet farre be it from us to condemn all their works to be drosse, because debased and allayed with superstitious intents: No doubt there was a mixture of much good metall in them, which God the good refiner knoweth how to sever, and then will crown and reward. (243–44)

Nevertheless, for many Protestant writers, the Crusades were touted as testament to the failings and duplicity of the papacy.

On the Continent, close proximity to the Ottoman threat had a strong influence on how the medieval crusades were perceived and judged. For many, the struggle against Muslim forces was ongoing, although at times politics and trade softened divisions with Muslims while creating new tensions among continental Christians. Some Catholic writers equated the Ottoman threat with that of the Protestants, and given the history of crusades against heretics, this was perhaps not surprising. Yet on the question of the medieval crusades, many, both Protestant and Catholic, did not query the initial genuineness of the crusaders but only what they perceived to be a later descent into avarice, corruption, and materialism. The Crusades were often praised for instigating a rise in western commerce and trade, thus forwarding the "progress" and development of European society. The notion of economic progress as a sign of civilization would become an important component in later perceptions of the Crusades and their professed contribution to Europe.

Views on Muslims and Islam itself were generally hostile during this period, again perhaps reflecting Europe's unease with Ottoman expansion. An exception was the west's perception of Saladin. Fuller, borrowing from an earlier historian, Richard Knolles (1545–1610), presented Saladin in a positive light, endowing the Muslim leader with knightly virtues. The west's admiration for the Kurdish sultan, which had begun after the Third Crusade, would continue to find expression in succeeding centuries.

THE ENLIGHTENMENT (CA 1650–1800)

The European Enlightenment was, in part, a product of revolutions in science, philosophy, and politics. It emphasized the ideals of freedom and human reason over what was seen as the unmerited hierarchy and religious dogma of the medieval period. Its adherents also demonstrated a marked preference for the ideas and forms of the classical period, dismissing medieval art and culture as primitive and unappealing. The Crusades were judged to be a typical episode of this archaic age, and many writers and thinkers characterized the movement as one of extreme fanaticism, slavish superstition, and boundless greed. The French writer and satirist Voltaire (1694–1778) branded them "*une maladie épidémiqué*," while his contemporary, the encyclopedist Denis Diderot (1713–89) defined them as "a time of the deepest darkness" and the "greatest folly" (see introduction to "David Hume on the Crusades," *CR*; Phillips 2010, 313).

Preference for the classical over the medieval was further aided by the rise of Orientalism, an admiration for eastern society, culture, and learning. Oriental styles of clothing and furnishings became popular during the eighteenth century, along with eastern art and literature (App 2010). The first European translation of the *Arabian Nights* was published between 1704 and 1717, while fashionable Orientalist clubs attracted well-known writers, artists, and other leading lights. All this served to consign the medieval crusades to a dim and inelegant past.

Edward Gibbon's (1737–94) monumental tome *The History of the Decline and Fall of the Roman Empire* (1776–88) confirmed the negative view of the Crusades, declaring that the west had learned nothing from its exposure to Islamic learning or to Byzantium's Greek heritage. Gibbon also emphasized what he saw as the Crusades' damaging effect on the economic development of the west, arguing that revenues were poured into the venture that should have been "employed in the improvement of their native country." He did concede some benefit, however, believing that the Crusades had undermined the wealth and power of "the iron weight of the martial aristocracy," thus paving the way for freedom of the non-noble classes. By this, he concluded, "[t]he conflagration which destroyed the tall and barren trees of the forest, gave air and scope to the vegetation of the smaller and nutritive plants of the soil" ("Edward Gibbon's Evaluation of the Crusades," *CR*).

These views were in agreement with the Scottish historian William Robertson (1721–93), who in detailing the final years of the Crusader States pronounced:

> Before the expiration of the thirteenth century, the Christians were driven out of all their Asiatic possessions, in acquiring of which incredible number of men had perished, and immense sums of money had been wasted. The only common enterprize in which the European nations ever engaged, and, which all undertook with equal ardour, remains a singular moment of human folly. (Robertson 1769, 25)

True to the Orientalist leanings of his day, Robertson held that the crusaders' encounter with "a more polished people" resulted in the channeling of eastern customs and comforts to a less sophisticated west:

> Accordingly we discover, soon after the commencement of the Crusades, greater splendour in the courts of Princes, greater pomp in public ceremonies, a more refined taste in pleasures and amusements, together with a more romantic spirit of enterprise spreading gradually over Europe: and to these wild expeditions we owe the first gleams of light which tended to dispel barbarity and ignorance. (27)

The philosopher David Hume (1711–76) echoed these views in his popular *History of England* (1754–62). Hume also proposed that the role of orthodox religion had been divisive, undermining the progress of humankind. To this end he believed that the spread of Islam was less disruptive, since in their efforts to expand, Muslims had "no leisure for theological controversy" and by this were less prone to "bigotry and persecution." Again, reflecting the Orientalism of his age, Hume viewed medieval Islamic culture as superior to both the Christian west and the Byzantines, judging the latter to be "indolent and speculative, ... continually refining on the several articles of their religious system" ("David Hume on the Crusades," *CR*).

It could be argued that these were the opinions of a small, elite circle of liberal-minded scholars. The Enlightenment thinkers had thrown doubt on the validity of the Crusades, but the movement was in no way forgotten or universally condemned. The more conservative royalists and those who ardently supported the papacy felt that in a climate of revolution and secularization, the Crusades represented the hierarchical stability and secure faith of the *ancien régime*. The old regime, however, was fading fast. Moreover, history itself was being repackaged to fit a more secular and global context. The Christian element of the Crusades would not be altogether sacrificed, but the movement would come to be defined in more generic moral terms rather than along strict Protestant/Catholic lines. This would allow for Protestant ownership of the Crusades without the associated "taint" of Catholicism. As we will see, it also enabled the movement's association with the secular ideals of nationalism and imperialism, as well as with notions of economic and social progress.

ROMANTICISM (CA 1770–1850)

Negative Enlightenment views of the Crusades were countered by the rise of Romanticism. With its emphasis on emotion and idealism, Romanticism led to the rejection of what was seen as the cold, unemotional stance of the previous "age of reason." This in turn produced a more positive view of the medieval past and the Crusades. Although there was no formal Romantic movement, those of this persuasion viewed the crusaders as the embodiment of mystic heroism. The notion of chivalry had never completely died out, but under the banner of Romanticism it gained a far greater respect, with the crusader knight held up as the ultimate example of this ideal. Crusading romanticism found expression in art, literature, poetry, drama, and music.

Sir Walter Scott (1771–1832) set four of his novels in the Holy Land of the Crusades (*Ivanhoe, The Betrothed, The Talisman*, and *Count Robert of Paris*). Scott himself expressed both criticism and praise for the Crusades, but the overall tenor of his works reinforced a romantic interpretation (Siberry 2000, 112–19; Siberry 2001, 375). Crusade literature would span the nineteenth and early twentieth centuries, with many works, such as George Alfred Henty's *Winning His Spurs: A Tale of the Crusades* (1882), aimed at the boys' adventure market, emphasizing the virtues of courage, duty, and piety. Certain crusader figures were highlighted in these works, the most popular being Richard I, Saladin, and Louis IX. In John Edgar's 1841 children's adventure *The Boy Crusaders: A Story of the Days of Louis IX*, the author explained that his purpose was to convey "the career and character of the renowned French Monarch who, in peril and perplexity, in captivity and chains, so eminently signalised his valour and his piety" (Edgar 1841, preface).

Further "stirring" tales of this genre included Margaret Yonge's *The Prince and the Page: A Story of the Last Crusade* (1866), F. Marion Crawford's *Via Crucis: A Romance of the Second Crusade* (1899), and H. Rider Haggard's *The Brethren* (1904). The Crusades were also fêted in poetry, as seen in William Wordsworth's *Ecclesiastical Sonnets* (1822; "William Wordsworth's Ecclesiastical Sonnets," *CR*), Eleanor Porden's epic *Coeur de Lion* (1822), and Elizabeth Barrett Browning's *The Romaunt of the Page* (1844).

Crusade-themed plays and "spectaculars" (the special-effects entertainment of their day) were also popular. *The Blood Red Knight* (1810) and *The Siege of Jerusalem* (1835) were well-received spectaculars of the period (Siberry 2001, 377–78). In 1841 *The Knights of the Cross; or, The Dog of the Blood-Stained Banner* was performed at the Royal Albert Saloon (see Illustration 5.1). The production offered a "Grand Eastern Procession," "Six Suits of Real Armour," a "Hermits' Cavern," a "Gothic Chapel and Chorus of Nuns," the "Crusader Camp" (with a distant view of Jerusalem), a "Grand Tournament" featuring "Broad-Sword and Shield Combat," and an ending that celebrated "the Pride and Glory of the English Crusaders."

Less sensational, but still popular, were the crusade-themed operas such as Rossini's *Count Ory* (1828) and Verdi's *Aroldo* (1857). Both featured storylines that pivoted on the return of a knight from the Crusades. This was a recurring story line that was taken up by numerous artists. William Bell Scott's painting *Return from a Long Crusade* (1861) and Karl Lessing's *The Return of the Crusader* (1835) each played up the drama of the theme.

NINETEENTH-CENTURY NATIONALISM, IMPERIALISM, AND CHRISTIAN MILITARISM

The nineteenth century saw the rise of European nationalism and imperialism. Once again, the Crusades were felt to have a role to play. Joseph François Michaud's (1767–1839) *Histoire des croisades* fused a nationalistic (primarily French) agenda with a romanticized version of crusade history. First published

ILLUSTRATION 5.1   **Playbill from the 1841 production of** *The Knights of the Cross; or,*
The Dog of the Blood-Stained Banner **(East London Theatre Archive).**

between 1812 and 1822, it was a product of its age, as is clear from the first and
last lines of its Introduction:

> The history of the Middle Ages presents no spectacle more imposing than the
> Crusades, in which are to be seen the nations of Asia and Europe armed against
> each other, two religions contending for superiority, and disputing the empire

127

of the world.... The present generation which has witnessed the outbreak of so many passions on the political scene, which has passed through so many calamities, will not see without interest that Providence sometimes employs great revolutions to enlighten mankind, and to ensure the future prosperity of empires. (Michaud 1853, xvix, xxiv)

The *Histoire* asserted that the Crusades were just such a "revolution" and that the prosperous empire in question was European, or more specifically French. Michaud is credited with setting out popular crusade misconceptions that still haunt us today. In true imperialist fashion, he believed the crusaders' primary aim was to subdue and civilize the east. The east itself was portrayed as decadent, misguided, and dangerous. Summing up the far-reaching impact of this work, the crusade historian Christopher Tyerman contends:

> Michaud was never and is not neutral. Perhaps uniquely among crusade historians, his ideas, work and their transmission in Europe, America, and the Muslim Near East over the following two centuries repay the serious attention of students of modern international affairs. A recent website commentary dedicated to crusader historians could not have been more wrong to say that "given Michaud's 'romantic' approach to the subject, his works are now mostly of value to modern scholars of medievalism." The author could, as easily, have added 'and to students of al-Qaeda.' (Tyerman 2011, 109; see also "Michaud, *History of the Crusades*," *CR*)

Michaud's *Histoire des croisades* did, indeed, have a wide influence and was translated into many languages, including Arabic. Gustave Doré contributed a hundred dramatic illustrations to the work in 1877 (see Illustration 5.2), adding to its romantic quality and helping to ensure its popularity well into the early twentieth century.

The Crusades were also seen as important to the education of Europe's young. Guhe, in her study of crusade narratives in French and German history textbooks between 1871 and 1914, notes that while French texts promoted internal nationalism, their German counterparts focused on the nation's imperial status. Thus French textbooks followed a theme of national superiority, as seen in the extract below:

> The French played the main part in the Crusades. They had carried out the First Crusade. They shared the second (1147) with the Germans, the third (1189) with the English and the fourth (1203) with the Venetians. The fifth (1217) and the sixth (1228) were insignificant. The seventh (1248) and eighth (1270) were exclusively French. The Crusades historian even entitled his book *Gesta Dei per*

ILLUSTRATION 5.2   Doré's illustration of Louis IX taken prisoner for Michaud's *Histoire des croisades* **(Gustave Doré [1997], Gustave Doré's Illustrations for the Crusades [Mineola, NY: Dover], plate 68).**

> *Francos*—'Deeds of God carried out by the Franks'. Even today, all Christians in the Orient go by one name, the Franks, regardless of which language they speak. (Victor Duruy, qtd. in Guhe 2013, 371–72)

German textbooks, on the other hand, laid claim to the nation's historical European and international standing:

> The name of Germany had never been more respected and feared as during the time of the Crusades. Frederick set off as a seventy-year-old man to seize Jerusalem back from the infidels.... A wail of grief was to be heard when the news of his death reached Europe. (Carl Krüger, qtd. in Guhe 2013, 376)

The west's renewed interest in the history of the Crusades inspired the establishment of military orders. This pseudo-revival merged nineteenth-century perceptions of medieval chivalry with the emerging agenda of imperialism. One of the supporters of this movement, Sir William Hillary (1771–1847), was a knight of the English Order of St. John. Hillary's response to the news that Acre had been taken by the sultan of Turkey in 1840 was a pamphlet entitled "Suggestions for the Christian occupation of the Holy Land, as a Sovereign State, by the

Order of St. John of Jerusalem." Nothing came of his proposals, but their message was clear: the work of the Crusades was yet to be completed, and Europe, under the banner of imperialism, was destined to fulfill the crusader vow. The understanding of this vow was, of course, much altered from its original intent. For Hillary, this was not to be a papal holy war, but a union of nations acting together as the Order of St. John to once more occupy and secure "peace and happiness" in the Holy Land ("William Hillary's Call for a New Crusade," *CR*). The dream of gaining the Holy Land was also cherished by the imperialist Cecil Rhodes (1853–1902). Although Rhodes's enterprises were focused in southern Africa, his second will (1877) included a clause for the creation a secret society, with the aim of bringing about the British occupation of the Holy Land (Knobler 2006, 313). Rhodes's vision of a British occupation foreshadows later developments in imperial aims, for while many European leaders would have agreed with his and Hillary's dream of a western presence in the Middle East, they were less inclined, as the century progressed, to cooperate and share the spoils.

National interests were often disguised in the rhetoric of imperialism. King Leopold II's (r. 1865–1909) notorious Congo Free State was built on the platitudes of progress and civilization. His speech at the opening of the International Geographical Conference on Africa (1876) called for a new, broader idea of crusade:

> The subject which calls us together to-day is one which deserves to interest, in the highest degree, the friends of humanity. To open to civilization the sole part of our globe which it has not yet penetrated, to pierce the darkness which envelopes whole populations is, I dare say, a crusade worthy of this century of progress, and I am happy to affirm how favourable public sentiment is to its accomplishment. (qtd. in Gibbons 2007, 430)

This stance was repeated by many as the nineteenth century drew to a close. J.A. Cramb, a London professor of modern history, declared in a lecture delivered in May 1900,

> All institutions are transfigured by the ideal which calls them into being. And this ideal of Imperial Britain—to bring the peoples of the earth beneath her sway the larger freedom and the higher justice—the world has known none fairer, none more exalted, since that for which Godfrey and Richard fought, for which Barbarossa and St Louis died. (Cramb 1915, 116)

Rulers and statesmen were keen to associate themselves with the crusading ideal. Perhaps the most theatrical example is that of Kaiser Wilhelm II of Germany (r. 1888–1918). In 1898, the Kaiser had organized a tour of the Middle East, in part to counter the imperial interests of France and Britain but also to cement a relationship with the Ottoman rulers of that region. His trip included a visit to Jerusalem, where he and his entourage were accommodated in luxury tents set up by the British tour company Thomas Cook & Son. The Kaiser entered Jerusalem through a gate in the walls made especially for his visit. Riding a white horse and dressed in a white pseudo-pilgrim costume, he was accompanied by retainers wearing the insignia of the Order of St. John. The Kaiser then changed into the mantle of a Teutonic Knight before attending a dedication ceremony for the city's Lutheran church. The tour then proceeded to Damascus, where Wilhelm laid a wreath at the tomb of Saladin. He later had a much grander marble tomb erected for the sultan, complete with a bronze wreath on which was inscribed the rather pompous dedication "From one great emperor to another" (Riley-Smith 2008a, 63–64).

Yet alongside the secular use of the Crusades there emerged a new religious application. We have seen how the Crusades were divorced from their Catholic legacy, making them more palatable for Protestants. In the mid-nineteenth century, British and American Protestant leaders were concerned over what has been termed the "feminization of religion." Male church attendance and participation had suffered a steady decline over the first half of the century, particularly among the working classes. Knobler sums up the urgency of the situation:

> This state of affairs posed both a spiritual and a financial problem for churches on both sides of the Atlantic, for while women filled the pews, men paid the clergymen's salaries. In order to redress this imbalance, churches tried to associate themselves with causes and rhetoric designed specifically to lure men back to services.... Most consistently, they attempted to incorporate manly and martial images into the presentation of religion, the church, and the life of Jesus. (Knobler 2006, 311)

The result was the cult of "Christian militarism," and the Crusades were an obvious accompaniment (see Anderson 1971). Crusade rhetoric and imagery were used to promote Christian manliness, whether on the playing fields of Eton and Rugby or in the working-class halls of the Young Men's Christian Association (YMCA) and Boys' Brigade. This was also the age of militant hymns, such as "Onward Christian Soldiers," "Stand Up, Stand Up for Jesus, Ye Soldiers of the Cross," and "The Son of God Goes Forth to War."

Tied closely to the ideal of muscular Christianity was the virtue of patriotism. The *Religious Tract Society*'s publication, *Boy's Own Paper*, highlighted modern-day "soldier-saints," likening them to crusading heroes of old. General Charles George Gordon (1833–85), who fell at the siege of Khartoum against Muslim forces, was instantly proclaimed a "Christian knight errant," with each of his three campaigns being lauded as a single "crusade" (qtd. in Knobler 2006, 314–15). As we will see, the promotion of the soldier-saint continued through to World War I.

Although involved with Christian militarism, nineteenth-century America did not generally go in for romanticizing the Crusades. This was in part because Americans "tended to shy away from anything that glorified the Old World" and, in truth, had little interest in depictions of nobility, chivalry, and foreign religious wars (Hillenbrand 2004, 204). The Crusades were also linked more clearly in America to Catholicism, at a time when tensions surrounding Irish and Italian immigration were sparking anti-Catholic propaganda and violence. Crusading imagery and rhetoric did eventually emerge, but this came later as a result of America's rising imperialism and the two world wars.

NINETEENTH-CENTURY ISLAM AND THE CRUSADES

Turning to the Islamic world, most contemporary historians contend that the Crusades, while not forgotten, did not hold the same degree of interest as they did for the west (at least not until the late nineteenth century). The extent to which the Crusades were an active memory for Muslims has recently been challenged by Cobb, who argues that evidence for this can be seen

> in the evocation of *jihad* that the Ottomans continued to use in their European campaigns; in the continued copying and circulation of medieval Arabic chronicles in which the Franks featured; in the folk epics about Baybars recited in public fora; in the panegyrics that made comparisons to the Ayyubid and Mamluk past; and in the silent, immovable presence of castles, walls, and ruins linked—sometimes by name—to a region's own experience with the Franks. (2014, 277–78)

The notion that Saladin had to be reintroduced to the east by the west has also been questioned (see Abouali 2011; Christie 2014, 113–14). Most would agree, however, that the first Arabic crusade histories did not appear until the mid-nineteenth century and that these were primarily translations from European accounts (such as Michaud's). The first true Islamic history of the Crusades, one that made almost exclusive use of medieval Islamic documents, was the *Book of the Splendid Stories of the Crusades* (*Kitab al-akhbar al-saniyah fi al-Hurub al-Salibiyah*), written by Sayyid 'Ali Hariri in 1899. 'Ali Hariri drew a direct line between the medieval crusades and the European imperialism of his day: "It is given that the kings of Europe are now colluding against our country (may God protect it) such that it resembles what those gone by had done. Therefore, our great [Ottoman] sultan, ... Abd al-Hamid II, said that Europe is once again waging a crusading war on us, in a political form" ("Sayyid 'Ali Hariri's *Book of the Splendid Stories of the Crusades*," *CR*). Just as Michaud promoted the continuation of the Crusades in the guise of imperialism, so 'Ali Hariri took him at his word, writing a Muslim history of the campaigns so that Muslims might "know the truth about them."

THE TWENTIETH CENTURY

The early years of the twentieth century and World War I confirmed the fears of Sultan al-Hamid II. During the Balkan Wars (1912–13), Ferdinand I of Bulgaria (r. 1887–1918) christened the conflict a "crusade," while the Indian Muslim political leader Mohammad Ali (1878–1931) compared Ferdinand to a modern-day Peter the Hermit (Knobler 2006, 320–21). Later, Britain's World War I campaign in the Middle East was hailed as "the Last Crusade." Major Vivian Gilbert's book *The Romance of the Last Crusade: With Allenby to Jerusalem* (1923) made no secret of his views on the matter: "At last Jerusalem was in our hands! In all the ten crusades organised and equipped to free the Holy City, only two were really successful,—the first led by Godfrey de Bouillon, and the last under Edmund Allenby" (1923, 171). On 11 December 1917, General Allenby (1861–1936) entered the city of Jerusalem as part of the campaign against the Turks. Prior to this event a Defense Notice had been issued to the British Press by the Department of Information, pointing out "the undesirability of publishing any article, paragraph or picture suggesting that military operations against Turkey are in any sense a Holy War, a modern Crusade, or have anything whatsoever to do with religious questions" (qtd. in Hammad and Peters 2015, 143).

Nonetheless, crusading rhetoric and imagery were very popular among the Allies, and the magazine *Punch* depicted Allenby as a second Richard I ("World War I Political Cartoons," *CR*). Allenby himself was not pleased, as many of his soldiers were Muslim. To downplay the allusion and to show respect, he entered the city on foot through the Jaffa Gate; this was also perhaps done in direct contrast to the German Kaiser's grand entry of 1898. Despite these gestures, Allenby's entrance and occupation were seen by both sides as a revival of the crusading spirit. Nearly 40 years later, Gamal Abdel Nasser (1918–70), the second president of Egypt, demonstrated the longevity of the crusading image brought about by Britain and France's Middle Eastern involvement:

It was England and France that attacked this region under the name of the Crusades, and the Crusades were nothing else but British-French imperialism ... it was no accident at all that General Allenby ... said on arriving in Jerusalem, "Today the wars of the Crusades are completed." Nor is it in any way an accident that when General [Henri] Gouraud [French World War I general (1867–1946)] arrived in Damascus, he said, "Behold we have returned Saladin." (qtd. in Knobler 2006, 322)

Soon after the war's end, the Ottoman Empire was partitioned by the western powers.

The British ruled Palestine from 1919 to 1948, during which time they faced opposition and attacks from radical Arabs and Jews alike. Writing during this period, the essayist and historian Hilaire Belloc (1870–1953) declared, "We have returned to the Levant, ... more as masters than ever we were during the struggle of the Crusades—but we have returned bankrupt in that spiritual wealth which was the glory of the Crusades." Belloc was an ardent Catholic who viewed the Crusades as "a continuous struggle between our civilization and the hostile world of Islam, which all but overwhelmed Europe.... [O]ne may speak of the Crusades in their deepest aspect as the conflict between Christendom and that undying Anti-Christ which desires to kill Christendom" (Belloc 1937, 1). For Belloc, British rule fell short of his vision of a new Levant; nor in his eyes was there any hope of a return to the security of a united Christendom (256–57). Britain withdrew from the region in May 1948. With the founding of the state of Israel that same year, new tensions arose in the Middle East.

Sayyid Qutb (1906–66) was a leading Islamic philosopher and political activist who equated the west's support of Israel with imperialism and what Qutb termed the "crusading spirit" (*ruh salibiyya*). According to Qutb, Israel was not simply a new political foundation but a religious and cultural assault on Islam by the west: "When we speak of the hatred of Islam, born of the Crusading Spirit, which is latent in the European mind, we must not let ourselves be deceived by appearances, nor by their pretended respect for freedom of religion" ("Sayyid Qutb's *Social Justice in Islam* and Muhammad Asad's *Islam at the Crossroads*," CR). In his writings, Qutb used the term "crusaderism" (*sulubbiya*), by which he meant a process, driven by hatred, that sought to destroy Islam, Islamic society, and Muslims. Qutb was a member of the Egyptian Muslim Brotherhood, but this movement was at odds with the Egyptian state and Qutb himself was imprisoned for many years. Although executed in 1966 by the Egyptian state, his works continued to have a significant role in shaping the more radical branches of the movement (Algar in Qutb 2000, 1–15).

During the middle decades of the twentieth century, the traditional notion of Arab nationalism gave way to the concept of pan-Islam, a worldwide Islamic society. Pan-Islam promoted a broader sense of Islamic culture and created a network of support for its varied and widespread members. The Arab–Israeli Wars of 1956, 1967, and 1973 further divided the Middle Eastern region, and in the latter half of the twentieth century these hostilities and tensions resulted in the creation of radical groups on both sides. Many were initially political in their aims, but over time more came to define themselves in terms of religious ideologies. In 1987, the Palestinian uprising known as the *intifada* gave rise to Hamas. Hamas (Arabic for "zeal") is the acronym of the Islamic Resistance Movement (*al-Harakat al-Muqawwama al-Islamiyya*), a group that has its roots in the Muslim Brotherhood. In its "Covenant" of 1988, Hamas made mention of the west's crusading imperialism, warning that "[t]he crusaders realized that it was impossible to defeat the Muslims without first having ideological invasions pave the way by upsetting their thoughts, disfiguring their heritage, and violating their ideals.... All this has paved the way toward the loss of Palestine" ("The Hamas Covenant," *CR*).

The instability of the Middle Eastern region, coupled with attacks on western targets by radical groups, alerted some western individuals and institutions to the growing gap between Islamic and traditionally Christian states (see, for example, "Pope John Paul II's Statements about Past Christian Actions," *CR*). Yet, for the most part, the divisions remained unresolved. Although relatively few in number, the most radical of Muslim groups were convinced of the west's "crusaderism," as evidenced by perceived interference in the Middle East and continued support for the state of Israel. At the same time, the west was seemingly unaware that the term "crusade" was now charged with explosive meaning.

THE TWENTY-FIRST CENTURY

On 11 September 2001, the terrorist group al-Qaeda hijacked four airplanes in the US, flying two of them into the World Trade Center's twin towers in New York City, one into the Pentagon in Washington, DC, and the last into a field in rural Pennsylvania. Thousands were killed, and in the aftermath President George W. Bush made the following statement: "This is a new kind of—a new kind of evil. And we understand. And the American people are beginning to understand. This crusade, this war on terrorism is going to take a while" ("Crusading Rhetoric after 9/11," *CR*; see also Illustration 5.3).

The use of the word "crusade" played right into the hands of al-Qaeda. In their eyes, here was an American president openly instigating crusaderism. To most non-Muslims of the west, "crusade" simply meant a cause, usually one with moral connotations. Within weeks there was a response from al-Qaeda leader Osama bin Laden (1957–2011): "Our goal is for our nation to unite in the face of the Christian Crusade.... The original crusade brought Richard from Britain, Louis from France, and Barbarus from Germany. Today the crusading countries rushed as soon as Bush raised the cross" ("Crusading Rhetoric after 9/11," *CR*; Ibrahim 2007, 271–73).

Still, there have been positive outcomes with regard to modern perceptions of the Crusades. Scholars have made determined efforts to separate crusade history from our own period and to focus not so much on the movement's rights or wrongs but instead on its significance within its own historical context. Rather than an ongoing injustice and source of pain, many Muslims have taken

ILLUSTRATION 5.3   Cartoon of President George W. Bush portrayed as crusader (*National Review*, 3 December 2001).

a second look at the Crusades, noting with pride the Islamic values of learning and culture that epitomized the Muslim states of that period. In this light the multiculturalism, scholarship, and relative tolerance found within medieval Muslim urban centers are seen to stand as a rebuke to the restrictive, anti-intellectual intolerance prescribed by modern terrorist groups. On a popular level, there has been a growing interest in central Muslim figures of the crusading period. Children's books such as Shahnaz Husain's *Muslim Heroes of the Crusades* and the Malaysian *Saladin: The Animated Series* seek to teach a younger Muslim generation that the Crusades are not the sole domain of the west (see El-Moctar 2012, 197–214 and also "Modern Uses of Images of Saladin," *CR*, which includes political appropriations).

BOX 5.1   *Matthew Schlimm's Analysis of Ridley Scott's* Kingdom of Heaven

Jonathan Lyons's book *Islam through Western Eyes* comments on the west's inability to recognize Islam's independent existence, noting that any "conversation" with Islam "has always been a one-sided affair, essentially a dialogue with itself, revealing much about the subject but little or nothing about the object in question" (2012, 4). Matthew Schlimm's critique of Ridley Scott's film *Kingdom of Heaven* (2005) perhaps offers an example of this self-regarding view.

Western films featuring the Crusades have been few and far between. Cecil B. DeMille's *The Crusades* (1935) and the 1954 film *King Richard and the Crusaders* both took the Third Crusade as their subject, focusing on the theme of peace and neutrality, a stance that reflected postwar sentiments of the 1930s and 1950s (Stock 2009). Non-western crusade films are even rarer, with the Egyptian *Saladin the Victorious* (1963) being the best known. Released at a time of Egyptian–Israeli conflict, the film promoted President Nasser's push for pan-Arab unity in its depiction of Saladin's unification of Muslim forces. Certain scenes were also created to mirror the conditions of Arabs within Israeli territory, showing crusaders raiding villages and displacing their inhabitants. None of the above films, however, made much of religious conflicts, focusing instead on the political issues of their own day.

Schlimm argues that Scott's *Kingdom of Heaven* is also a product of its time. The film follows the fortunes of Balian, a clear nod to Balian of Ibelin, who participated in the battle of Hattin and negotiated with Saladin for the surrender of Jerusalem. There, however, the similarities end, for this Balian is a self-made crusader (originally a blacksmith), who brings to the east his religious doubts and utopian dreams. The film was initially praised in both Muslim and western circles for its messages of tolerance and multiculturalism. Even the Council on American-Islamic Relations lauded its avoidance of "the usual stereotyping or dehumanizing of Muslims." Yet despite these qualities, Schlimm contends that *Kingdom of Heaven* is not as "benign" as it appears. Indeed, "[t]he movie rewrites the Crusades (and similar colonizing efforts in the Middle East), rationalizing western occupation of Middle Eastern lands and transforming one of Islam's greatest heroes into a spokesperson for western values" (Schlimm 2010, 130–31).

It does this, he argues, in several ways. Released at a crucial point in the Iraq War (2003–11), Schlimm sees within the film scenes that "closely align with how the Bush Administration sought to frame its military engagement in Iraq" (134). More generally, he contends, the film promotes "benevolent colonialism" (135), offering two types of colonizers/crusaders that can be easily distinguished. The villains include Raynald of Châtillon, Guy of Lusignan, and the fanatical, war-mongering military orders. Balian, on the other hand, represents the more acceptable face of imperialism, voicing the honorable message, "We fight for the people—their safety and freedom" (137).

Balian is not merely an idealistic occupier; he is also an improver. In a series of scenes the crusader is shown bringing water to a wasteland. Schlimm continues: "The movie tells us that this blacksmith from France is able to do far more with the land than Arabs ever could, transforming this desert into a virtual Garden of Eden" (141). He also maintains that this is a device seen in many Hollywood films, and further supports his claim by citing Raka Shome's 1996 study on race and popular cinema:

> Such representations of the white man as being able to make a home for himself in stark living conditions, and emerging as a champion of those who constitute those conditions is a characteristic trait of colonialism that enables the white imperial adventurer to assert his manliness and become a hero. (142)

Schlimm goes on to link this argument with evidence from the Bush administration's directives for the occupation of Iraq (2004): "Current projects will provide running water to 75% of the [Iraqi] population—more than at any time in Iraq's history" (142).

Schlimm's final point concerns the film's portrayal of Saladin, calling on Edward Said's classic work *Orientalism* (1978) to show how the Orientalist depicts Islam "not on its own terms but on Western terms" (143). In this way Saladin is made harmless, even admirable, as he parrots what Schlimm calls "post-Christian religious belief" (143). In the film, Saladin's faith is akin to Balian's in that neither relies upon religion to direct his policy or actions. This is, Schlimm notes, "*Realpolitik*" (143), with a smattering of humanist moralizing. *Kingdom of Heaven* thus portrays a fantasy world where neither historical nor current realities hold sway. One of Said's central principles is that the Orient is seen as something to be either feared or controlled. With this in mind Schlimm concludes:

> *Kingdom of Heaven* provides a mechanism whereby Western audiences can shift from their fear of Islam to a sense that they have control of Islam. It uses, encapsulates, and manipulates one of Muslim's most feared heroes, robbing him of his core beliefs and making him a mouthpiece for Western conviction.... In short, *Kingdom of Heaven* is classic colonial rhetoric repackaged for a post-9/11 audience. Its liberating message of religious tolerance is fully negated by its justification of violent and imperialistic practices. (146–47)

There are, and probably always will be, those who exploit negative perceptions and memories of the Crusades to suit their own religious or political ends. The diplomat and writer Umej Bhatia (b. 1970) has argued, however, for a more constructive approach to the history of this movement:

> By now, it should be quite clear that the notion of the Crusades as a recurring ideological and physical invasion of the Dar-ul Islam (the Abode of Islam), particularly in the majority Sunni world, merely promotes a permanent and debilitating sense of victimhood that fuels violent reprisal. Against this trend, it is a worthwhile task for historians and opinion-shapers in the Muslim world to develop a deeper understanding of the historical forces at play during the Crusades.... In the clash over historical perspectives, an accent should be placed on finding concrete examples of positive cooperation instead of merely highlighting instances of conflict. ("Umej Bhatia's Analysis of the Crusades and Modern Muslim Memory," *CR*)

Bhatia rejects Samuel Huntington's "clash of civilizations" thesis: the idea that that relations between groups from different civilizations are rarely close and are inevitably hostile when brought into contact with one another (Rose 2013). The concept was first proposed by the historian Bernard Lewis in 1990 and further developed in 2002 in his post-9/11 analysis *What Went Wrong? Western Impact and Middle Eastern Response* (Lewis 2002). Lyons, in his *Islam through Western Eyes: From Crusades to the War on Terror* (2012), takes Lewis to task, however, paraphrasing Edward Said's *Orientalism*, which holds that "one of the overriding characteristics of such scholarship is the complete disregard for what Muslims actually say and do in favour of what the Islam expert [the western Orientalist] says that they say and do—and mean" (Lyons 2012, 116).

The clash of civilizations thesis does not recognize the value of dialogue. Instead it proposes that both past and present (and this includes the Crusades) can be safely interpreted within the comfort of our own culture. Bhatia, Cobb, Christie, and others have suggested that, while the Crusades were indeed violent, this is only "half the story," and to concentrate solely on the conflicts and irrevocable differences "completely neglects the periods of peaceful interaction" (Christie 2014, 118). To conclude, with Bhatia:

> ... promoting a better understanding of the [crusade] period may offer the scaffolding for an informed dialogue between the west and the Muslim World. As the poster conflict of civilizational clash, the history of the Crusades is an ideal subject for the foregrounding of such dialogue. ("Umej Bhatia's Analysis of the Crusades and Modern Muslim Memory," *CR*)

QUESTIONS FOR REFLECTION

What were the factors that came together to make the First Crusade a reality? Which of these was the most significant?

What accounts for the success of the First Crusade, and why was it never repeated?

How did the crusaders divide and rule the Holy Land? In what ways did the Crusader States differ from the kingdoms of Europe?

What role did trade play in the Crusades of the Levant? How important were the merchants of Europe to the success of the Crusades?

What enabled the Islamic forces to unite and challenge the Crusader States?

How did the papacy justify crusades within Europe? In the long run, were these domestic crusades beneficial or harmful to the Church?

What was the *Reconquista* of the Iberian Peninsula? Were the Baltic campaigns crusades or an organized land-grab? What of the crusades against heretics, such as the Cathars/Albigensians?

How did one go about calling, recruiting, planning, and paying for a crusade? What were the challenges faced by individuals who decided to take the cross?

What are the uses and limits of manuscript evidence? What role might archaeological evidence play in our understanding of the crusading period? Discuss with reference to Chapter Three.

What part did diplomacy and negotiation play in the Crusades? Why were both Christians and Muslims willing to make truces and treaties with one another?

Who do you believe benefited most from their contact with the other: the crusaders or the Muslims? What did each gain and/or lose by the experience?

What is the legacy of the crusades? How should the Crusades be taught, and what are the dangers of this subject given the world's current political climate?

CHRONOLOGY

The following is a limited Chronology reflecting events and persons covered in the text. Please note that there may be some discrepancies with other sources as to exact dates, but the majority of these differ by no more than a year.

BEFORE THE CRUSADES

132–135 CE	Jews are exiled from Jerusalem following a revolt against Roman rule
ca 325	Emperor Constantine I undertakes the construction of the Church of the Holy Sepulcher in Jerusalem
ca 400	Augustine, bishop of Hippo, proposes Christian theory of just war
613	The Prophet Muhammad begins to preach Islam
632	Death of Muhammad
638	Byzantine Jerusalem falls to Muslim forces
656–661	First major war dividing Muslims into Sunni and Shi'a factions
661	Sunni Umayyad Dynasty begins
711	Muslim forces invade the Iberian peninsula, initiating Islamic rule in Spain
749	Overthrow of the Umayyads by the Abbasid Dynasty
800	Charlemagne crowned Roman emperor of the west by Pope Leo III
910	The foundation of the reforming monastery Cluny
ca 989	Peace of God movement recognized and supported by the Church
ca 990	The Seljuk Turks of Central Asia convert to Islam
1009	The Egyptian Fatimid caliph al-Hakim orders the destruction of Jerusalem's Church of the Holy Sepulcher In France, persecution of Jews blamed for the event follows
1027	Truce of God initiated at the Council of Elne

1048	Byzantine restoration of the Church of the Holy Sepulcher completed
1054	Schism and mutual excommunication between eastern and western churches
1061	Popes offer penance to Normans fighting Muslims in Sicily
1070	Seljuk Turks take Jerusalem from the Fatimids
	Beginnings of the Order of Knights of the Hospital of St. John of Jerusalem (Hospitallers)
1071	Battle of Manzikert—Seljuk Turks defeat Byzantine forces and take Anatolia
	Normans take remaining Byzantine lands in Italy
1074	Pope Gregory VII calls for a military force to "liberate" the Byzantine eastern Christians from a "pagan race" (offering of heavenly rewards and the reconciliation of eastern and western churches)
1081	Alexius I Comnenus begins his reign as Byzantine emperor
1085	The Muslim city of Toledo falls to King Alfonso VI
1095	Alexius I sends an envoy to a church council held in the Italian city of Piacenza, asking the pope for military support against the Seljuk Turks

THE CRUSADING AGE

1095	Pope Urban II calls for the First Crusade at the Council of Clermont
1096	Launch of so-called People's or Peasants' Crusade from northern France and Germany
	Massacre of Rhineland Jews by certain factions of the Peoples' Crusade
	Remains of People's/Peasants' Crusade obliterated by Seljuk forces in Anatolia
	Forces making up the First Crusade gather and leave for the Holy Land.
1096–97	First Crusade forces arrive in Constantinople
1097	Crusading armies are forced to surrender Nicaea to Alexius I
1098	Baldwin of Boulogne gains Edessa
	Fall of Antioch to forces under Bohemund of Taranto
	Fatimids take Jerusalem from the Seljuk Turks
1099	Fall of Jerusalem to the crusaders and massacre of its inhabitants

Beginning of the Crusader States (Edessa, Antioch, Tripoli, and Jerusalem)

1105 Al-Sulami composes *The Book of the Jihad*, a call to arms in response to the crusader threat

1113 The papacy recognizes Knights of the Hospital of St. John of Jerusalem (Hospitallers) as a religious military order

1114 Beginning of sanctioned crusades in Spain

1120 Knights Templar established as a religious military order

1123 First Lateran Council offers Spanish crusades equal privileges as those in the Holy Land

1144 Zengi, emir of Mosul and Aleppo, captures Edessa

1145 Pope Eugenius III calls for the Second Crusade

1146 Zengi assassinated and succeeded by his son, Nural-Din

1147 First crusade against the Wendish Slavs
Muslim Lisbon falls to crusaders fighting for Duke Afonso of Portugal

1148 Second Crusade forces defeated at Damascus

1164 Nural-Din's forces, under his Kurdish general Shirkuh, invade Shi'a Egypt

1169 Shirkuh dies, leaving his nephew, Saladin, as new ruler of Egypt
Saladin consolidates Sunni power in Egypt and defeats crusader forces under Amalric I, king of Jerusalem

1171 The Shi'a Fatimid caliph dies leaving Saladin in control of Egypt
Pope Alexander III calls a crusade against pagans in the east Baltic region

1174 Death of Nural-Din
Saladin takes control of Damascus

1187 Battle of Hattin—crusader army defeated
Saladin takes Jerusalem
Pope Gregory VIII calls the Third Crusade

1190 Attack on Jewish communities in England in the wake of preparations for the Third Crusade
Foundation of the military order of the Teutonic Knights

1191 Third Crusade; siege of Acre

1192 Treaty of Jaffa between Richard I and Saladin concludes Third Crusade

1193 Death of Saladin and division of his territory among relatives

1095 German crusade launched by Emperor Henry VI

1198	Innocent III calls for both the Fourth and Livonian crusades
1199	Innocent offers indulgences equal to those of crusades to oppose Markward of Anweiler (seen as one of the early "political crusades")
1204	Fourth Crusade; sack of Constantinople
1208	Beginning of the Albigensian Crusade
1212	The Children's Crusade
1213	Pope Innocent III calls Fifth Crusade
1215	The Fourth Lateran Council
1217	The Fifth Crusade begins
	Pope Honorius III calls a crusade against the Prussians
1226	Rekindled Albigensian Crusade
1228	Emperor Frederick II departs on crusade despite excommunication by Pope Gregory IX
1229	Emperor Frederick II gains Jerusalem by means of a treaty with Sultan al-Kamil Ayyubid
	Peace of Paris formally ends Albigensian Crusade
1231	Beginning of crusades against Byzantium over western holdings in Greece
1239	Beginning of political crusades against the Holy Roman Emperor, Frederick II
	Mongol invasions reach eastern Europe
1244	Jerusalem falls to the mercenary forces of the Khwarizmians
	Crusaders defeated at battle of La Forbie
1248	Louis IX of France begins his first crusade
1250	Louis IX's crusaders defeated at battle of Mansourah in Egypt
	Mamluks seize power from Egyptian sultan Turan-Shah in the midst of hostage negotiations with Louis IX
1251	First Shepherds' Crusade with attacks on Jewish communities and clerics
1260	Mamluks defeat the Mongols at battle of Ayn Jalut
	Baybars, former Mamluk slave, seizes the sultanate of Egypt
1261	Constantinople is recovered by Byzantium under self-proclaimed emperor, Michael VIII
1267	King Louis IX begins his second crusade
1268	Sack of Jaffa and Antioch by Baybars's Mamluk forces
1271	The crusader stronghold Crac des Chevaliers surrenders to Baybars
1291	Fall of Acre to Mamluk forces and end of crusader rule in the Holy Land

1306   Hospitallers begin their conquest of Rhodes
1307   Beginning of the trial and suppression of the Templars
1309   Crusade of the Poor
        Hospitallers transfer their headquarters to Rhodes
        Beginning of the Avignon papacy
1320   Second Shepherds' Crusade
1378   End of the Avignon Papacy and beginning of the Great
        Western/Papal Schism, which lasts to 1417
1396   Battle of Nicopolis: crusade force defeated by the Ottoman
        Turks
1402   Battle of Ankara: the Ottomans are defeated by Timur's
        Mongol-Turkish army
1420   Beginning of the Hussite Crusades
1444   The Crusade of Varna: crusade force defeated by the
        Ottoman Turks
1453   Constantinople falls to the Ottoman Turks
1460   Pope Pius II fails in his efforts to gather a crusade
1472   A crusading naval league successfully attacks the Ottoman
        held cities of Antalya and Smyrna
1492   Muslim Granada falls to Christian Spanish forces
1517   Ottoman Turks take Egypt
        Martin Luther publishes his "Ninety-five Theses"
1520   The Field of the Cloth of Gold, cementing the crusading
        truce between King Henry VIII of England and Francis I of
        France
1522   Rhodes falls to Turks, who displace Hospitaller rule
1525   Lands ruled by Teutonic Knights in Prussia become secular
        principalities
1529   Ottoman sultan Suleiman unsuccessfully lays siege to the
        city of Vienna
1530   Hospitallers establish rule in Malta
1562   Lands ruled by Teutonic Knights in Livonia become secular
        principalities

AFTER THE CRUSADES: MODERN EVENTS, PERCEPTIONS, AND IDEOLOGIES

1841   Publication of the final edition of Joseph Michaud's *History
        of the Crusades*
1898   Kaiser Wilhelm II of Germany tours Jerusalem and the Holy
        Land

1899	Publication of the first Islamic history of the Crusades, Sayyid 'Ali Hariri's *Book of the Splendid Stories of the Crusades*
1917	The British general Allenby's occupation of Jerusalem
1948	Creation of the State of Israel
1949	The term "crusaderism" (*sulubbiya*) is popularized by Sayyid Qutb in his work *Social Justice in Islam*
1987	Palestinian *intifada* and foundation of Hamas
1990	Beginning of the Gulf War
1992	Erection of statue of Saladin in Damascus featuring defeated crusaders
2000	Pope John Paul II's Day of Pardon
2001	Al-Qaeda 9/11 attacks on the United States US President Bush declares a "crusade" on al-Qaeda terrorism The term "crusade" is echoed by Osama bin Laden to describe the west's conflict with Islam
2003–11	Iraq War

GLOSSARY

Abbasids: Sunni dynasty at the time of the Crusades. It succeeded the Umayyad dynasty in 750 and established the capital at Baghdad. Ousted by the Mongols in 1258, but reinstated in Cairo by Baybars in 1261. The dynasty ended with the Ottoman defeat of the Mamluks in 1517.

al-Aqsa Mosque/Temple of Solomon: constructed around the same time as the Dome of the Rock, this Islamic place of worship was converted by the crusaders into a palace for the new Latin rulers and renamed the *Templum Salomonis*—the Temple of Solomon. A wing of this complex later became the residence of the master of the Temple (Templars), while another section was used as stables.

Albigensian Heresy/Catharism: a heretical neo-Manichean dualist religion professing two opposing divine forces or gods that developed in southern France in the twelfth and thirteenth centuries. Things spiritual were seen to be good, while the material world was considered evil. Innocent III called a crusade against the sect in 1208.

Allah: the Arabic word for God in the Islamic religion.

al-Qaeda: an extremist Islamic terrorist movement founded in 1988 by Osama bin Laden. The group was responsible for the 9/11 attacks in the United States in 2001.

Anatolia/Asia Minor: the peninsula of western Asia between the Mediterranean Sea and the Black Sea, roughly corresponding to modern-day Turkey.

Avignon papacy: (1309–78) also known as "the Babylonian Captivity" (of the papacy), when popes were based in Avignon, France, rather than Rome. The Avignon papacy damaged the reputation of the Church, as Avignon popes were believed to be under the control of French kings and nobles.

Ayyubid: Muslim dynasty founded by Saladin, which lasted until the mid-thirteenth century.

Balkans: the territories found within southeast Europe between modern-day Greece and the Black Sea. These included Bosnia, the Serbian and Bulgarian states, Wallachia, Transylvania, and Hungary.

Baltic region: home to the Slavs, its main territories around the Baltic Sea included Prussia, Livonia, Lithuania, Estonia, Finland, Pomerania, Russian holdings, and smaller tribal groupings.

caliph: meaning "successor," it is the name given to leaders of a Muslim community or state. During the time of the Crusades, caliphates were, in principle, dynastic.

chivalry: a code of conduct for the landed classes of Europe that emphasized courage, honor, courtesy, justice, and protection of the weak. Its association with crusading began in the thirteenth century.

Christendom: generally, the community of Christians, but more specifically an ideal put forward by reforming popes, such as Gregory VII and Urban II, of a federation of secular states whose leaders and subjects were to be obedient to the authority of the papacy and the Church.

clash of civilizations thesis: the theory proposed by Samuel Huntington (1992) that relationships between groups from different civilizations will almost always be antagonistic and detached. Different cultures and civilizations are, by this theory, more prone to conflict than dialogue.

crusaderism: defined as the deliberate policy of the west to destroy Islam, Islamic society, and Muslims. Crusaderism was advanced by Sayyid Qutb in his 1949 work *Social Justice in Islam*.

Crusader States: states established in the Holy Land by the First Crusaders. These included the kingdom of Jerusalem, the principality of Antioch, the county of Edessa, and the county of Tripoli.

dhimma: an agreement between the Islamic state and "People of the Book," that is, Jews and Christians living under Muslim authority. By this agreement those known as *dhimmis* are accorded protection as long as they pay the poll tax/*jizya* and adhere to set laws.

Dome of the Rock/Temple of the Lord: a holy Muslim shrine built in 692 to commemorate the Prophet Muhammad's Night Journey from earth to heaven. After the fall of Jerusalem to the crusaders in 1099, the site became a Christian church called the *Templum Domini*, the Temple of the Lord.

Dominicans: founded by Saint Dominic (1170–1221), they were mendicant friars, that is, uncloistered and begging brothers, preaching, teaching, and dependent on charity. The order was formally recognized by Honorius III in 1216. They were involved in preaching crusades and investigating heresy, including the Albigensians. This latter role earned them the title *Domini canes*—hounds of the Lord. Dominicans were also sent out as missionaries to Muslims and Mongols.

emir: a Muslim political or military leader.

excommunication: the barring of a Christian from the sacraments and any contact with others of the faith. The purpose was to encourage sinners to confess their transgressions so that they might do penance and be reincorporated into the Church community.

Fatimid: Isma'ili Shi'a dynasty that ruled in Qayrawan (modern Tunisia) and Egypt. The caliphate was brought to an end by Saladin in 1171.

Franks/Ifrang: a term used by Muslims and those of the Byzantine Empire to refer to western Europeans at the time of the Crusades. The word originally referred to the Germanic tribe, the Franks, but by the time of the Crusades it designated the French or Europeans.

futuwwa: an Arabic term translated as "youthful manliness." In the medieval period, it referred to a code of behavior extolling the virtues of piety, fidelity, truth, justice, courage, generosity, as well as magnanimity toward enemies, reverence for women, and protection of the poor. *Futuwwa* brotherhoods of single men were formed in urban areas, with members taking oaths of fidelity and supporting chivalric virtues. There were also groups that took on military and policing roles within cities.

Great Schism: a reference to the formal schism and mutual excommunication in 1054 of the eastern and western churches.

Great Western/Papal Schism: a period in western Europe (1378–1417) when there were two, and at times three, rival popes.

Hamas: an organization that had its origins in the Palestinian branch of the Muslim Brotherhood. It emerged as an active political movement at the time of the Palestinian uprising (*intifada*) of 1987.

heresy: the term used by the medieval Church to distinguish any belief or practice that deviated substantially from accepted Christian doctrine. Non-Christians were given other titles such as pagans, or infidels.

Holy Land: a term used by Christians to designate the land where Jesus lived and died. This includes the city of Jerusalem and its surrounding region.

Holy Roman Empire: also called the German Empire, this was a fragmented group of territories under the loose control of the "Roman" Emperor. Emperors were traditionally crowned by the papacy.

Holy Sepulcher: the most sacred site for Christians in Jerusalem, it is believed to mark the site of Jesus' burial and resurrection. A church was built on the site in the fourth century and became the most important pilgrimage destination for both eastern and western Christians.

Hospitallers: see Knights of St. John

Hussites: followers of the declared heretic John Hus. The movement, originating in fifteenth-century Bohemia, took on political overtones which escalated into a revolt in 1420. A crusade was called against the Hussites that year.

Iberia/Iberian Peninsula: the region that includes modern-day Spain and Portugal.

imam: a spiritual leader of a Muslim community or one who leads prayers. The term is commonly found within Shi'a groups.

indulgences: the Church's promise of the soul by-passing all or part of the required time spent in purgatory before progressing to heaven. Those crusaders who fulfilled their vows were granted this privilege by the papacy. By the early thirteenth century, those who were not able to go on crusades themselves could purchase indulgences that gave full or partial remittance of time in purgatory.

infidel: from the Latin *infidelis*, unfaithful, the term was applied by those in the Christian west to Muslims.

Inquisition: the papal judicial system created in 1184 by Pope Lucius III and the German Emperor Frederick Barbarossa. The purpose of the Inquisition was to enquire into the heretical beliefs and practices of individuals and, if possible, bring them back into the fold of the Church. During the Albigensian Crusade, the Inquisition was entrusted to the Dominicans.

interdict: a papal punishment against communities in response to heresy or the excommunication of their ruler. An interdict forbade communities to participate in church sacraments (which could include the Eucharist). Those under interdict were still considered to be members of the Church.

jihad: the Arabic term for "striving," *jihad* refers to two practices. These are "the greater *jihad*," that is, the internal struggle against sin and the external defense of one's Islamic faith, and "the lesser *jihad*," which involves defense of Islam by military means. During the medieval period, Muslim religious scholars formalized the regulation of this lesser *jihad*, forbidding attacks on non-combatants, destruction of property, or suicide in the course of conflict.

jizya: a tax paid by non-Muslims living in Muslim-controlled states that granted rights of protection.

just war: the notion of what constituted just war was first put forward by Augustine, bishop of Hippo, around the year 400. According to Augustine, just war must be initiated by a recognized leader, reflect "right intention" (no gratuitous violence), and embody a just cause.

Ka'ba: the most holy shrine in Islam, the Ka'ba is located in Mecca and is believed to have been created by Abraham and Ishmael.

khan: Turkish title for a lord or prince (subordinate to a sultan).

Khwarazmians: Turkish mercenaries originally displaced by the Mongols, they settled in Anatolia and Mesopotamia, serving various political factions, and played a role in the conflicts surrounding Syria and Palestine in the mid-thirteenth century.

knight: a mounted warrior in western medieval society; the lowest rung of the nobility.

Knights of St. John/Hospitallers: the Order of the Hospital of St. John of Jerusalem, the Hospitallers, initially cared for pilgrims in the Holy Land and Jerusalem. With the success of the First Crusade, the group became more involved with military activity, occupying castles within and on the borders of the region. It was recognized as a military order in 1113.

Knights Templar: one of the military orders of the Holy Land, the Templars were founded by Hugh of Payns in 1119. The order prospered thanks in part to the patronage of Bernard of Clairvaux, who wrote the order's Rule and the treatise, "In Praise of the New Knighthood."

Kurds: one of many ethnic groups found within the crusade regions, the Kurds converted to Islam in the ninth century, with early dynasties ruling areas within Anatolia and western Iran. The Kurdish Ayyubid dynasty came to power through the conquests of Saladin.

Levant: in reference to the sunrise (in the east), this twelfth-century French term applied to the area of the Crusader States. Later, in the thirteenth century, the term would come to encompass all of the territories between Greece and Egypt.

Mamluks: the Arab term indicating one who is a slave. Mamluks were originally obtained from the borders of Muslim territories and trained as soldiers. Although granted freedom once they reached adulthood, Mamluks continued to serve their former owners and were the heart of the Muslim forces fighting against the crusaders. The Mamluk Sultanate refers to the dynasty that came to power in 1250 and ruled Egypt and Syria up to 1517.

mangonel: see trebuchet

military orders: crusaders who took monastic vows yet engaged in military activity. The three main crusading military orders were The Hospitallers (Knights of St. John of Jerusalem), the Templars, and the Teutonic Knights.

minaret: the tower of a mosque from which the call to prayer is sounded.

Mongols: nomadic tribal peoples originating from the steppes of eastern Asia. Under their leader Chingis (Genghis) Khan (r. 1206–27) a federation of tribes was formed. The khans believed they were destined for world domination and, over the thirteenth century, the Mongol army created a vast empire that spread from the Black Sea to the western shores of China.

Moor: a Christian European term for north African and Iberian Muslims.

mosque: an Islamic place of public worship, usually with at least one minaret.

mujahid: a title for one who engages in military *jihad*. Also known as "jihadist."

Muslim: a follower of Islam; the term means "surrender" in Arabic.

Muslim Brotherhood/Ikhwan: an Islamic political movement founded in Egypt in 1928 by Hassan al-Banna. Its stated aim is to create a state ruled by Islamic law (Sharia).

Near East: the region including modern Egypt, Israel, Palestine, Lebanon, Syria, Turkey, and Greece.

Nizaris/Assassins: from the Isma'ili Shi'a sect, the Assassins were a terrorist group that emerged in the twelfth century. The sect carried out a program of political assassination, primarily against Sunni targets.

Normans: originally a term applied to the Scandinavian peoples (Northmen) who settled in Europe during the ninth and tenth centuries, the name came to refer to the lords of Normandy. In the eleventh century, the Norman Robert Guiscard established a kingdom in Sicily, while England was subjected to the rule of the Norman duke William the Conqueror.

oath of fealty: an oath made by a vassal to his lord, usually signifying an exchange of protection from the lord for military service and/or taxes from the vassal. This contract could apply to individuals, groups, or states.

Ottomans: a Turkish tribe that settled the area of Anatolia in the mid-thirteenth century and attacked and sacked the Byzantine city of Constantinople in 1453, establishing the Ottoman Empire, which lasted until 1922 when it was replaced by the republic of Turkey.

Outremer: meaning "across the sea," the term was used to describe the Crusader States.

pagans: a term used by both Muslims and Christians, usually refering to polytheists.

Palestine: used in reference to the region corresponding to the lands between Egypt and Syria.

papal bull: an official letter or decree from the papacy.

papal legate: a Church official acting for the pope.

passagium generale: referring to the more traditional crusade, with links to penitential pilgrimage, the Holy Land, and conflicts with Muslim forces.

passagium particulare: The "lesser" crusade of the fourteenth century. This defines smaller campaigns directed against a variety of perceived enemies of the Church and papacy.

patriarch: a bishop of the eastern Church, the highest-ranking patriarch being the patriarch of Constantinople.

Peace of God: a religious movement that emerged in the tenth century in response to the violence of the times. The aim was to protect clergy and the poor from hostilities between warring landed families.

penance: the undertaking of a pious act to gain forgiveness for a confessed sin. Participation in the Crusades was seen as an act of penance by the Church.

penitential/holy war: the notion of holy or penitential war that had its origins in Augustine of Hippo's theory of just war. By the end of the eleventh century, acceptance of the papacy's authority to call holy wars and the penitential nature of such ventures was an established concept.

People of the Book: a reference from the Qur'an to Jews and Christians in the context of Islamic rule. The distinguishing of Jews and Christians from other non-Muslims created an Islamic policy of tolerance for those who shared the same religious heritage (although with certain restrictions and the payment of a tax known as *jizya*).

*perfecti***:** the religious leaders of the Albigensian heresy, the *perfecti* were expected to live sin-free lives of extreme asceticism. *Perfecti* shunned the evils of the material world to focus on their future spiritual reunion with God. Those of the faith ("believers") were made *perfecti* through the ceremony known as *consolamentum*.

pilgrimage: a journey to a holy site or object with the purpose of serving penance or gaining spiritual aid.

Pillars of Islam: the five required ritual practices of Muslims: 1) *shahada*, the declaration of faith, 2) *salat*, prayer, 3) *zukat*, almsgiving, 4) *sawm*, fasting, and 5) *hajj*, the "greater pilgrimage" to Mecca.

pope: the bishop of Rome and head of the medieval western Church.

Purgatory: a middle ground of purgation between heaven and hell for souls waiting for the Last Judgment, where souls undergo a period of suffering and penance.

Qur'an/Koran: the holy book of the Islamic faith, the Qur'an is held to be Allah's Word as revealed to the prophet Muhammad.

*Reconquista***:** an eleventh-century European term designating the wars fought in Iberia by Christians to take back lands from Muslims. The wars ran from the ninth to the very end of the fifteenth century, resulting in the expulsion of all Muslims and Jews from the peninsula in 1492. From the 1090s, the campaigns shared similar features and privileges to the Near Eastern crusades, with official recognition of this status granted from the twelfth century onward.

relic: the mortal remains (in part or full) of a holy figure, or objects associated with that individual. Medieval Christian relics were the object of pilgrimages, and their veneration was believed to facilitate penance, miracles, and God's aid.

Romans/Rhomaioi: what the Byzantines called themselves. The term demonstrates their perception of themselves as the continuation of the Roman Empire.

Rule: rules for an order, setting out how its members should live and organize the community.

Rum: the Arabic name for the Byzantines, deriving from the Greek word for Rome.

Rum sultanate: the western portion of Asia Minor at the time of the First Crusade. Its name derived from the fact that the region had previously been under Byzantine control and a large portion of its inhabitants were eastern Christians.

Saladin tithe: a crusading tax imposed in 1188 by Henry II of England and Philip the II of France for the Third Crusade.

Saracens: a medieval word for Muslims used by both Byzantines and Europeans.

Seljuk Turks: a Turkish tribe originating in central Asia that expanded west in the tenth century and converted to Sunni Islam. Named "Seljuk" after one of their leaders (Saljuqs), the Seljuks were made up of Mamluks (slaves) and Turkmen (free men and their families). Seljuk Turks challenged both Muslim held lands and the Byzantine Empire. They defeated the latter at the battle of Manzikert in 1071, prompting the first Byzantine call for aid from the west.

Shi'a: the sect of Islam that recognizes the descendants of Ali (the prophet Muhammad's cousin and son-in-law) as the rightful heirs of Islamic leadership.

sultan: the title used by Muslim rulers to denote independent political power, although it was originally applied to Seljuk sub-rulers of the Abbasid caliph.

Sunni: one of the two main sects of Islam. Unlike Shi'a Muslims, the sect does not believe that Muslim leadership must be passed down from the line of Muhammad.

Sword Brothers: a military order that was created in 1202 to assist crusading activities in Livonia. It merged with the Teutonic Knights in 1237.

Syria: territory between Anatolia and Palestine.

Teutonic Knights: the German military order founded in 1198 by Hermann of Salze and supported by the German emperor Henry IV. The order did not achieve the same status in the Crusader States as the Templars or Hospitallers, but it did play a significant role in the northern crusades.

trebuchet: a counterweight catapult used in siege warfare for throwing stones and other missiles, powered manually or by counterweights. Also known as a "mangonel," although this can refer to a tension-based rather than counterweight machine.

Truce of God: an extension of the Peace of God, the Truce of God movement sought to prohibit hostilities on certain holy days and seasons.

Umayyads: the dynasty of caliphs that ruled from 661 to 750, when they were deposed by the Abbasids.

vassal: the subject of a lord who provided military service in exchange for protection and a fief of land or money. The term could apply to groups and realms as well as individuals.

vizier: a Muslim term for second-in-command to the ruler, one who holds high office.

Wends: a shared name for the various Slavonic tribes settled on the shores of the Baltic Sea. Their lands and pagan religion instigated armed missionary ventures into the territory and, in 1147, at the instigation of Bernard of Clairvaux, a crusade.

WHO'S WHO IN THE CRUSADING WORLD

Please note that spellings of names can vary across different sources.

Adhemar (d. 1098): bishop of Le Puy, appointed papal legate for the First Crusade by Pope Urban II, served as unifying force for the disparate crusading armies, and died after the fall of Antioch.

Al-Ashraf Khalil (r. 1290–93): Mamluk sultan of Egypt who took the city of Acre in May 1291, an event seen as the conclusion of the Crusades in the region.

Alexius I Comnenus (r. 1081–1118): Byzantine emperor who sent an appeal to Pope Urban II for help against the Seljuk Turks, which resulted in the First Crusade.

Al-Hakim (r. 996–1021): caliph of Egypt who persecuted Christians and Jews, and also ordered the destruction of the Church of the Holy Sepulcher in Jerusalem in 1009.

Al-Kamil (r. 1218–38): Ayyubid sultan of Egypt who defended the region from the advances of the Fifth Crusade and negotiated a treaty with Frederick II for the return of Jerusalem to Christian hands.

'Ali ibn Tahir al-Sulami (ca 1040–1106): Damascus religious scholar, one of the first to call for *jihad* against the crusaders.

Allenby, Edmund (1861–1936): British general who led the Sinai and Palestine Campaign during World War I, including the capture of Jerusalem from the Ottoman Turks on 9 December 1917.

Amalric (r. 1163–74): king of Jerusalem, younger brother of Baldwin III who died childless. Led several unsuccessful campaigns to capture Egypt. Died of dysentery and succeeded by his 13-year-old son, Baldwin IV (r. 1174–85).

Anna Comnena (1083–ca 1153): daughter of Emperor Alexius I who was witness to the crusaders arriving in Constantinople and wrote the *Alexiad*, with information on the Byzantine imperial court and their interactions with the early crusaders.

Baldwin of Boulogne (r. 1100–18): first king of Jerusalem, who succeeded his brother Godfrey, who had founded the Christian county of Edessa in 1098.

Baldwin Count of Flanders (1172–1205): a leader of the Fourth Crusade who was chosen to be the first Latin emperor of Constantinople. Died in captivity after the battle of Adrianople.

Baldwin IV (r. 1174–85): the "leper king" and son of Amalric who ascended the throne of Jerusalem at 13.

Balian of Ibelin (ca 1140–93): a crusader whose family rose from the lower ranks of knights to become lords of Rama (Ramlah). He was a participant in the battle of Hattin in July 1187 and negotiated with Saladin for the surrender of Jerusalem.

Baybars (r. 1260–77): Mamluk slave who served as a commander under the Ayyubid sultan of Egypt and then as sultan. Responsible for a successful campaign against the Franks, retaking much of the remaining Latin territory in the Levant.

Bayezid (r. 1389–1402): "The Thunderbolt," the Ottoman sultan who defeated the crusaders at the battle of Nicopolis in 1396. Later captured and killed at the battle of Ankara (1402) against the Turkish-Mongol khan Timur.

Bernard of Clairvaux (ca. 1090–1153): Cistercian abbot and reformer, the author of the "Rule of the Templars" and "In Praise of the New Knighthood," a treatise extolling the virtues of the Templars. The principal preacher of the Second Crusade and crusading in the Baltic.

Blanche of Castile (1188–1252): queen of the French king Louis VIII, she became regent to her son Louis IX from 1226–34. Responsible for the "Peace of Paris," which brought about the end to the Albigensian conflict.

Bohemund of Taranto (1050–1111): son of Robert Guiscard, he was one of the leaders of the First Crusade and was instrumental in the capture of Antioch. Took the title of prince of Antioch in 1198; held prisoner in Aleppo from 1100 to 1103, was unable to make gains against the Byzantine emperor, and was forced to sign a treaty recognizing the suzerainty of Alexius Comnenus.

Chingiz/Genghis Khan (d. 1227): Mongol chief of the eastern Asian steppes, who came to power in 1206, uniting several tribes in a campaign that saw the conquest of northern China and central Asia. After his death, his sons and grandsons continued the expansion of the empire, attacking eastern Europe and the regions of Anatolia, Khwarismian Persia, Syria, and Palestine.

Clement V, pope (r. 1305–14): first of the Avignon popes, pressured by the French king Philip IV to investigate and condemn the Templars. Also ordered an investigation into the deeds of the Teutonic Knights.

Conrad III (r. 1138–52): king of Germany who undertook the Second Crusade. Much of his army was destroyed in Anatolia, leaving Conrad and his depleted force to join Louis VII's army in 1147. Abandoned the crusade after the failure of the siege of Damascus (1148).

Constantine XI (r. 1449–53): the last Byzantine emperor, Constantine led the defense of Constantinople against the Ottoman Turks in 1453, dying in the ensuing battle.

Daimbert (1050–ca 1107): archbishop of Pisa who accompanied Pope Urban II to Clermont in 1095. Deposed Arnulf, patriarch of Jerusalem, and took the title in 1100. Sought to rule Jerusalem on the death of Godfrey. Exiled by Baldwin, and banished from Jerusalem. Reinstated twice, but died on the way back to Jerusalem ca 1107.

Dandolo, Enrico (r. 1193–1205): doge (chief magistrate) of Venice who directed the Fourth Crusade toward Constantinople which ended with the crusaders' siege and capture of the city and the beginning of the Latin Empire of Constantinople.

Dominic of Calaruega (ca 1170–1221): founder of the Dominican Friar Preachers who undertook a preaching campaign against the Albigensian heretics in the early thirteenth century.

Edward of England (1239–1307): son of the English king Henry III who headed a crusade to Palestine from 1270 to 1271.

El Cid/Rodrigo Díaz de Vivar (or Bivar) (ca 1043–99): member of the lesser nobility of Castile, El Cid (from the Arabic *sidi*, "lord") fought as a mercenary for both Muslim and Christian leaders of the Iberian region. Became the prince of Valencia from 1094 to 1299. The epic poem "Cantar del Mio Cid" ("The Poem of the Cid") offers a dramatic retelling of his life.

Eleanor of Aquitaine (1122–1204): queen to the French king Louis VII from 1137 to 1152. Accompanied her husband on the Second Crusade, where a quarrel led to the later annulment of their marriage. Went on to marry King Henry II of England and was mother to Richard I, a leader of the Third Crusade.

Emich of Flonheim (*fl.* 1096): with his followers, led attacks on Rhineland Jewish communities before the First Crusade in late spring 1096. Went on to lead a popular crusading force via Hungary, but his army was defeated and disbanded on the Hungarian frontier and he returned home.

Eugenius III, pope (r. 1145–53): called for the Second Crusade and asked Bernard of Clairvaux to aid him in preaching the crusade. Also proclaimed a crusade against the pagan Wends in 1147.

Eugenius IV, pope (r. 1431–47): called the fifteenth-century Varna Crusade. Negotiated with the Byzantine emperor John VIII for the unification of the eastern and western churches under the authority of the papacy.

Ferdinand II of Aragon (r. 1479–1516): king of Aragon, married to Isabella of Castile. Conquered the Muslim state of Granada in 1492 and expelled Muslims and Jews from the kingdom.

Francis of Assisi (1181–1226): Founder of the Franciscan order of preaching friars who preached a spiritual crusade to convert the Muslims. In 1219 he traveled to Egypt but failed to convert the sultan.

Frederick I, Barbarossa (r. 1155–90): German emperor who tightened control over his German territories and re-established good relations with the papacy. A key leader of the Third Crusade; drowned in Asia Minor en route to Palestine.

Frederick II (1194–1250): "Stupor Mundi" ("Wonder of the World"), inherited the kingship of Sicily, although still an infant, in 1197. German emperor from 1212, and king of Jerusalem from 1226. Delays in embarking on crusade brought an excommunication, but he gained Jerusalem in 1229 through negotiations with al-Kamil, Ayyubid sultan of Egypt.

Genghis. See Chingiz

Geoffrey of Villehardouin (ca 1160–1213): participant and chronicler of the Fourth Crusade and its aftermath.

Godfrey of Bouillon (d. 1100): duke of Lorraine, prominent leader of the First Crusade, became Jerusalem's first Latin ruler.

Gregory VII, pope (r. 1073–85): Cluniac and papal reformer who called in 1074 for a military force to liberate the Byzantine eastern Christians from Muslim forces, offering heavenly rewards for military service. Promoted the reconciliation of eastern and western churches, but died in exile without achieving his goals.

Gregory IX, pope (r. 1227–41): nephew of Pope Innocent III who promoted the authority of the papacy, especially against Frederick II, whom he excommunicated.

Guy of Lusignan (r. 1186–94): a French noble, king of Jerusalem and Cyprus, who married Sibylla, the sister of the king of Jerusalem, and later ruled the city jointly with his wife. Defeated by Saladin at the Battle of Hattin, captured, then released and later ruled Cyprus.

Honorius III, pope (r. 1216–27): ordered Frederick II to undertake a crusade, worked to maintain peace within Europe, and continued Innocent III's crusades against the Albigensians.

Hugh of Payns (ca 1070–1136): founder and first grand master of the Knights Templar; asked Bernard of Clairvaux to write the Order's Rule.

Hugh of Vermandois (1054–1102): count of Vermandois and brother of the king of France. One of the principal leaders of the First Crusade. After failing to lure Emperor Alexius to Jerusalem, he abandoned the crusade for France. Returned to the crusade but died at the Battle at Tarsus in 1102.

Hus, John (ca 1372–1415): Czech religious reformer and university lecturer, influenced by the writings of Wycliffe. Excommunicated by the pope in 1411, arrested, tried, and burned as a heretic in 1415.

Iftikhar al-Dawla (*fl.* 1099): the Fatimid governor of Jerusalem, he negotiated safe passage to Ascalon for himself and his garrison upon the fall of the city to the forces of the First Crusade.

Innocent III, pope (r. 1198–1216): administrative pope, an active supporter of the Crusades, who instigated the Fourth Crusade, proclaimed the Albigensian Crusade, and promoted crusading in the Baltic regions and Spain.

Isabella of Castile (r. 1474–1504): queen who ruled Spain with her husband, Ferdinand of Aragon, from 1481. Expelled Jews and Muslims after 1492.

Isabella of Jerusalem (r. 1190–1205): gained the crown of Jerusalem upon her half sister Sibylla's death in 1190. Married to Conrad of Montferrat in this year and, upon his death (1192), remarried first to the nephew of Richard I, Henry of Champagne, and on his death in 1198 to King Amalric of Cyprus.

James of Molay (ca 1243–1314): the last grand master of the Templars, who moved the order to Paris after their expulsion from Palestine. He and his order were accused of heresy and witchcraft by the French crown. Condemned as a heretic and burned in 1314.

John VIII (r. 1421–48): Byzantine emperor who sought aid from Pope Eugenius IV against the Ottoman Turks and signed a document agreeing to the unification of eastern and western churches under the authority of the papacy.

John Hunyadi (d. 1456): lord of Transylvania and later regent for the king of Hungary, led forces in the Crusade of Varna and defeated an Ottoman force in the 1456 siege of Belgrade.

John of Joinville (1224–1317): knight in the service of Louis IX who accompanied his king on crusade to Egypt and wrote the *Life of Saint Louis*.

Kilij Arslan I (r. 1092–1107): Seljuk sultan of Rum Anatolia who was responsible for the destruction of the People's Crusade but lost his capital Nicaea to the First Crusade in 1097.

Louis VII (r. 1137–80): French king and husband of Eleanor of Aquitaine who led the Second Crusade along with Conrad III of Germany. His army suffered heavy losses and he was forced to retreat after failing to gain Damascus.

Louis VIII (r. 1223–26): king of France and husband of Blanche of Castile who helped to launch the Albigensian Crusade.

Louis IX (1226–70): French king and son of Blanche of Castile who took up the crusader call in 1244, attacking Egypt, but was defeated and taken prisoner. Ransomed and returned home after fortifying Christian-held sites in the Holy Land; initiated a second crusade in 1270 (again via Egypt) but died on campaign. Recognized as a devout Christian and canonized in 1297.

Markward of Anweiler (d. 1203): made a count by the German emperor, administered Sicily, and became regent for the infant Frederick II in 1198. Pope Innocent III offered indulgences to anyone who opposed him, instigating one of the first "political crusades."

Martin V, pope (r. 1417–31): pope whose election to the papacy ended the Great Western/Papal Schism. Declared the Hussite Crusade in 1420.

Mathilda (1046–1115): countess of Tuscany and protector of the papacy who fought against the German emperors Henry IV and Henry V and also supported a select group of clergy to develop the idea of holy or penitential war.

Mehmed II (r. 1451–81): Ottoman ruler known as "the Conqueror," who united Turkish forces and took Constantinople in 1453.

Murad II (r. 1421–44 and 1446–51): Ottoman sultan known for his conquests in the Balkans and in particular his victory against the crusaders at the Battle of Varna in 1444.

Nicholas of Cologne (*fl.* 1212): a German youth who led one of the two so-called Children's Crusades.

Nur al-Din (r. 1146–74): son of Zengi, captured Damascus in 1154 and consolidated Muslim rule in Syria. A Sunni ruler, he suppressed Shi'a teachings and practices. Was unable to check the rise of Saladin in Egypt.

Nyklot (d. 1160): Wendish overlord of the pagan Abotrites who fought with Christian neighbors over bordering territory, the cause of the Wendish Crusade of 1147. Was killed by the forces of Henry the Lion, duke of Saxony.

Osama bin Laden/Usama ibn Ladin (1957–2011): born in Saudi Arabia, condemned foreign western powers, participated in the Afghan war against the Soviet takeover of Afghanistan, and in 1988 founded the terrorist movement al-Qaeda ("the Base"). Orchestrated 9/11 attacks in 2001. Killed by American Special Forces in 2011.

Pelagius (d. 1224): cardinal and papal legate for the Fifth Crusade who controlled the funding for the campaign and clashed with King John of Jerusalem over negotiations with al-Kamil, the Ayyubid sultan of Egypt.

Peter Bartholomew (d. 1099): Provençal pilgrim of the First Crusade who had a vision of the location of the Holy Lance at Antioch. Later found a lance head in the city's cathedral and claimed it as the relic.

Peter the Hermit (ca 1050–1115): leader of the Peasants' or People's Crusade, a popular movement that preceded the official First Crusade. Survivor of the Seljuk ambush in Anatolia that destroyed his people, but went on to meet up with the First Crusade and was with the crusaders when they took Jerusalem in 1099.

Philip II Augustus (r. 1180–1223): French king who undertook the Third Crusade in 1189 along with Richard I and Frederick Barbarossa. Left the crusade after the surrender of Acre to the crusaders in 1191, and returned home seizing Richard's French lands; supported the Albigensian Crusade but took no part in the campaign.

Prester John: fabled Christian king and priest who was believed to rule a large and wealthy empire somewhere in the east.

Qutb, Sayyid (1906–66): influential Islamic philosopher and political activist and member of the Egyptian Muslim Brotherhood who wrote on "crusaderism," defined as a deliberate policy on the part of the west to destroy Islam, Islamic society, and Muslims.

Qutuz (d. 1260): usurped the Mamluk sultanate in Egypt in 1259, marched his army into Syria, and defeated the Mongols at the Battle of 'Ayn Jalut in 1260.

Raymond III (ca 1140–87): count of Tripoli, the first cousin of King Amalric of Jerusalem, appointed regent for Amalric's son, Baldwin IV, and later wounded at the battle of Hattin in 1187.

Raymond IV (ca 1041–1105): count of Toulouse from 1093 who was a senior leader of the First Crusade, refused to be crowned King of Jerusalem, but went on to establish the Latin county of Tripoli in 1101.

Reynald of Châtillon (r. 1153–87): prince of Antioch from 1153 to 1160, and lord of the Transjordan from 1177 to 1187. Took part in the Second Crusade but was captured at the Battle of Hattin by Saladin and executed.

Richard I (r. 1189–99): son of King Henry II and Queen Eleanor of Aquitaine, known as "the Lionheart" (Coeur de Lion). Became king of England in 1189 and set out on the Third Crusade with the aim of retaking Jerusalem. Took Cyprus from the Byzantines but failed to take Jerusalem and signed a treaty with Saladin in 1192.

Robert II (1065–1111): count of Flanders who was one of the key leaders of the First Crusade, took part in the siege and capture of Jerusalem in 1099, and returned home to Flanders in 1100.

Robert Curthose (1054–1134): duke of Normandy, a leader of the First Crusade who returned to Normandy in 1100.

Robert Guiscard (r. 1057–95): duke of Apulia from 1057, conquered the island of Sicily in 1072 with his brother Roger I. Completed his conquest of Byzantine holdings in southern Italy by 1076.

Saladin/Salah al-Din (r. 1169–93): nephew of the Kurdish general Shirkuh who became sultan of Egypt at his uncle's death in 1173. Leader of the Ayyubid dynasty, he fought the Zengids, defeated the crusading forces at the Battle of Hattin, and took Jerusalem, prompting the Third Crusade.

Shirkuh (d. 1169): Kurdish general in the service of Nur al-Din, vizier of Egypt in 1169, and succeeded by his nephew Saladin.

Sibylla of Jerusalem (r. 1186–90): sister of Baldwin IV, king of Jerusalem, and later queen of Jerusalem who participated in negotiations between the kingdom and Saladin.

Simon of Montfort (1150–1218): lord who abandoned the Fourth Crusade after its attack on Zara. Later led the Albigensian Crusade, gaining the lands of noble families throughout southern France and becoming count of Toulouse in 1213.

Stephen of Blois (1045–1102): count of Blois and son-in-law of William the Conqueror who took part in the First Crusade, deserted during the siege of Antioch, returned to the First Crusade in 1101, but was killed at the battle of Ramla in 1102.

Stephen of Cloyes (*fl.* 1212): one of two leaders of the so-called Children's Crusade, a young French shepherd who had a vision of Christ and made his way to Paris with a large entourage of young and older followers.

Suleiman I (r. 1520–66): Ottoman sultan known as "the Magnificent" who extended the Ottoman Empire, taking Rhodes and besieging Vienna.

Tancred of Hauteville (d. 1112): nephew of Bohemund of Taranto, he joined him on the First Crusade, became prince of Galilee, and later served as regent and then prince of Antioch.

Timur/Tamerlane (r. 1370–1405): warrior of Turkish origin, proclaimed khan, attacked Persia, and plundered and destroyed the kingdom of Delhi in India. Defeated the Ottoman forces at the battle of Ankara in 1401.

Urban II, pope (r. 1088–99): a reforming, monarchical pope who trained as a monk of Cluny and was made cardinal in 1080. Served as Gregory VII's legate to Germany and France. Called the First Crusade at the Council of Clermont in 1095.

Yosuf ibn Tashfin (r. 1061–1106): sultan of the Berber dynasty, the Almoravids, who conquered the region of Morocco, founding the city of Marrakesh in 1062. Invaded Spain at the invitation of the Abbasids of Seville, and defeated Alfonso VI's Castilian army in 1086. Went on to conquer all of Islamic Spain (except Saragossa).

Zengi, Imad ad-Din (r. 1127–46): son of a Turkish emir and governor of Mosul in 1127, he worked to expand his territory, including the negotiated takeover of Aleppo. Took Edessa in 1144 from crusader hands, an act that precipitated the Second Crusade.

BIBLIOGRAPHY

There has been a significant increase in scholarship on the Crusades over the past 10 years and it is hoped that students will find, in the sources listed below, opportunities for further study.

Abouali, D. 2011. "Saladin's Legacy in the Middle East before the Nineteenth Century." *Crusades* 10: 175–89.

Allen, S.J., and E. Amt, eds. 2014. *The Crusades: A Reader*. 2nd ed. Readings in Medieval Civilizations and Cultures VIII, ed. P. E. Dutton. Toronto: University of Toronto Press.

Anderson, O. 1971. "The Growth of Christian Militarism in Mid-Victorian Britain." *English Historical Review* LXXXVI (CCCXXXVIII): 46–72. http://dx.doi.org/10.1093/ehr/LXXXVI.CCCXXXVIII.46.

App, U. 2010. *The Birth of Orientalism*. Philadelphia: University of Pennsylvania Press.

Asbridge, T. 2012. *The Crusades: The War for the Holy Lands*. London: Simon & Schuster.

Asbridge, T. 2013. "Talking to the Enemy: The Role and Purpose of Negotiations between Saladin and Richard the Lionheart during the Third Crusade." *Journal of Medieval History* 39 (3): 275–96. http://dx.doi.org/10.1080/03044181.2013.787542.

Barber, M. 2012. *Crusader States*. New Haven, CT: Yale University Press.

Bartusis, M. 1997. *The Late Byzantine Army: Arms and Society, 1204–1453*. Philadelphia: University of Pennsylvania Press.

Belloc, H. 1937. *The Crusades: The World's Debates*. Milwaukee: Bruce Publishing. Reprinted TAN Books, 1992.

Bennett, M. 2001. "Virile Latins, Effeminate Greeks and Strong Women: Gender Definitions on Crusade?" In *Gendering the Crusades*, ed. S. Edgington and S. Lambert, 16–30. Cardiff: University of Wales Press.

Bettenson, H. 2003. *Saint Augustine's City of God*. London: Penguin Books.

Bhatia, U. 2008. *Forgetting Osama bin Munqidh, Remembering Osama bin Laden: The Crusades in Modern Muslim Memory*. Singapore: S. Rajaratnam School of International Studies.

Billings, M. 2010. *The Crusades: The War against Islam 1096–1798*. Stroud, UK: The History Press in Association with the British Library.

Boas, A. 1999. *Crusader Archaeology: The Material Culture of the Latin East*. New York: Routledge.

Boas, A. 2001. *Jerusalem in the Time of the Crusades*. London: Routledge.

Bohn, H. 1848. *Chronicles of the Crusades*. London: Henry G. Bohn.

Byrom, J., and M. Riley. 2013. *The Crusades*. London: Hodder Education.

Caspi-Reisfeld, K. 2001. "Women Warriors during the Crusades, 1095–1254." In *Gendering the Crusades*, ed. S. Edgington and S. Lambert, 94–107. Cardiff: University of Wales Press.

Cassidy-Welch, M., and A. Lester. 2014. "Memory and Interpretation: New Approaches to the Study of the Crusades." *Memory and the Crusades: Rethinking Past and Present*, special issue of *The Journal of Medieval History* 40 (3): 225–36.

Catlos, B. 2014. *Muslims of Medieval Latin Christendom, c. 1050–1614*. Cambridge: Cambridge University Press. http://dx.doi.org/10.1017/CBO9780511843518.

Chazan, R. 2006. *The Jews of Medieval Western Christendom 1000–1500*. Cambridge: Cambridge University Press. http://dx.doi.org/10.1017/CBO9780511818325.

Christiansen, E. 1997. *The Northern Crusades*. London: Penguin Books.

Christie, N. 2014. *Muslims and Crusaders: Christianity's Wars in the Middle East, 1095–1382*. New York: Routledge.

Christie, N. 2015. *The Book of the Jihad of 'Ali ibn Tahir al-Sulami (d. 1106): Text, Translation and Commentary*. New York: Routledge.

Claster, J. 2009. *Sacred Violence: The European Crusades to the Middle East, 1095–1396*. Toronto: University of Toronto Press.

Cobb, P., ed. 2008. *The Book of Contemplation: Islam and the Crusades*. By Usama Ibn Munqidh. London: Penguin Books.

Cobb, P. 2014. *The Race for Paradise: An Islamic History of the Crusades*. Oxford: Oxford University Press.

Constable, G. 2002. "Medieval Charters as a Source for the History of the Crusades." In *The Crusades, The Essential Readings*, ed. T. Madden, 129–153. Oxford: Blackwell Publishing.

Cramb, J. 1915. *The Origins and Destiny of Imperial Britain and Nineteenth Century Europe*. New York: E.P. Dutton and Company.

David, C. 2001. *De expugnatione Lyxboniensi: The Conquest of Lisbon*. New York: Columbia University Press.

Delaney, C. 2012. *Columbus and the Quest for Jerusalem*. London: Duckworth.

Dennis, G., trans. and ed. 2001. *Maurice's Strategikon: Handbook of Byzantine Military Strategy*. Philadelphia: University of Pennsylvania Press.

Dennis, G. 2009. *Three Byzantine Military Treatises.* Washington, DC: Dunbarton Oaks.

Dennis, G. 2010. *Taktika of Leo VI.* Washington, DC: Dunbarton Oaks.

Dickson, G. 2008. *The Children's Crusade: Medieval History, Modern Mythistory.* London: Palgrave MacMillian. http://dx.doi.org/10.1057/9780230592988.

Dickson, G. 2015. "Shepherd's Crusade, First (1251)" and "Shepherd's Crusade, Second (1320)." In *The Crusades to the Holy Land: The Essential Reference Guide*, ed. A. Murray, 216–19. Santa Barbara: ABC-CLIO.

Doré, G. 1997. *Gustave Doré's Illustrations for the Crusades.* Mineola, NY: Dover.

Edgar, J. 1841. *The Boy Crusaders: A Story of the Days of Louis IX.* Edinburgh: Gall and Inglis.

Edgington, S. 2013. *Albert of Aachen's History of the Journey to Jerusalem:* Volume 1: Books 1–6, The First Crusade 1095–1099. Crusade Texts in Translation 24. Burlington: Ashgate.

Eihmane, E. 2009. "The Baltic Crusades: A Clash of Two Identities." In *The Clash of Cultures on the Medieval Baltic Frontier*, ed. A. Murray, 37–52. Farnham: Ashgate.

Ekdahl, S. 2006. "Warfare: The Baltic Crusades." In *The Crusades: An Encyclopedia*, vol. 4., ed. A. Murray, 1241–49. Santa Barbara: ABC-CLIO.

Ellenblum, R. 2007. *Crusader Castles and Modern Histories.* Cambridge: Cambridge University Press. http://dx.doi.org/10.1017/CBO9780511497247.

El-Moctar, M. 2012. "Saladin in Sunni and Shi'a Memories." In *Remembering the Crusades: Myth, Image and Identity*, ed. N. Paul and S. Yeager, 197–214. Baltimore: The Johns Hopkins University Press.

Elukin, J. 2007. *Living Together, Living Apart: Rethinking Jewish-Christian Relations in the Middle Ages.* Princeton, NJ: Princeton University Press.

Esposito, J. 2003. *The Oxford Dictionary of Islam.* Oxford: Oxford University Press.

Fine, J.V.A. 1994. *The Late Medieval Balkans: A Critical Survey from the Late Twelfth Century to the Ottoman Conquest.* Ann Arbor: University of Michigan Press. http://dx.doi.org/10.3998/mpub.7807.

Fonnesberg-Schmidt, I. 2006. *The Popes and the Baltic Crusades, 1147–1254.* Leiden: Brill. http://dx.doi.org/10.1163/ej.9789004155022.i-287.

France, J. 1999. *Western Warfare in the Age of the Crusades 1000–1300.* Ithaca, NY: Cornell University Press.

France, J. 2006. "Warfare: Outremer." In *The Crusades: An Encyclopedia*, vol. 4, ed. A. Murray, 1261–62. Santa Barbara: ABC-CLIO.

France, J. 2015. *Great Battles: Hattin.* Oxford: Oxford University Press.

Friedman, Y. 2001. "Captivity and Ransom: The Experience of Women." In *Gendering the Crusades*, ed. S. Edginton and S. Lambert, 121–139. Cardiff: University of Wales Press.

Friedman, Y. 2015. "How to End Holy War: Negotiation and Peace Treaties between Muslims and Crusaders in the Latin East." *Common Knowledge* 21 (1): 83–103.

Fulcher of Chartres. 1969. *A History of the Expedition to Jerusalem, 1095–1127.* Trans. F. Ryan. Knoxville: University of Tennessee Press.

Fuller, T. 1639. *The historie of the holy warre; by Thomas Fuller, B.D. prebendarie of Sarum, late of Sidney Colledge in Cambridge.* Ann Arbor, MI; Oxford: Text Creation Partnership, 2003–01 (EEBO-TCP Phase 1). http://name.umdl.umich.edu/A01342.0001.001.

Gabrieli, F. 1984. *Arab Historians of the Crusades.* Berkeley and Los Angeles: University of California Press.

Gibb, H. 2002. *The Damascus Chronicle of the Crusades: Extracted and Translated from the Chronicle of Ibn Al-Qalānisī.* Mineola, NY: Dover.

Gibbons, R. 2007. *Exploring History 1400–1900: An Anthology of Primary Sources.* Manchester: Manchester University Press.

Gilbert, V. 1923. *The Romance of the Last Crusade: With Allenby to Jerusalem.* London: D. Appleton and Company.

Goldsmith, L. 2015. "Louis IX of France (1214–1270)." In *The Crusades to the Holy Land, The Essential Reference Guide,* ed. A. Murray, 163–66. Santa Barbara: ABC-CLIO.

Grandin, T. 2008. *The Castle of Salah ad-Din: Description, History, Site Plan & Visitor Tour.* Geneva: The Aga Khan Trust for Culture. http://archnet.org/system/publications/contents/5215/original/DPC1952.pdf?1384788818.

Guhe, I. 2013. "Crusade Narratives in French and German History Textbooks, 1871–1914." *European Review of History* 20 (3): 367–382. http://dx.doi.org/10.1080/13507486.2012.756854.

Hagenmeyer, H. 1902. *Die Kreuzzugsbriefe aus den Jahren 1088–1100.* Innsbruck.

Hallam, E., ed. 2000. *Chronicles of the Crusades: Eye-witness Accounts of the Wars Between Christianity and Islam.* New York: Welcome Rain, Salamander Books.

Hamas. 1988. "The Covenant of the Islamic Resistance Movement." Trans. Yale Law School Avalon Project. http://avalon.law.yale.edu.

Hammad, M., and E. Peters. 2015. "Islam and the Crusades: A Nine Hundred-Year-Long Grievance?" In *Seven Myths of the Crusades,* ed. A. Andrea and A. Holt, 127–49. Indianapolis: Hackett.

Heidemann, S. 2013. "Memory and Ideology: Images of Saladin in Syria and Iraq." In *Visual Culture in the Modern Middle East: Rhetoric of the Image,* ed. C. Gruber and S. Haugbolle, 57–81. Bloomington: Indiana University Press.

Henty, G. 1895. *Winning His Spurs: A Tale of the Crusades.* London: Sampson Low, Marston & Company.

Hillenbrand, C. 2000. *The Crusades Islamic Perspectives*. New York: Routledge.

Hillenbrand, C. 2004. "The Legacy of the Crusades." In *Crusades: The Illustrated History*, ed. T. Madden, 200–11. London: Duncan Baird.

Hodgson, N. 2006. "Women." In *The Crusades: An Encyclopedia*, vol. 4. ed. A. Murray, 1285–91. Santa Barbara: ABC-CLIO.

Horden, P. 2011. "How Medicalised Were Byzantine Hospitals?" *Medicina & Storia* [S.l.]: 45–74. ISSN 1828–6224. http://www.fupress.net/index.php/mes/article/view/10356.

Housley, N. 1996. *Documents on the Later Crusades, 1274–1580*. London: MacMillan Press.

Ibrahim, R. 2007. *The Al-Qaeda Reader*. New York: Broadway Books.

Jordan, W. 1979, reprint 2015. *Louis IX and the Challenge of the Crusade: A Study in Rulership*. Princeton, NJ: Princeton University Press.

Kedar, B. 1990. "The Subjected Muslims of the Frankish Levant." In *Muslims under Latin Rule, 1100–1300*, ed. James M. Powell, 135–74. Princeton, NJ: Princeton University Press. http://dx.doi.org/10.1515/9781400861194.135.

Kennedy, H. 2015. "Castles." In *The Crusades to the Holy Land, The Essential Reference Guide*, ed. A. Murray, 49–53. Santa Barbara: ABC-CLIO.

Khalidi, T. 2003. *The Muslim Jesus: Sayings and Stories in Islamic Literature*. Cambridge, MA: Harvard University Press.

Knobler, A. 2006. "Holy Wars, Empires, and the Portability of the Past: The Modern Uses of Medieval Crusades." *Comparative Studies in Society and History* 48 (2): 293–325.

Krey, A. 1943. *William of Tyre's A History of the Deeds Done Beyond the Seas*. New York: Columbia University Press.

Latiff, O. 2011. *The Place of Fada'il al-Quds (Merits of Jerusalem) Literature in the Muslim Effort to Recapture Jerusalem during the Crusades*. PhD thesis, Royal Holloway, University of London.

Levy, R. 1929, reissued edition 2011. *A Bagdad Chronicle*. Cambridge: Cambridge University Press.

Lewis, B. 2002. *What Went Wrong? Western Impact and Middle Eastern Response*. New York: Oxford University Press.

Lewis, R. 2015. "Crusader Battlefields: Environmental and Archaeological Perspectives." In *The Crusader World*, ed. A. Boas, 460–89. New York: Routledge.

Lyons, J. 2012. *Islam through Western Eyes: From the Crusades to the War on Terrorism*. New York: Columbia University Press.

Meri, J., ed. 2006. *Medieval Islamic Civilization: An Encyclopedia*, vol. I and II. New York: Routledge.

Michaud, J.F. 1853. *The History of the Crusades*. Trans. W. Robson. New York.

Milner, N. 1997. *Vegetius: Epitome of Military Science. Translated Texts for Historians*. Liverpool: Liverpool University Press.

Mitchell, P. 2004. *Medicine in the Crusades: Warfare, Wounds and the Medieval Surgeon*. Cambridge: Cambridge University Press.

Mitchell, P. 2015. "Intestinal Parasites in the Crusades: Evidence for Disease, Diet and Migration." In *The Crusader World*, ed. A. Boas, 593–608. New York: Routledge.

Mitchell, P., Y. Nagar, and R. Ellenblum. 2006 "Weapon Injuries in the 12th Century Crusader Garrison of Vadum Iacob Castle, Galilee." *International Journal of Osteoarchaeology* 16: 145–55. http://dx.doi.org/10.1002/oa.814.

Mitchell, P., and E. Stern. 2000. "Parasitic Intestinal Helminth Ova from the Latrines of the 13th Century Crusader Hospital of St John in Acre, Israel." In *Proceedings of the XIIIth European Meeting of the Paleopathology Association, Chieti, Italy 2000*, ed. M. La Verghetta and L. Capasso, 207–13. Teramo: Edirafital SpA.

Morton, N. 2013. *The Medieval Military Orders*. Harlow: Pearson Education.

Murray, A., ed. 2001. *Crusader Conversion on the Baltic Frontier, 1150–1500*. Farnham: Ashgate.

Nicholson, H. 2003. *Medieval Warfare: Theory and Practice in Europe 300–1500*. New York: Palgrave Macmillan.

Nicholson, H. Reprint 2010. *The Chronicle of the Third Crusade: A Translation of the Itinerarium Peregrinorum et Gesta Regis Ricardi*. Farnham: Ashgate.

Nicolle, D. 2004. *Crusader Castles in the Holy Land 1097–1192*. Oxford: Osprey Publishing.

Nicolle, D. 2006a. "Warfare: Iberia." In *The Crusades: An Encyclopedia*, vol. 4. ed. A. Murray, 1251–54. Santa Barbara: ABC-CLIO.

Nicolle, D. 2006b. "Warfare: Muslim Armies." In *The Crusades: An Encyclopedia*, vol. 4. ed. A. Murray, 1255–58. Santa Barbara: ABC-CLIO.

Nicolle, D. 2007. *Crusader Warfare. Vol I: Byzantium, Western Europe and the Battle of the Holy Land* and Vol. II: *Muslins, Mongols, and the Struggle against the Crusaders*. London: Hambledon Continuum.

Nicolle, D. 2011. *Hattin 1187: Saladin's Greatest Victory*. Oxford: Osprey.

Paul, N. 2012. *To Follow in Their Footsteps: The Crusades and Family Memory in the High Middle Ages*. Ithaca, NY: Cornell University Press. http://dx.doi.org/10.7591/cornell/9780801450976.001.0001.

Phillips, J. 2010. *Holy Warriors: A Modern History of the Crusades*. London: Vintage Books.

Qutb, S. 2000. *Social Justice in Islam*. Trans. J. Hardie, rev. trans. H. Algar Oneonta. New York: Islamic Publications International.

Ragab, A. 2015. *The Medieval Islamic Hospital: Medicine, Religion and Charity.* Cambridge: Cambridge University Press. http://dx.doi.org/10.1017/CBO9781316271797.

Rautman, M. 2006. *Daily Life in the Byzantine Empire.* Santa Barbara: Greenwood Press.

Riley-Smith, J., ed. 1991. *The Atlas of the Crusades.* New York: Guild Publishing.

Riley-Smith, J. 1995. "The State of Mind of Crusaders to the East: 1095–1300." In *The Oxford Illustrated History of the Crusades*, ed. J. Riley-Smith, 66–90. Oxford: Oxford University Press.

Riley-Smith, J. 2008a. *The Crusades, Christianity and Islam.* New York: Columbia University Press.

Riley-Smith, J. 2008b. *The First Crusaders, 1095–1131.* Cambridge: Cambridge University Press.

Riley-Smith, J. 2014. *The Crusades, A History.* 3rd ed. London: Bloomsbury.

Robertson, W. 1769. "A View of the Progress of Society in Europe, from the Subversion of the Roman Empire, to the Beginning of the Sixteenth Century." In *The History of the Reign of the Emperor Charles V.* Edinburgh: W. and W. Strahan.

Rodriguez, J. 2015. *Muslim and Christian Contact in the Middle Ages.* Readings in Medieval Civilizations and Cultures, XVIII. Ed. P.E. Dutton. Toronto: University of Toronto Press.

Rose, G., ed. 2013. *The Clash of Civilizations? The Debate: Twentieth Anniversary Edition.* New York: Foreign Affairs Magazine.

Ross, J., and M. McLaughlin, eds. 1981. *The Portable Medieval Reader.* Harmondsworth: Penguin Books.

Rossabi, M. 2012. *The Mongols: A Very Short Introduction.* Oxford: Oxford University Press. http://dx.doi.org/10.1093/actrade/9780199840892.001.0001.

Rousseau, C. 2001. "Home Front and Battlefield: The Gendering of Papal Crusading Policy (1095–1221). In *Gendering the Crusades*, ed. S. Edgington and S. Lambert, 31–44. Cardiff: University of Wales Press.

Rubenstein, J. 2011. *Armies of Heaven: The First Crusade and the Quest for Apocalypse.* New York: Basic Books.

Said, E. 2003. *Orientalism.* 25th anniversary ed. Orig. pub. 1978. New York: Vintage Books.

Schein, S. 2001. "Women in Medieval Colonial Society: The Latin Kingdom of Jerusalem in the Twelfth Century." In *Gendering the Crusades*, ed. S. Edgington and S. Lambert, 140–53. Cardiff: University of Wales Press.

Scheindlin, R. 2008. *The Song of the Distant Dove: Judah Halevi's Pilgrimage.* Oxford: Oxford University Press.

Schlimm, M. 2010. "The Necessity of Permanent Criticism: A Postcolonial Critique of Ridley Scott's *Kingdom of Heaven.*" *Journal of Media and Religion* 9 (3): 129–49. http://dx.doi.org/10.1080/15348423.2010.500967.

Sharf, A. 2007. "Byzantine Empire." In *Encyclopaedia Judaica.* Second Edition. vol. 4, ed. M. Berenbaum and F. Skolnik, 324–28. Detroit: Macmillan Reference.

Shaw, M.R.B. 1977. *Joinville & Villehardouin, Chronicles of the Crusades.* London: Penguin Books.

Siberry, E. 2000. *The New Crusaders: Images of the Crusade in the 19th and Early 20th Centuries.* New York: Routledge.

Siberry, E. 2001. "Images of the Crusades in the Nineteenth and Twentieth Centuries." In *The Oxford Illustrated History of the Crusades,* ed. J. Riley-Smith, 365–85. Oxford: Oxford University Press.

Sibly, W.A., and M.D. Sibly, trans. 1998. *The History of the Albigensian Crusade: Peter of les Vaux-de-Cernay's Historia Albigensis.* Woodbridge: The Boydell Press.

Slack, C., and H. Feiss, eds. 2001. *Crusade Charters, 1138–1270.* Tempe: Arizona Center for Medieval and Renaissance Studies.

Somerville, R. 1972. *Decreta Claromontensia.* Amsterdam: Adolf M. Hakkert.

Somerville, R. 2011. *Pope Urban II's Council of Piacenza.* Oxford: Oxford University Press. http://dx.doi.org/10.1093/acprof:oso/9780199258598. 001.0001.

Stock, L. 2009. "Now Starring in the Third Crusade: Depictions of Richard and Saladin in Films and Television Series." In *Hollywood in the Holy Land: Essays on Film Depictions of the Crusades and Christian-Muslim Clashes,* ed. N. Haydock and E. Risden, 97–115. Jefferson, NC: MacFarland & Company.

Sumption, J. 2002. *Pilgrimage.* 2nd ed. London: Faber and Faber.

Tyerman, C. 2004. *The Crusades: A Very Short Introduction.* Oxford: Oxford University Press.

Tyerman, C. 2007. *God's War: A New History of the Crusades.* London: Penguin Books.

Tyerman, C. 2011. *The Debate on the Crusades.* Manchester: Manchester University Press.

Tyerman, C. 2015. *How to Plan a Crusade.* London: Allen Lane.

Urban, W. 1994. *The Baltic Crusades.* Chicago: Lithuanian Research and Studies Center.

Wallis, F., ed. 2010. *Medieval Medicine: A Reader.* Readings in Medieval Civilizations and Cultures, XV. Ed. P.E. Dutton. Toronto: University of Toronto Press.

Wasserstein, D. May 24, 2012. "How Islam Saved the Jews." Jordan Lectures in Comparative Religion at the School of Oriental and African Studies

(SOAS), London. Audio file: https://www.soas.ac.uk/religions/events/
jordan-lectures-in-comparative-religion/14may2012-opening-lecture-how-
islam-saved-the-jews.html. Adapted text: "So What Did the Muslims Do for
the Jews?" *The Jewish Chronicle Online*. http://www.thejc.com/comment-
and-debate/comment/68082/so-what-did-muslims-do-jews.

Whalen, B. 2009. *Dominion of God: Christendom and Apocalypse in the Middle
Ages*. Cambridge, MA: Harvard University Press. http://dx.doi.org/
10.4159/9780674054806.

Whalen, B., ed. 2011. *Pilgrimage in the Middle Ages: A Reader*. Readings in
Medieval Civilizations and Cultures, XVI. Ed. P.E. Dutton Toronto:
University of Toronto Press.

SOURCES

Figures

Figure 2.1: Baggage cart. From the *Morgan Bible* (New York: Pierpont Morgan Library), MS M. 638, ca. 1240. The Morgan Library & Museum/Art Resource, NY.

Figure 3.1: Kneeling Crusader. From the *Westminster Psalter* (London: British Library), MS Royal 2A XXII fol. 220, ca. 1250. © British Library Board/Robana/Art Resouce, NY

Figure 3.2: The arms and armor of Baron Adhemar of Beynac. Photo by Stephen Bowden

Figure 3.3: Islamic forces attacking Byzantine garrison. From John Scylitzes. *Synopsis historianum* (Madrid: Biblioteca Nacional), Madrid Matritiensis Vitr. 26–2. Album/Art Resource, NY

Figure 3.4: Greek fire. From the *Codex Skylitzes Matritiensis* (Madrid: Biblioteca Nacional de Madrid), Vitr. 26–2, Bild-Nr. 77, f 34 v. b. Biblioteca Nacional, Madrid, Spain/ Bridgeman Images

Figure 3.5 Twelfth-Century Islamic incendiary grenade (Sévre: Musée National de la Céramique), Aj 1. RMN-Grand Palais/Art Resource, NY

Figure 3.6 Siege scene with manual trebuchet. From the *Morgan Bible* (New York: Pierpont Morgan Library), MS M 638, ca 1240. The Morgan Library & Museum/Art Resource, NY

Figure 3.7: The siege of Antioch. From the *Historia Rerum in Partibus Transmarinis Gesarum* (Lyons: Bibliothéque Municipale), MS 828. Thirteenth Century. Art Resource, NY

Figure 3.8: Sappers protected by moveable shield. From *Les Grandes chroniques de France* (London: British Library), Royal MS 16 GVI f. 74, between 1332 and 1350. British Library, London, UK © British Library Board. All Rights Reserved/Bridgeman Images

Figure 3.9: Siege of Jerusalem. From William of Tyre, *Histoire d'Outremer* (Paris: Bibliothéque Nationale), MS Fr. 9081, Thirteenth century. Pictures from History/Bridgeman Images

Figure 3.10: From Manuscript of Matthew of Paris's Chronica Majora (ca 1255), Parker Library, Corpus Chrisi College Cambridge. Courtesy of the Master and Fellows of Corpus Christi College Cambridge.

Figure 3.11 The Hospitaller Castle of Crak des Chavaliers, Syria. De Agostini Picture Library/C. Sappa/Bridgeman Images

Figure 3.12 From Roger of Frugard, The Practice of Surgery (ca 1180), Trinity College Cambridge. Images from MS O.1.20. Reprinted by permission of the Master and Fellows of Trinity College Cambridge.

Figure 5.1: *Playbill: The Knights of the Cross* (London: Victoria and Albert Museum). Every effort has been made to contact copyright holders; in the event of an error or omission, please notify the publisher.

Figure 5.2: Louis IX taken prisoner. From Gustave Doré's *Illustrations for the Crusades* (Mineola, New York: Dover Publications, Inc), Plate 68. Private Collection Ken Welsh/Bridgeman Images.

Figure 5.3 National Review 3 December 2001. Copyright National Review. Used with permission.

INDEX

Illustrations and maps are indicated by page numbers in italics